TOWN OF BAR:
Jewish Pages Through The Prism Of Time

By M. B. Kupershteyn

Original Book in Ukrainian:

К 92 M. B. Kupershteyn *Town of Bar: Jewish Pages Through The Prism Of Time.* –

Vinnytsia: LLC "Nilan-LTD", 2019 - 344 pages.

Book proofreader: A. M. Krentsina

Published by JewishGen

An Affiliate of the Museum of Jewish Heritage—A Living Memorial to the Holocaust
New York

TOWN OF BAR:
Jewish Pages Through The Prism Of Time

Translated from Ukranian By M. B. Kupershteyn
Town of Bar: Jewish Pages Through The Prism Of Time.
Vinnytsia: LLC "Nilan-LTD", 2019 - 344 pages.

The Original publication was carried out with the financial support of the Charity
Fund " Christians for Israel-Ukraine"

Author: M. B. Kupershteyn
Bar Kehila Leader: Stefani Elkort Twyford
Cover Design: Rachael Kolokoff Hopper
Name Indexing: Jonathan Wind

Published by JewishGen, Inc.
An Affiliate of the Museum of Jewish Heritage
A Living Memorial to the Holocaust
36 Battery Place, New York, NY 10280

Printed in the United States of America by Lightning Source, Inc.

Library of Congress Control Number (LCCN): 2020952482
ISBN: 978-1-954176-00-3 (hard cover: 292 pages, alk. paper)

Cover Credits:

Front Cover:

> Photograph of Bar synagogue, main facade, 18th century from original Bar Book (page 44)

> Original artistic texture and graphic design by Rachel Kolokoff Hopper

Back Cover:

> Photograph of M. B. Kupershteyn from original book

> Background: Map of Podolia province, 19th century from the original book, page 22

> Original artistic texture and color by Rachel Kolokoff Hopper

JewishGen and the Yizkor Books in Print Project

This book has been published by the **Yizkor Books in Print Project**, as part of the **Yizkor Book Project** of JewishGen, Inc.

JewishGen, Inc. is a non-profit organization founded in 1987 as a resource for Jewish genealogy. Its website [www.jewishgen.org] serves as an international clearinghouse and resource center to assist individuals who are researching the history of their Jewish families and the places where they lived. JewishGen provides databases, facilitates discussion groups, and coordinates projects relating to Jewish genealogy and the history of the Jewish people. In 2003, JewishGen became an affiliate of the **Museum of Jewish Heritage—A Living Memorial to the Holocaust** in New York.

The **JewishGen Yizkor Book Project** was organized to make more widely known the existence of Yizkor (Memorial) Books written by survivors and former residents of various Jewish communities throughout the world. Later, volunteers connected to the different destroyed communities began cooperating to have these books translated from the original language—usually Hebrew or Yiddish—into English, thus enabling a wider audience to have access to the valuable information contained within them. As each chapter of these books was translated, it was posted on the JewishGen website and made available to the general public.

The **Yizkor Books in Print Project** began in 2011 as an initiative to print and publish Yizkor Books that had been fully translated, so that hard copies would be available for purchase by the descendants of these communities and also by scholars, universities, synagogues, libraries, and museums.

These Yizkor books have been produced almost entirely through the volunteer effort of researchers from around the world, assisted by donations from private individuals. The books are printed and sold at near cost, so as to make them as affordable as possible. Our goal is to make this important genre of Jewish literature and history available in English in book form, so that people can have the personal histories of their ancestral towns on their bookshelves for themselves and for their children and grandchildren.

A list of all published translated Yizkor Books in the project with prices and ordering information can be found at:
http://www.jewishgen.org/Yizkor/ybip.html

Lance Ackerfeld, Yizkor Book Project Manager
Joel Alpert, Yizkor-Book-in-Print Project Coordinator
Susan Rosin, Yizkor-Book-in-Print Project Associate Coordinator

This book is presented by the
Yizkor-Books-In-Print Project
Project Coordinator: Joel Alpert

Part of the Yizkor Books Project of JewishGen. Inc.
Project Manager: Lance Ackerfeld

These books have been produced solely through efforts of volunteers
from around the world. The books are printed using the Print-on-Demand technology and sold at
near cost, to make them as affordable as possible.

Our goal is to make this intimate history of the destroyed Jewish shtetls
of Eastern Europe available in book form in English, so that people can
experience the near-personal histories of their ancestral town on their
bookshelves and those of their children and grandchildren.

All donations to the Yizkor Books Project, which translated the books,
are sincerely appreciated.

Please send donations to:

Yizkor Book Project
JewishGen, Inc.
36 Battery Place
New York, NY, 10280

JewishGen, Inc. is an affiliate of the
Museum of Jewish Heritage
A Living Memorial to the Holocaust

Notes to the Reader:

We apologize ahead of time for the poor quality of images in the book. Often these images had been scanned from the original Yizkor books which were of poor quality to begin with, being copies of old photographs. Each transfer results in loss of quality. We have done the best we could, given the original material and the resources and technology at hand. Even though images often appear of higher quality on computer screens, that does not transfer to high quality images in print. A reader can view the original scans on the web sites listed below.

Within the text the reader will note "{34}" standing ahead of a paragraph. This indicates that the material translated below was on page 34 of the original book. However, when a paragraph was split between two pages in the original book, the marker is placed in this book after the end of the paragraph for ease of reading.

Also please note that all references within the text of the book to page numbers, refer to the page numbers of the original Yizkor Book.

In order to obtain a list of all Shoah victims from the town of Bar, the reader should access the Yad Vashem web site listed below; one can also search for specific family names using family name option. These lists are continually updated by Yad Vashem, so it is worthwhile to periodically search these lists.

There is much valuable information available on this web site, including the Pages of Testimony, etc.
http://yvng.yadvashem.org

A list of this book and all books available in the Yizkor-Book-In-Print Project along with prices is available at:
http://www.jewishgen.org/Yizkor/ybip.html

Geopolitical Information:

Bar, Ukraine is located at 49°04' N 27°40' E and 158 miles SW of Kyyiv

Period	Town	District	Province	Country
Before WWI (c. 1900):	Bar	Mogilev	Podolia	Russian Empire
Between the wars (c. 1930):	Bar	Vinnitsa	Ukraine SSR	Soviet Union
After WWII (c. 1950):	Bar			Soviet Union
Today (c. 2000):	Bar			Ukraine

Alternate names for the town:
Bar [Rus, Ukr, Yid]

Nearby Jewish Communities:

Volkovintsy 9 miles N

Yaltushkiv 9 miles SW

Verkhivka 10 miles S

Popovtsy 13 miles SSE

Staryi Zakrevskiy Maydan 14 miles NNW

Kopaihorod 15 miles SSE

Mezhirov 16 miles E

Derazhnya 17 miles NW

Snitkov 18 miles S

Snitivka 19 miles NNW

Zamikhiv 19 miles SW

Zhmerynka 20 miles E

Vinkivtsi 20 miles W

Stanislavchyk 22 miles ESE

Letychiv 22 miles N

Brailiv 23 miles E

Nova Ushytsya 24 miles SW

D'yakovtsy 24 miles NNE

Murovani Kurylivtsi 24 miles SSW

Luchynets 25 miles SSE

Verbovets 25 miles SSW

Lityn 26 miles NE

Zinkiv 27 miles W

Medzhybizh 28 miles NNW

Vil'khovets' 29 miles SSW

Sharhorod 29 miles SE

Novokostyantyniv 29 miles N

Myn'kivtsi 30 miles WSW

Voroshylivka 30 miles E

Hnivan 30 miles E

Jewish Population in 1900: 5,773

Map of Ukraine with Bar

Preface

Back in 2016 I took on the responsibility for being JewishGen's Kehila Leader for the town of Bar Ukraine. My grandfather was from Bar and I had very little information about his family and hoped that by learning more and connecting with other Bar descendants, I would find my way to learning about that family. I built a KehilaLinks website, started a records translation project, and developed a mailing list of other Bar researchers that I kept in touch with as new records became available and were translated.

In May of 2019, I was contacted by Stefan Ostrach, one of my researchers, who had returned from Bar with a newly published book about the history of Bar, or what we refer to as a Yizkor Book. It was published in 2019 by a Mikhail Kupershtein, a resident of Bar and local historian. Stefan asked me if it was possible to have the book translated into English and I said, of course! I was able to find contact information for Mikhail and emailed him, asking him if he would be willing to make the book available to US researchers and have it translated into English. He agreed and sent me his manuscript.

Quite a lot had already been written about the city of Bar, but aside from mentioning that there were Jews living there, nothing really detailed the life and experiences of the Jewish people. Mikhail chose to write this story so other Jews could read and understand the breadth and depth of the Jewish contribution to Bar over hundreds of years. It took Mikhail three years of visiting archives, meeting and interviewing people and groups, and a lot of hard work to bring this book to fruition. Mikhail is a proud of the fact that this book reflects his own commitment, along with a long history of other Jews, on the vision and understanding of this important city.

Initially available as a PDF to my researchers, I am so thrilled to finally see an English version of this book available in hardcover. I would like to thank Aleksandra Khaskin for her wonderful translation of the book and the time she took re-wording certain concepts for an American audience. I also am indebted to Gregg Tracton for his generous and enthusiastic support in the formatting of the English version. He developed a program that allowed us to create a name index as well as repaginate the Table of Contents and the Index of Images as I further edited and refined the document. Thank you to all my Bar researchers for your financial support of the project which paid for the translation. Thank you to JewishGen and their Yizkor Book volunteers who work tirelessly to make these books available to an international audience. And finally, a heartfelt thank you to Mikhail Kupershtein, whose generosity in sharing his knowledge has allowed us to learn so much about Bar. It is an extraordinary work of dedication, love and scholarship.

Stefani Elkort Twyford
Bar Kehila Leader

TOWN OF BAR:

Jewish Pages Through The Prism Of Time

By M. B. Kupershteyn

Vinnytsia-**2019**

The publication was carried out with the financial support of the Charity Fund " Christians for Israel-Ukraine"

K 92   M. B. Kupershteyn ***Town of Bar: Jewish Pages Through The Prism Of Time.*** - Vinnytsia: LLC "Nilan-LTD", 2019 - 344 pages.

This book tells about the town of Bar, namely the life of the Jewish population through the prism of historical events. When writing this book archival, historical, memoir, public materials, historical and ethnographic dictionaries, reference books, works of historians, local historians, as well as memories and stories of direct participants, living witnesses of history, photos from the album "Old Bar" and from other sources were used. The book is devoted to the Jewish people of Bar, the history of contacts between ethnic groups, which were imprinted in the people's memory and monuments of material culture, will be of interest to both professionals and a wide range of readers who are not indifferent to the history of the Jewish people and its cultural traditions.

Layout and cover design: L. M. Kupershtein

Book proofer: A. M. Krentsina

ISBN 978-617-7742-19-6

TABLE OF CONTENTS

- Let's sit on the porch and talk for a while. I don't know who you are or how you got to shtetl. Yes, do not be surprised, Jews live here! We've lived here for five hundred years. Although it seems to us that we have always been. We live in those shtetls, we pray to God, we will live.

-You still haven't left? Are you interested? Do you want me to tell you about life, about the "shtetl"?

- I see! All this is familiar to you! Surely you also have a hard time!

- Listen, and stay with us, we will live in our shtetl!

INTRODUCTION

In this work I describe the main events of the Jewish community in the town of Bar, Vinnytsia region. These historical events took place in Ukraine, in Podolia, and documents the life of the Jewish people from the moment when they first appeared in Bar. At the same time, I describe their life without any accents.

One of the oldest and strongest Jewish communities in Ukraine was in the town of Bar. This Jewish community had a hard fate: to be constantly disadvantaged and bullied.

The history of this Jewish community dates back about 500 years. It was a period of self-affirmation involving destruction and revival.

On our land of Bar during its centuries-old history there were rivers of blood of all who lived here during the various battles, revolts, pogroms, revolutions, repressions and Holodomor. And the reason for this was hatred, bitterness, intolerance.

To those who have eyes and mind, understand and see: a man's blood is not water; everyone's blood is red color. Everybody's eye drop is salty, and the grief - all disappointing. The memory could not be selective. It must be one and eternal.

The lights of the menorah and the lamp show all living people how to be. This light is a guide to the feelings in souls and hearts, to charity and love, to compassion and harmony.

It is necessary to always remind ourselves, remember, pray. And everyone can do it in the way he can, as he wants, as he knows. And then all these words will reach those to whom they are intended, who are waiting for them.

The Jewish writer Sholem Aleichem wrote:

I, of course, understand that the book, like any creation of human hands, is not without flaws. I put into it the most precious thing I have – my own heart. Read this book from time to time. Perhaps it will teach you or your children something – teach them how to love our people and appreciate the treasures of their spirit, which are scattered in all the remote corners of the vast world.

I believe that this work must be both light and heavy for the reader at the same time, it should bring light, make you smile, and worry.

I express my deep gratitude to my family – wife Svetlana, daughter Alla and son Leonid for their patience and help in preparing the book.

I am also sincerely grateful to the charitable Foundation "Christians for Israel-Ukraine" and separately to its founder Karlir Kun for financial support in the publication of this book.

HISTORICAL BAR

The land of Bar literally breathes history. It seems, if you just touch with a palm to the smallest mound of soil, your hand will be filled out with powerful bio-currents. And immediately in your imagination will appear, as living, visions of the past: here is, on the well familiar to all, the conquerors Kuchmansky path, rush on prey Crimean Tatars, and from Turkish torches ignited ancient Rov - ancestor of Bar. And there, on prepared trade route from Shargorod to Bar, slowly go carts of Moldavian merchants carrying the wine, honey and other products.

This land is generously watered with Cossack and Jewish blood. Here, traditions are still alive in the people's memory about the Haidamaks and Koliyvschina. Peter I was here when he went to the Prut campaign. Here, the tireless Frenchman Guillaume Le Vasseur de Beauplan designed and built numerous fortifications and fortresses. Who has not set foot on this ancient land. What else she didn't hide in herself!

To get acquainted with the history of the city of Bar, you need to walk along the old walls on the banks of the river Rov, as well as the streets that are adjacent to them.

Sometime ago the settlement that was on the steep bank of the river Riv bore the same name. Deep water, swamps, reeds, earth mounds, stone walls – all these defensive fortifications were used to protect the settlement from the enemy's hordes that came from the vast steppes.

The first time the outpost Rov was mentioned in historical documents in 1401. Since 1434 Polish rule begins here. Podolia was captured by Poland. The town entered the Podolian Voivodeship. In 1443 Stogniew Reya became the owner of Rov. In 1452 the town was destroyed by the Tatar conquerors. Part of the population fled to Zinkov, on the Ushitsya river; the other part was destroyed or taken into slavery.

Only in the first half of the 16th century Rov was rebuilt again, but on the opposite, low and swampy bank of the river. Since then, the town has been called Bar.

According to one version, the name of the town comes from the word "bar" in the old Ukrainian language, which means a wetland. In Slovenian, Serbian languages - "bar" is a swamp. This word also occurs in non-Slavic languages, where it means the same thing.

From other sources, the town was so named by Bona Sforza, the wife of king Sigismund I of Poland. She bought the outpost Rov in 1537 at the Krakow Sejm, after the last member of the family of Stanislaus Odrovonja that owned Rov died in 1523. Then the equal wealth went to the Royal Treasury and by that time was devastated.

Bona Sforza, an Italian by birth, was from the city of Bari in Italy. Perhaps these two versions together led to the fact that the city began to be called Bar.

The purchase of the town was sealed by the decision of the Polish Sejm of March 14, 1538.

In the first book of "Chronicles", A. Guagnini describes as follows: "80 thousand Tatars with Bakai and Seoz came under Bar in Podolia and burned dozens of towns and villages and returned with a great prey, but the Kamyanetz headman Buchatsky beat them part of the prey and beat them up".

In the third book of "Chronicles" it is written about Bar: "the town is surrounded by a fence and lies on the plain. It was built by order of the Polish Queen B. Sforza, daughter of a Prince of Milan. Bar, a city in Ukraine, is widely spread, its stone castle stands on a high mountain, surrounded by marshy and wide lakes, across which it is difficult to get."

An excursion into the history of Bar reveals the creation of the Podolia area, the appearance of the name "Podolia" (previously, in the 13th century, it was called "Ponizzya"- a place that lies lower than others).

So, Bona Sforza ordered to build a fortress on the left bank of the river Rov, where now Bar is located. In 1540 Bar was granted Magdeburg law, thanks to which the settlers received many benefits, including exemption from taxes for 16 years, the coat of arms with the sign "BS" and a seal.

In 1540, with the permission of the king, the first few families of Armenian and Jewish merchants settled in Bar.

Coat of arms of Bar, 1540

Seal Of Bona Sforza, 1540.

In 1546, Bar became the center of the old town, which included 30 surrounding villages. Later, a plaque was placed on the wall of the fortress, on which the following text is carved in Latin: "Bona Sforza d'Aragona, Queen of Poland, Grand Duchess of Lithuania, owner of Russia, Prussia, Mazovia, and other possessions of God 1537, during the reign of the best king of Poland Sigismund I, her husband, settled this region by this time, totally devastated by the constant enemy attacks, introduced to him for the settlement of the inhabitants and founded the town and fortress, created calm and peace surrounding residents and strengthened it according to local customs with wood walls, and the name of the city was given in the name of her hometown Bari".

The fate of Bona Sforza was such. After the death of Sigismund I the Old in 1548, his son Sigismund II Augustus, decides to take revenge on his mother for the death of his beloved Barbara Radziwill (modern historians proved that Barbara died of cancer).

Bona was put under a kind of "house arrest". She bought off her son with a gift signature for her land possessions, and then returned to her native town Bari, where she died on November 19, 1557. She was poisoned by her own doctor who was bribed by the Spanish monarch Philip II of the Habsburg family. The king owed Bona Sforza 420 thousand ducats. He did not know that the son inherited the land from his mother, and the young Polish king still knocked out most of the Habsburg debt.

Bona Sforza, wife of King Sigismund I.

The town grew rapidly. From the beginning it was divided into three parts: Polish Bar, Russian Bar, Gorsky Bar, each of which had not only a separate name, but also owned different rights.

Thus, the population of the Russian Bar was made up of the inhabitants of the ancient Rov, who hid from the Tatars in neighboring Zinkov and Yaltushkiv. Now, returning to their former places, they received a tax exemption for 6 years. Other settlers (Russians, Armenians and Jews were allowed to settle in the vicinity of this part), received benefits for 12 years, while the inhabitants of Polish Bar - for 16 years.

Gorsky Bar was inhabited by Chemeris people, the family of Nevid had the power over them (Nevid's descendants inherited this position of ownership). Now the village is called Barskie Chemerisy.

Each part of the town had a separate jurisdiction, as indicated in the Royal privileges granted them Magdeburg rights. In particular, one of them noted that the coat of arms of the Russian Bar is considered common with the Polish Bar, that is, the letters "BS", meaning "Bona Sforza". It was the first coat of arms of the town.

Magdeburg law in the town was incomplete. It was limited to the power of the Royal presidency, which was vested with legislative power and embraced the office of President (judicial power). The town administration was elective, unlike the rules under full Magdeburg law.

From 1540 to 1552 the head of the town of Bar was Bernard Pretvych. He was the viceroy of the king in Bar territories. Pretvych had great military talent, he participated in 70 battles, and won the victory in all of them. Polish historians called Pretvych "wall of the Podolia lands", and the population of Podolia – "behind Pretvich the land is free from Tatars".

It sounded at the time as follows: Merus Podoliae (wall Podoliaaya) Terror Tartarorum (Fear of the Tatars).

In 1558 the town and the castle were destroyed by the Tatars and were not restored for a long time. After that, during the uprising under the leadership of S.Nalyvaika the Cossacks destroyed the castle completely.

In the 17th century, the headquarters of the Polish Hetman Stanislaw Koniecpolski together with an arsenal and town fortifications were built in Bar; the town had an impregnable fortress by that time. The assortment of military equipment of the castle, built by General Krzysztof Artsishevski, was one of the largest and had a great importance for Poland.

The manor castle was further strengthened by the French military engineer Guillaume Levasseur de Beauplan. In the early 17th century Bar became a stronghold of Catholicism.

Various historical events happened in Bar during this time, including the activities of Bar Confederation, and the struggle of ordinary people under the leadership of Ustim Karmelyuk and many other events. Here, since the 16th century, Jews began to settle and their lives were closely intertwined with the local population.

I want to pay attention to the personality of Ustim Karmelyuk. He was almost the only leader of the rebel movement in which Jews took part, not taking into account the Jewish department UGA and the army of N. Makhno, where the situation was different. By the way, one of the languages spoken by Ustim, was Yiddish, because since childhood he has lived close to Jews.

Ustim Karmanyuk (and this was his family name, later converted to Karmelyuk), apparently was the last figure in the Ukrainian history, his name was mentioned in poems and idealized by the Ukrainian people themselves. The idealized image of a certain Ukrainian "Robin hood" of the 19th century is quite far from what was a real robber from Podolia, undoubtedly outstanding in his temper, strength and courage. Thus, according to the materials of the investigation, in the surrounding villages of Bar, where Karmelyuk was, 2000 oxen and 400 horses were stolen from rich people in the town. Part was given to poor peasants, and part was sold to tavern owners for sale. In contrast to the peasant movements of the previous time, the activities of Ustim Karmelyuk had no national orientation: robbed the same extent as the poles-gentry, Jews-tavern keepers, and peasants-Ukrainians.

On the other hand, among those who took a direct part in the robberies or provided support to the robbers (sheltered them, bought stolen goods from them), there are representatives of the same three main national groups of the inhabitants of Podolia. Judicial acts of that time testify that the most favorite objects for attacks of Ustim Karmelyuk throughout all its activity as the robber, were rural, and especially roadside inns and taverns that often settled down in the wood at a certain distance from settlements: travelers with money stopped there, sometimes with quite a considerable amount of money. The Jewish tenants and tavern-keepers of most of these establishments in Podolia became victims of robberies because of this. Ustim Karmelyuk never committed attacks on small-town Jews. The first tavern robbery involving Karmelyuk was a tavern of his native village Holovchyntsi from Lityn district. In August 1814, tavern keeper Chaimovich from village Petrani, Lityn County was robbed. After being several times in a jail and escape from the hard labor in Siberia, Karmelyuk robbed Hanovetska tavern on November 8, 1826. On November 22 of the same year in village

Sakhny of Letichev district he robbed the road-by tavern that was rented by Lazar Shlomovich. During the first half of 1827 Karmelyuk made the attack on Gerkaska tavern rented by Jonah Itskovich, it belonged to village Grishki of Letichev district, And later he pounced the tavern of village Komarovtsy of Lityn district. The attacks on the taverns were usually accomplished by a small gang of robbers, about 3-7 people, rarely more people were involved. Jewish innkeepers, as a rule, saved their own lives by giving away their money and possessions. However, there were cases of murders of tenants, as occurred in 1827 during the taverns' robberies in villages Guta and Grishki.

The number of taverns' robberies declined toward the end of 1832 and the beginning of 1833. In spite of the numerous attacks on taverns and the material and human losses suffered by the Jewish population, Ustim Karmelyuk was not a national enemy for the Jews of Podolia. Moreover, Jews en masse are on trial as accomplices of the robber with charges of granting him asylum, buying stolen property, warning of danger and direct participation in the attacks committed by Karmelyuk. The right hand of Karmelyuk, the direct participant of the majority of robberies and attacks made by him in the period from 1822 to 1827 was the Jew by origin Vasily Dobrovolsky. He was baptized in 1822 in the church of the small town Zinkov of the Letichev district. After that he married the daughter of a nobleman Chernelevsky in village Letechintsy of New Letychiv district, and lived there in a rented house. In February 1823, he was convicted together with Ustim Karmelyuk and imprisoned in the Letichev prison. Dobrovolsky's imprisonment lasted until early 1826, when his was amnestied by the highest manifesto. Subsequently, by the agreement with landowner Staroripinsky, he became the owner of the tavern, which belonged to the village Khodaky Letychiv district. Karmelyuk, upon returning from penal servitude in the second half of 1826, finds Dobrovolsky and they turn the tavern in Khodaky into their headquarters, where new attacks were planned and the loot was hidden. Besides, Karmelyuk falls in love with Dobrovolsky's wife. On June 17, 1827, Dobrovolsky with Karmelyuk were captured in village Kal'nya. On February 29, 1828, the high court in Podolia passed a final sentence, according to which Dobrovolsky publicly received 50 lashes from the executioner in Lityn, was branded and exiled to penal servitude, from where he did not return. He was 30 years old at the time of his arrest in 1827.

The Jews of Bar also helped U. Karmelyuk. Thus, in the Karmelyuk case of 1827-1828, a Jew from Bar of Mogilev district, a townsman Aron Shmulevich Klebansky, was wanted.The scale of involvement of the Jewish population of Podolia in the Karmelyuk case is evidenced by the following generalized data. As accomplices, 405 peasants together with the gentry and 205 Jews were involved in the investigation in 22 villages and 9 towns of Lityn, Letychev, Proskurov and Vinnytsia districts. According to the Polish historian of the 19th century, I. Rolle (perhaps they relate to the early 30s of the

19th century), the proportion of Jews in the total number brought for complicity in the Karmelyuk case was even higher: out of the 618 accused were 5 noblemen, 309 peasants and 304 Jews.

A noticeable trace remained in the national memory of the Jews of Podolia in the form of a certain folklore heritage. In particular, according to the Rolle, it is known that in the 19th century itinerant Jewish klezmers performed the dance Mazurka, which was called "Karmelyuk".

In 1909 in the storage of Museum of Antiquities in shtetl Kamenetz-Podolsky was found an embroidered portrait of Karmelyuk, which belonged to a lady from Bar who personally knew the rebel from Podolia.

In 1653 Bar became the residence of B. Khmelnytsky. Here the Hetman received, through his messenger, l. Kapusta letter from the Russian Tsar, which said that he " took a strong hand in Ukraine."

The town of Bar was called the "key" to the Eastern Podolia. With the annexation of the right-bank Ukraine to Russia, Bar in 1793 became part of its Bratslav governorate, and in 1797 became a provincial town of Mogilev district in Podolia province. Bar was also the center of one of the 4 police districts (states) of the county.

In 1793, Bar became a Russian possession. From 1793 to 1796 Bar is a main district town of Podolia province. According to the revision of 1797, in there were only 9982 people, out of them 5773 were Jews.

The tumultuous events of 1648-1659, as well as the Polish-Turkish war of 1672-1699, led to the destruction of the town and the fortress. The castle lost its strategic importance and was never rebuilt.

In 1997 in France the Ukrainian historian Ya. Matviyishin found Bar's plan of the second half of the 17th century, made by an unknown French military engineer, who was in the service of the Polish king during the Polish-Turkish war. This plan was called "a true, accurate and orthographic plan of the town and castle of Bar." Here are depicted: the town, which has already been destroyed (A) and the castle with modern fortifications (B); fortification of the town (C); the dam, about 6 km long and 0.8 km wide (D); water mills; dam (on the pond); two bridges on dam (N); Kamenetz and Polish roads (T); Polish Gates; forests; ruins of the settlement of Polish Tatars (D). In the plan, the North is at the bottom. Bar was considered by the Turks as an important fortress in the central Podolia. This plan was sent by French ambassador Charles Marie Francois Olier, marquis de Nointel in a dispatch to king Louis XIV of France from Istanbul on 28 January 1678.

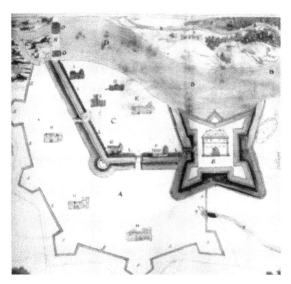

*A true, accurate, and orthographic plan of
the town and castle of Bar, 1677.*

Bar saw dramatic changes in the socio-economic development of the town in the second half of the 19th century. In 1880 the population was 8,277 inhabitants. Since 1880, the steam-water mill began to work, the reconstruction of the distillery took place. In 1892, 11 other large enterprises were added:

1. Soap factory. Founded in 1886. Belonged to Aron Borukhovich Khariton, petty bourgeois from Bar.

2. Tannery. Founded in 1892. Belonged to Aron Moshkovich Moreynis, petty bourgeois from Bar.

3. Tannery. Founded in 1858. Belonged to Leyb Friedman, petty bourgeois from Bar.

4. Tannery. Founded in 1846. Belonged to Moyshe Gilman, petty bourgeois from Bar.

5. Honey factory. Founded in 1879. Belonged to Pesya Shamshonovna Levitova, petty bourgeois lady from Bar.

6. Honey factory. Founded in 1866. Belonged to Sheyndl Lipovna Kiperman, petty bourgeois lady from Bar.

7. Brick factory. Founded in 1840. Belonged to Borukh Rosenblatt, petty bougeois from Bar.

8. Brick factory. Founded in 1840. Belonged to Srul Averbukh, petty bourgeois from Bar.

9. Brick factory. Founded in 1850. Belonged to Gershko Felberg, petty bourgeois from Bar.

10. Brick factory. Founded in 1876. Belonged to Sheyna Seltzer, petty bourgeois lady from Bar.

11. Water roller mill. Built in 1884. Rented by Yankel Katz, merchant.

Bar gradually turned into an industrial town with a developed social infrastructure. The further rise of the town's economy was facilitated by the commissioning in August 1892 of the railway Zhmerinka - Mogilev-Podolsky, on which the station Bar was built (6 km from the town).

At first the railway track did not to go through Bar. Thanks to the maximum efforts of the Chairman of the joint stock company "Barsky sand-refined sugar plant "(as it was called at the time) Ye. Ashkenazi and merchant S. Marants managed to solve the issue of construction of the station near Bar, despite the fact that this track makes a large loop.

In the town there was a large industrial enterprise – the sugar plant that produced the first products in 1900. The development of agriculture required new, more advanced technology, so near the town, in village Luka-Barskaya at the end of the 19th century began to operate a powerful iron foundry. Development of the following crafts continued in Bar: sewing business, black smithing and carpentry-pottery.

Notable steps had taken place in the development of education and culture. Since 1888, the city operated a two-class school (now the building of the Greek Catholic Church). In 1906, the real school (now school No. 4) was opened, in 1911 — a private gymnasium for girls (now school No. 2). On April 7, 1899, the opening of the town public library, which was maintained at the expense of the town, took place.

In the early 20th century Bar was a town of contrasts. On the one hand it was a developed industrial place, and on the other - crooked unsealed streets with very poor lighting. In the spring, when the snow fell, they had a drooping appearance and turned into mud. Water logging of the lowland and the town was caused by a dam on the river Rov, which raised the water level by 1.5 - 2 m. As early as 1861, the writer A.Svidnitsky (originally from Podolia in the magazine "Basis" wrote:

"Barskaya dam - a common dam in the town of Bar. It is very long, goes in curves and in the spring is filled with mud that it is very difficult to go on it and even dangerous. In the summer, potholes are promoted, and it is really necessary to ask God for salvation from this dam."

In 1911, the population of Bar was 22,620 inhabitants, the confessional composition:

Jews - 10,450 (46.2%), Orthodox and old believers - 9052 (40%), Roman Catholics - 3106 (13.7%).

Bolshevik-Soviet power in the town was finally established on June 24, 1920 and the territory started to belong to the Ukrainian SSR, which on December 30, 1922 "United" with the three Soviet republics in the USSR.

Immediately after the end of the civil war, the persecution of people suspected by the Bolshevik regime began. Industry and agriculture also began to be restored. Alcohol and sugar factories are being reconstructed, a machine-building plant is being built, new enterprises are being opened: brick factories, a bakery, a clothing factory, a power plant, a machine and tractor station. In 1925, a mechanical college was opened. The Jewish population of the city in 1926 was 5,720 (55%).

In 1938, Bar was classified as a city.

Geographically, the town is located in the South-West of Ukraine, on the Podol hill, on the Ukrainian crystal shield in the forest-steppe zone on the river Rov, in its middle course. Its length along the river bank is 5 kilometers.

The most dynamic period of development of the town fell on 1970-1980 and was associated with the strategic project REV - construction of gas pipelines "Soyuz" (Orenburg-Western border, 26 billion cubic meters / year), commissioned in 1979, " Urengoy-Uzhgorod"(28 billion cubic meters / year), which was completed in 1983 and "Progress" (Yamburg-Western border, 26 billion cubic meters/year), commissioned in 1988. All pipes have a diameter of 56 inches (1420 mm). Specialists from the German Democratic Republic, Czechoslovakia and other countries that were to become gas consumers took part in the development of the town. During this period, the town developed at an unprecedented pace, perhaps since the time of Queen Bona. A gas compressor station and a gas outlet from the main highway to Bar (total on the Ukrainian section 9 stations). The reliable control system in Bar LVU MG "Cherkassytransgaz" was created on March 24, 1978.

But, since 1993, active de-industrialization, liquidation of large enterprises of food industry which the city was saturated with, was carried out. This managed economic collapse significantly improved the ecology of the area.

The town of Bar is going through hard times in its development. But still there is hope that the glory of the glorious town will be restored, because here live good, decent people of different nationalities, who are not indifferent to the fate of the town. But it will probably take many more years.

The main historical and chronological events in the life of Bar that make it possible to understand the conditions in which the population of the town, including the Jewish, lived:

- 1240 - the ancient Russian settlement of Rov, burned by the Mongol-Tatars of Batu Khan.
- 1362 - defeat of Tatars by Lithuanians near the river Syni Vody, Podolia fells under the reign of Lithuanian princes.
- 1401 – Rov becomes the property of A.Rovsky (the certificate was issued.
- 1434 - Poland captured Rov.
- 1452 - Tatars devastated the town.
- 1456 - Rov becomes the property of S. Odrovonzha.
- 1537 - Polish queen Bona Sforza bought town.
- 1540 - completed the construction of the fortress, the town received its current name Bar and the Magdeburg right.
- 1558 - Tatars destroyed the town and fortress.
- 1565 - 1576 - construction of a stone fortress
- 1594 - the uprising under the leadership of S. Nalyvaiko, Bar and the fortress were captured.
- 1616 - Jesuits settled in the town and opened a Collegium (school) in 1635.
- 1630 - de Beauplan fortifies the fortress.
- 1648 - Bar is a residence of Hetman Konetspolsky.
- 1648 - beginning of the liberation war under the leadership of M. Krivonos, the town has a population of 5200 inhabitants.
- 1649 - again the town was owned by Poles.
- 1651 - the town is captured by the Cossack Colonel I. Glukh.
- 1653 - Bar is a residence of B. Khmelnitsky, here he received a letter from the Russian Tsar on the reunification of Ukraine with Russia.
- 1654 - after Pereyaslav Council Bar remains under the power of Poland 1672-1699 - Bar is under the Turkish rule.
- 1702 - liberation of Bar with rebellious Cossacks and peasants under the leadership of S. Paliy.
- 1703 - again invasion of Polish magnates.
- 1757 - town has 1,500 inhabitants.
- 1768 - established Bar Confederation.

- 1772 - defeat of Confederation.

- 1793 - Bar under the rule of the Russian Empire.

- 1822-1835 - Ustim Karmelyuk's activities in the area.

- 1880 - steam mill was built.

- 1883 - Bar has 13580 inhabitants, of them 58% - were Jews.

- 1892 - the Duma in Bar was established.

- 1900 - a sugar factory was built.

- 1905-1917 - revolutionary events swept Bar, the town's Duma was overthrown and the power of the Soviet authority was established.

- 1918 - troops from the imperial Germany occupy Bar.

- 1919 - 1st Bogunsky regiment under leadership of Nikolay Schors liberated the town.

- 1920 - Petlyuras' military and the Poles were exiled from the town, the civil war ended.

- 1923 - Bar becomes a district center.

- 1929 - agricultural cartel "Jewish agriculturist" was organized.

- 1932 - the machine-building plant began to operate.

- 1936 - power plant was built.

- 1937 - water supply was built.

- 1941-1944 - Bar was occupied by Hitler's troops.

- March 25, 1944 - town of Bar was liberated from the Nazi occupiers.

After the liberation, the town began its restoration and construction of new facilities.

Modern view of the entrance to Bar from Vinnytsia

The modern coat of arms of Bar depicts the contours of the fortress

Modern view of the entrance to Bar from Kamenetz-Podolsky

1980's view of Bar from above

The   following   are   some   photographs   of   Bar   in   the   18th-19th   centuries:

Map of Podolia province, 19th century

Bar's fortress outside the town center

View of the fortress from the river Ditch, author Napoleon Orda, writer, musician, artist, researcher Podolia, 1850

Fortress wall remnants, 1900

Fortress remains, Western part, 1930

Fortress ruins, early 20th century

Entrance to the town through the dam, 19th century

Castle entrance, 19th Century

General view of the town, 1900

The town's entrance gate, 18th century

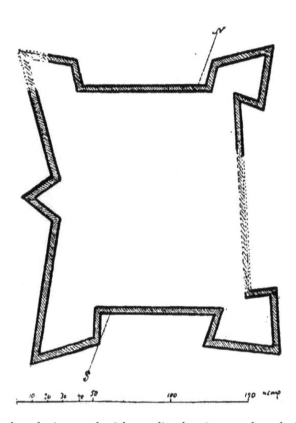

Fortress plan designated with cardinal points and scale in meters

FROM THE DEPTHS OF HISTORY

The ashes of Jewish places, overgrown with sagebrush, silently knocking to this day in the heart

The ethnic group of Jews in Ukraine and on the territory of our region belongs to one of the oldest and most numerous, the size of which fluctuated sharply in some historical periods, as well as in forms of settlement: from compact areas to small groups. In the 12th century Ashkenazi Jews from the Southern Germany and Czech Republic resettle in Galicia - Volyn Principality. Eretz Ashkenazi – the territory of Germany was called such once in ancient times, and, accordingly, these Jews were called Ashkenazi. Today there is a hypothesis that the Jews came to the territory of present-day Ukraine through the Balkans and Crimea. The Jews of Kievan Rus were probably free people engaged in trade. Their trade activity is mentioned in the Kiev letter of 10th century - a registered letter issued to Yakov Ben Hanukkah by the Jewish community of Kiev, in which local Jews appeal to other communities with a request to help redeem a person from a debt pit.

Jewish migration continued from Central Europe into the 16th and 17th centuries. Further their resettlement was promoted by three partitions of Poland as a result of which the considerable part of the Jewish population of the Belarusian lands moves to the South of Ukraine, on the right bank of the Ukraine, including Podolia and Volyn.

After the Union of Kreva in 1385, by which Poland was United with Lithuania, Polish feudal lords went to Podolia, together with them the first Jews arrived. The first Jewish artisans settled in 1434 in cities and large villages of Podolia Voivodeship.

The first mention of Jews in Bar dates back to 1537, and the first Jewish settlement - to 1542, that means the Jewish community of Bar is about 500 years old. In 1542, there were already 145 households, and if we multiply by 6 (this is the average number of people living in one house), we will have 870 people. Already in the 16th century in Bar was a Jewish street (shtetl), by lustration in 1556, so called one of the three streets inside the city walls. It had 34 stone houses. Other streets were called Gorodska (town street), which had 10 stone houses and Kostelnaya, where 24 stone houses were located.

In the Polish part of Bar as of March 1, 1566 house-owners were Jews: Isaac, Moshko, Israel, Volko and Shloyme, and on the Jewish street – Tsimlya, Zhivachina, Manko, Khavka, Faybish, Sablika, Moshechko, Noelchko, Yudka, Kostsina, Marechko, Biskova, David. This gives us an idea of the names of the Jews, because they did not have surnames at that time. Each house paid a tax of 15 pennies (hroshy).

The famous "Kiev letter", 10th century.

SHTETL

What was a shtetl? This is such a small town in the city. Shtetl - "Jewish town", the important small world with small houses, invisible stalls, narrow streets and noisy market. Shtetl was poor. Its voice was always heard – an old "Singer" tapped out characteristic sounds, there was a creak of a dray, timpani of tinsmiths, sounds of shoemakers. The aromas, the aromas... Saturday-Shabbat!

In terms of outward simplicity and modesty, the deep meaning and philosophy of the meaning of life, love, joy and celebration was hidden here. It was a hymn to goodness and humanity, despite the oppression and suffering. Here, on this earth, a religious trend of Judaism, Hasidism, was created. Here, in shtetl Medzhybizh, preached his doctrine legendary Israel Baal Shem Tov ("Master of the Good Name" - from Hebrew), (BESHT is the acronym). Here, in Zolochiv, Shargorod, Uman, Chernobyl, and Bar lived the famous tzadiks - the righteous of this world, whose main concern was the bright souls of believers. In Bar lived a disciple of BESHT and one of the first members of his community Rav Menachem-Mendel (?-1765), there also lived David Leykes, Zeev Wolf, Shmarel Verkhivker and student of Dove-Ber from Mezhyrich Rabbi Zalich, it was so called Chevra Hasidim. The literature in Hebrew of Chaim Nachman Bialik and Shaul Chernikhovsky, literature in Yiddish of Mendele Moykher Sforim, Sholem Aleichem and Yitzhak Peretz was created here. The list goes on... We must preserve this unique history of our people, the history of shtetl. Let's listen to the voices of its inhabitants and feel them: the all-pervading prayer, the tender lullaby, the Sabbath blessing and the merry wedding melody, the sounds of the violin and the unsteady choir of the cheder boys. Here are the wise grandfather Haim's eyes and the boy Motl's mischievous eyes, the attentive parental gaze and the mother's eyes full of love and anxiety, the sly and beautiful eyes of Esther. And this is our Jewish Bar. Although there is nothing left of shtetl in the town, it lives in each of us, in memory, in old family albums, in memories and behavior, words, jokes, gestures... Here's what you could hear in a Bar in Yiddish: *dry viber zitsn oyfn shtein. Eine zugt: "yo", di andere zugt: "Nein", di drite zugt: "fun vanen iz gekomen, ayn zols gein!* The translation is: "Three women sit on stones, one says, 'Yes,' the second, 'No,' and the third, ' where these diseases came from, let them return.' This was the whole shtetl. The Jews built houses (shtiblach) in the shtetl at the crossroads of the roads that led to the market, to the county, to the church. In addition to the inns, hostels, there were stalls (keitlah). Skillful hands and talented heads responded to all requests. The shtetl was a socio-ethnic-cultural group, which merged with the external environment in a single ecological unit. It was also in Bar, the center of which was where the bus station and the surrounding area is now located. It was an independent town - Jewish Street, which was based on the idea of an independent town in the city. The heart of shtetl is a synagogue, the lungs are a fair, the brain is religiosity. In shtetl all the houses were built with their faces to the street, because everyone wanted to have access there, so that they could place their shops or workshops, and the cost of land was high. When children, grandchildren married, from the rear to the house was attached a small room.

There were no street names in the little shtetls. The indicators were houses that belonged to different dynasties, by occupation. Everyone in town knew each other, but sometimes one of the newcomers asked for an address. To the question: "Where does Chaim the shoemaker live?" they used to answer:" Do you know where the seamstress Dvoyra lives? It's across the street."

Jewish housing developed with families, 18ᵗʰ -19ᵗʰ centuries

But the Jews did not live by bread alone. There was a Moishe-Rabeinu and Aron-ha-Koen, that is, a spiritual pastor, a teacher for children (Melamed), a synagogue, a cemetery, a market, shoikhet Reb Simche. Here were their batlounim – people with certain disabilities, have kaptsunim – poor, for which collected tsdoku (alms). There was such a Rabbi Srul, who was famous constantly for his saying: "Ven ich valt geveyn zayn azoy klig aynt, vie main veib morgen." It is translated: "If I could be as smart today as my wife is tomorrow."

A shtetl is a concept without which it is impossible to understand the life of Jews in Eastern Europe. The word shtetl evokes a thousand images, each of which is essentially an expression of Jewish life. The rhythm of life in shtetl was dictated by Jewish traditions. The Jewish community of Bar grew from the second half of the 16ᵗʰ century to the first half of the 17ᵗʰ century.

The largest shtetls of Podolia province

In 1556, a special treaty between the townspeople and the local Jews took place. Here is how it is described in the Jewish encyclopedia of Brockhaus and Efron: "by virtue of this agreement, the latter are permitted to continue to save for themselves the number of houses they owned. Jews undertook to pay the town obedience, and in the wartime to give 1 horse from each house. Instead of it, Jews were provided to use the rights, privileges common to all citizens; they were not allowed to accept strange Jews to live in their residences. For violation of the agreement, the guilty party paid to a magistrate a penalty in the amount of 10 marks. The agreement was confirmed on 11 December 1556. King Sigizmund at the General Sejm in Warsaw, and as representatives of the Jews were present Abraham Koshka and Cheya". In 1556, there were 17 Jewish houses out of 107 in Bar; by 1570-1571 there were 23 houses.

In 1648, the Jewish community of Bar consisted of 600 families, but this year there was an uprising against the Polish yoke which was supported by ataman M. Krivonos. The cities and towns of Podiolia and Bratslav area, which were at the epicenter of the Cossack war of 1648-1654, were repeatedly plundered and destroyed by the Cossack-peasant detachments of Krivonos and Nechay. For Jewish communities, these years were a disaster. Colonel Krivonos captured the town of Bar and the fortress. During this period, more than two thousand Jews were killed in Bar.

In the South Russian chronicle (Belozersky publishing house) it is written: "Krivonos, Khmelnitsky adviser, claimed there were more than 15 thousand of Lyakhov and Jews in Bar". However, in Nathan Hanover's book *The Bottomless Pit* (1653) it is stated that at that time there were only 600 families in Bar. However, in the same book "Tit ha-Yeven" there is an indication that "they were killed along with other Jews who sought refuge in Bar, in the total number of dead was 15 thousand." This figure may be exaggerated, but given the fact that to Bar, where the fortress was well fortified, Jewish communities were fleeing from Vinnytsia, Tulchin, Mogilev-Podolia, Shargorod and the surrounding towns, it may correspond to reality. Three years later, in 1651, Cossacks and Tatars on the way to Zboriv burned and destroyed Bar, while beating Jews and Poles. Thus, according to the census of Podolia, which was conducted by the Polish authorities during the temporary cessation of hostilities, in 1661 there were only a few Jewish houses in Bar and Medzhybish. At the end of 1661 Bar had only 20 Jewish homes. In lustration of Bar's old age, there are number of names of Jews who paid from each house 15 pennies (15 hroshey) a year to magistracy. In 1662, the number of Jews paying the poll tax was 16.

SYNAGOGUE

"And they will build me a sanctuary that I May dwell among them."
(Shmot 25: 8)

Now back to the structure of the shtetl. Its heart was a synagogue. Synagogue from the Greek, "house of assembly", but its main purpose is to gather for prayer. However, in the Talmud only once the synagogue is called "Beit Tfila", that is, the house of prayer. From the distant depths of history to our times it is called Beit Knesset - house of assembly. The functions of the synagogue are much broader. At the synagogue there was a school (cheder), where children studied the Torah. There also were meetings and celebrations of Bar Mitzvah, Brit-Mila, redemption of the firstborn, as well as a rabbinical court and much more that needed the Jewish community of the town. The synagogues were completely autonomous. Any group of Jews could organize a synagogue. Each synagogue was independent and governed by an elected government. But the ordinances of the Rabbi of the community were binding on all members of these communities, although the style of some rites may have been different.

I will briefly focus on cheder. This is an elementary school where children were taught. Jews, teaching and educating their children, primarily cared about their religious education, which consisted in the study of the Torah, Talmud and other religious books. It was for this that they held cheder at their own expense. Training was conducted in Hebrew, because all the Holy books were written in Hebrew, and the Jews spoke Yiddish. Hebrew was considered a sacred language, so every Jew studied this language.

Here the boys studied all day, studying the Torah, the Talmud, all the commandments of the Jewish people in the cramped and stuffy rooms, reading each his own and all together aloud. This general noise was included in the proverbs (noise, as in cheder), sometimes only broke through the sleepy voice of the teacher - Melamed.

Secular subjects were studied in cheder beginning in the 19th century. On November 13, 1844, the Minister of Public Education issued a decree "on the establishment of special schools for the education of Jewish youth", which specified the creation of cheders of the first category (a type of parish school) and second category (a type of County school). A rabbinical commission issued certificates for the right to create cheders in Bar and in surrounding towns. In 1852, the state demanded that cheders begin to teach the Russian language and arithmetic. Bar contained several cheders of the first and second categories in accordance with the Emperor decreeing an allowance of one school per 30 houses. Both cheder and yeshiva were located in the synagogue annexes. These extensions were built on all sides except the East. They were called "kloyzi", later "kloizami", and became known as the Hasidic synagogues.

Jewish children study in cheder

During the Polish-Lithuanian Commonwealth, the construction of the synagogue required the permission of the bishop. In 1717, the Bar's Jewish community contributed 100 thalers to the construction of the Roman Catholic Church and received permission to build a new large synagogue in Bar.

The Bishop of Kamenetz outlined his requirements for the construction of the synagogue. From Polish:

We agreed to preserve and tolerate the Jewish community at the newly built Bar's synagogue. Jews should recognize themselves in all their affairs and actions subordinated to the Christian population. By no means to express disrespect even to the most insignificant of Christians, as well as in relation to the faith of the Roman Catholic or Slavic.

The synagogue should be neither higher nor richer than the parish, and only what is permitted by the Bible can be placed in it. On great holidays, do not open neither windows, nor doors of houses and dwellings and do not leave them on the market during divine service or other Catholic processions. Do not sell vegetables, bread, guns, gunpowder or other things to Turks or Tatars, and do not to help them in any other way. Exclude Christians and Christian women from services.

On Sunday and other Christian holidays, vodka, smoking, cooking with beer and honey, and other work are prohibited.

This is the decree of the Church of the Lord. So that no one is not justified by ignorance of this post, the Jewish community should send its student to the chaplain of the Church for information regarding Christian holidays.

The threat of losing the right to the synagogue will serve as a guarantee of the implementation of the above regulations.

For this permission they took a hundred broken thalers donated by the Jews to build a church in Bar.

A large stone synagogue in the Polish Baroque style was built in the center of the town (the current territory of the bus station). Baroque pediments were used in the compositions of the Western and Eastern facades of Bar's synagogue. They were built in the form of a fancy spinning wheel. It was called "the great synagogue." Stone synagogues have always shown the strength of the Jewish community. And Bar was one of the oldest and strongest communities at the time.

Bar was the second center of Jewish religious teaching after Medzhybizh.

At that time Abraham Ben Baruch of Zamist was the rabbi in the 18th century. He was a famous Talmudist, a scientist. Abraham Ben Baruch was the author of the biblical commentary almost to the entire Bible - "Bederech Alshech", printed in 1727.

Jewish communities were proud of the achievements of their Talmudists. In Medzhybizh lived Yosel Sirkis (1561-1640), whose notes in the Talmud are included in most modern editions.

Also at that time, Rabbi Abraham Meir and Rabbi Nachman Halevi gave an interpretation of the Talmud in the book "Bederch Alshech".

In addition to the great synagogue, 5 smaller synagogues operated in Bar.

Since 1881, the Rabbi at Bar has been Sholem Muterperil. In 1920-1935 the rabbis were David Zaidman and Barlbarlach Zeidi, these were the last rabbis in the life of the Jewish community of Bar. In 1935, the Soviet authorities closed the synagogue and no longer allowed it to open. The closure of the synagogue was held under the slogan - "religion is the opium for the people." And also, the reasons for closing of the temple could be different: the room under club, a warehouse, a kindergarten and other is necessary. And all this was carried out under the well-known expression: "at the request of the working people." In Bar the closing of the synagogues took place "at the request of the believers themselves", so it was stated in the decree of the local government. They were converted into apartments, because there was no free housing in the town.

In the 1930s, during a campaign to close the synagogues, an active participant in the event, Yakov Samoilovich , collected all the Torah scrolls and carried them with pathos to the attic of the house on Lenin Street, 4 (now Soborna Street). Previously, there were some classes of the Jewish school and one of the synagogues (from the memoirs of S. Dunaevich).

At the closed door there is a silence on the clock. As before, the Jew doesn't come to yearn at the foot of the Torah at a late time. And praying benches are waiting for prayers for a long time in vain.

- wrote the poet M. Svetlov in his poems.

The rabbis Zaydman and Barlbarlach were executed by the Nazis on 19 August 1942 in the tract near the village Guyove.

The great synagogue was destroyed during World War II. As an inhabitant of Bar Nahum Anopolsky told, a barrel with gasoline was brought there and it was set on fire by shutsmany, and the occupants dismantled the metal figured fence for their needs, for fencing of birch crosses on graves of the killed fascists. Thus ended the existence of the great synagogue in the town of Bar. Only the photos of this structure are left. M. Svetlov has these words in his poem "Poems about the Rabbi" – "and in a bright fire, the synagogue asked for mercy from G-O-D".

The Ukrainian scholar P. Zholtovsky was engaged in the study of the synagogues in Podolia. He was in the town of Bar in October 1930; thanks to him the remains of the synagogue were preserved.

It was believed that the synagogue in the holiness was second only to the Temple, and it was called "mikdash katan" - "small sanctuary." After the destruction of the Jerusalem Temple, the synagogues became the main source of preservation of the Jewish tradition. It was the spiritual and cultural center of the community.

The period from 1580 to 1648 was called the "Golden" years of Podolia Jewry. Some economic growth and development of self-government gave impetus to the development of national traditions and culture. It was a period of rapid construction of synagogues.

The construction of synagogues was regulated by certain rules: it should not have been higher than a Roman Catholic Church or a Protestant Church, but inside the premises should always have been high and bright, with a balcony for women. The synagogues were still to be a defensive building, and therefore were built on a high place so that they could observe the approach of the enemy.

The synagogue's modern look makes it an architectural monument in Sharhorod. Funds are currently being raised to restore it.

The synagogue in Sataniv Khmelnytsky until its restoration in the early 21st century

Modern view from above of the restored synagogue in Sataniv

Such were the synagogues. In Shargorod, a synagogue had survived to our times, but needs restoration (built in 1589). The oldest Ukraine's synagogue located in Sataniv was restored with the efforts of many sponsors. The year of its construction is 1514 (according to other sources - 1532).

In Kopaihorod the synagogue was built in the 19th century in the center of the town. After its closure in 1930s, a bakery was lately placed there. At present time, the building is destroyed. Jews do not live in this town.

The sides of the world also had a certain importance in the construction of the synagogue, because the inner view of the Jew from inside of the synagogue was always to the East, towards Jerusalem, from where the Messiah was to come. On the Eastern side of the synagogue was the cabinet of Aron Kodesh, where the Torah was kept. Above the Aron Kodesh was a text where it was written in Hebrew "in the East the sun rises" and then "from the East to the West the name of G-d is glorified." These are the words from the Torah.

The synagogue began with the waiting room, people gathered there and they discussed certain events of life, there the Rabbi met with his assistants and various gatherings took place.

The central place in the synagogue was occupied by a Torah scroll. They kept the Torah in a special place, a Torah ark, Aron Kodesh. To the right or to the left of Aron Kodesh there was the menorah. This is a special seven-branched candelabrum, which was constantly burned in Jerusalem's Temple. The menorah in the synagogue is a reminder of the events that took place in the Temple in those distant times.

In Bar's synagogue directly in front of Aron Kodesh stood two wooden carved pillars with three-dimensional figures of seahorses on top. The whole Aron Kodesh was carved, the cabinet doors were closed by a curtain of cloth on which were Jewish symbols from the Torah.

Stylistically, this "living" portal was solved in a single connection with tectonics and carving and was an example of the deep emotional power of love for one's God.

The women in the synagogue prayed separately from the men in a special room. A balcony was set aside for them, sometimes a side or rear trailer.

The staff of the synagogue was as follows: Rabbi, Chazan, Shamash, Gabay, Cohen.

Shamash is a person who looks after the order, cleanliness, safety of property in the synagogue. Sometimes he served as a Torah reader.

Gabay or Parnassus is a community leader who deals with financial and administrative matters. Usually, there are several gabays in the synagogue.

The Cohanims are the priests of Israel, descendants of Aaron - the high priest on the paternal side, so the Cohen could only be the son of Cohen. During the time of Temple, besides performing the main function – to lead the service in there - the Cohanim were also the spiritual mentors of the Jews, their teachers. In our times, the Cohanim continue to fulfill only part of the prohibitions that are specified in the Torah for them. So, Cohen has no right to go to the cemetery. For them in front of the cemetery were built special premises at a certain height so that they can observe, a Cohen has no right to go into the premises where there is a dead man, as well as to marry a divorced woman. In our time, their duty is to conduct the ablution of the firstborn and the blessing of the people.

Chazan is a cantor, a person who conducts prayers, which is very important in the life of Jews. The Chazan leads the prayers in the Sabbath and holidays. Requirements for the Chazan: he must be polite, honest, clearly know the laws of the Torah and fulfill them, have a good voice, be an educated person, understand the meaning of prayers.

Cantorial singing was very important in the life of the shtetl. This can be seen in the example of creativity Sholem Aleichem in his works: "Yosele-Nightingale", "Motl the boy", "Twinkling stars". Sholem Aleichem was a great connoisseur of cantor chants, as he told in his stories. If the famous cantor – guest performer was visiting the shtetl, the synagogue was filled with people.

Probably, a cantor-chazan also was in Bar, but nothing is known about it.

In addition to the synagogue in Bar, there was a kloyz for believers in Hasidism. After all, there lived a student of the BESHT Menachem Mendel and Rabbi Zalich, who preached Hasidism. There was also a shul for Orthodox Jews.

Each house of worship was a separate religious community. Here for example, some of those that were in the city: "Mezhyrivs'ky prayer house", the Jewish religious community "of Enteles", "Snaidershis" and others. All of them existed in the early 1930s until they were closed by the Soviet government.

The rich and the poor had different synagogues. And it is the great synagogue that does not have to be for the rich. Usually the rich built a small synagogue for themselves, leaving the poor a large one. So it was in Bar, where the first synagogue was stone and was used by the majority of the community.

The German traveler Ulrich von Werdum visited Bar at the end of the 17th century after the town was destroyed. On August 23, 1671 he recorded in his diary that there was a synagogue near the dilapidated town hall (in the area of Polish Bar), which was fully destroyed, leaving only the pieces of masonry with Jewish symbols, and only a small synagogue was in town.

Jews in Poland and Ukraine could not hide their synagogues. Therefore, the synagogue was one of the best buildings in the city. A Jewish school (cheder) was closing in on them. An example of such a building could be a synagogue in the city of Vinnytsia.

*The main synagogue in Vinnytsia near the
Central market, 19th century*

Melamed (teacher) conducts classes in the cheder at the synagogue

Inside the synagogue was a large painted prayer hall, instead of the ceiling – was a dome, at the base – a quadrangular, which then goes into the octagonal. The dome was painted with the zodiacal signs of the Jewish months. This is clearly seen in the photos of Bar's synagogue. The painting of the synagogue was carried out with glue paints in living, major tones. There were floral ornaments, various iconographic plots.

Also on the walls you can see paintings on the history of Babylon, Jerusalem and so on. The decoration of the synagogue was carried out by famous Jewish artists who were invited to perform these works, or there were local artists who performed all this as well as the famous ones. During the construction of Bar's synagogue, Isaac Leib Ben Yehuda Ha-Cohen from Yaryshev decorated with picturesque images many synagogues in Podolia. Perhaps it was he who created the inner world of the synagogue in Bar. Zholtovsky pointed out that the walls of the synagogue were original in content and style of painting.

*Fragments of the painting of the walls and ceiling
in Bar's synagogue, 1930*

Bar synagogue, West facade. 18th century

Bar synagogue, main facade, 18th century

View of Aron-Kodesh in the synagogue, Bar, 18th century

View of the prayer hall with a large Chanukah
menorah in Bar's synagogue. 18th century

In 1904, there were 168 active synagogues in Podolia, including 6 in the town of Bar. Jews in Bar led an active religious life, some of them were Hasidim.

There are no remains of the great synagogue house in Bar, there is only one building left where there was a shul (small synagogue), but now it is rebuilt and people live there. It is located on street Marat (now it is called street Shpakovich).

The road from the synagogue to the cemetery was such an invisible axis, on which the traditional institutions of the town were strung, and this is a bath - mikvah, a room for ritual and hygienic body washing, a Jewish hospital, which also served as a shelter for children and elders, and more.

The mikvahs of pious rabbis and tzadiks had a healing effect. Many pilgrims from Podolia and Volhynia came, for example, to Berdichev to dive into the water of the mikvah of Tzadik Lieber and cure eye diseases.

In Bar, the mikvah was closed along with the closure of the synagogue in the 1930s.

Top view of an ancient mikvah, 12th century

Bar in 1942. The synagogue is missing, destroyed by the Germans

Since 2001 and until now Shaul Horowitz is the Rabbi of Vinnytsia and Vinnytsia region, he represents the Orthodox Hasidic direction of Judaism. If necessary, he visits the Jewish communities of the region. He was in the town of Bar. Shaul Horowitz created Vinnytsya regional Jewish religious community "Beys Menachem Lubavitch Vinnytsia", which includes the Jewish community of Bar.

Although there is no synagogue in Bar, it lives in the memory of the Jews. Through eyelids she looks at everyone with tenderness and care, she meets newborns, brings up and lets out in life, helps not to stray from a vital way, not to be lost in a whirlpool of events and reminds of who you are, where you came from and where you go. The number of centuries has not destroyed her. Perhaps she, while seeing how few of her children remained in this once large Jewish town, as a mother, will shelter those who remained and, most important – will wait, that someday a flamboyant and turbulent life will return here. The synagogue is always protected by Heaven.

CEMETERY

The cemetery was one of the shtetl's public institutions. The place for the cemetery was chosen on the edge of the city, behind some natural barrier. The cemetery is one of the holiest places in style. No Jew allowed himself to sit on a tombstone or to block the passage to the grave.

The Jewish name of the cemetery is "House of Life." It had a deep philosophical meaning. And to this day, people go to the graves of the tzadiks, and to the deceased relatives, in search of a way out of difficult situations, go for advice, for help, go for the wisdom of the ages. Tsadik Rabbi Leib Yehuda ben Yosef (also called Leib Sarah's) from Rivne is buried in village Yaltushkiv of Bar area. Over his grave is built a small chapel ("ohel" in Hebrew), where Jews can come and worship him and leave their requests.

Stone urn with requests from visitors to the grave of Leib Sarah's

Rabbi Leib ben Sarah (1730-1791) was a famous Hasidic figure of the second half of the 18th century. In folk legends, he is an all-knowing tzadik who traveled around Poland, Volhynia, Podolia. Always helped the poor, did wonderful feats, fought with the powerful of this world.

With a special prayer, the Jew must enter the cemetery and with a prayer he must leave it. Thus the Jew has to enter through one gate, and to leave through other. Many folk beliefs are connected with the cemetery, everything connected with the ever-existing soul of the deceased is consecrated by ritual.

In those ancient times Jews were buried without a coffin. The body of the deceased was wrapped in a shroud. The shroud should be linen and white colored. It was considered offensive to expose the body of the deceased to public view, so the entire body and face of the deceased were covered. The dead man should lie in the grave facing East (to Jerusalem). It was customary to wash hands before exiting from a cemetery, but not to wipe them with a piece of cloth. Close relatives tore the edges of the clothes they wore. There was no wake. Returning from the cemetery, neighbors and distant relatives brought relatives of the deceased "a meal of sympathy."

During mourning, all mirrors were covered with rags or pieces of clothes, candles were lit, and they burned day and night. The mourning (so called "shiva" from Hebrew "sheva" – which means number 7) lasted seven days. It was not allowed to work during this period and not leave the house. The greetings and words of goodbye weren't allowed to use. All 7 days the prayers were said. Close relatives weren't allowed to wash, shave or cut hair during shiva. Everybody in the house sat on a low bench or on the floor.

Deceased were buried, and after, visited without flowers or wreaths, only a small stone was placed on the grave. Leaving flowers is not a traditional Jewish custom. A tradition that is widely held is to place a small stone on the grave with the left hand, even on the grave of one whom visitors have never known. This shows that someone visited the site of the grave and is a form of care for it. In biblical times Jews did not use tombstones, and graves were designated with mounds of stones, so by placing them or moving them, they perpetuate the existence of the burial place.

There is a legend about why stones are brought to the graves. Rabbi Kalonimus, who is buried in the Jewish cemetery at the foot of Mount of Olives, near the grave of the prophet Zechariah, miraculously saved the Jews of Jerusalem from the consequences of a bloody attack. Arabs killed one of their children and dumped the body in the courtyard of the synagogue. This happened on Shabbat, but Rabbi Kalonymus deliberately went to the violation. He wrote one of the Holy Names of God on a piece of parchment and placed it on the forehead of the murdered child. A formidable crowd of Arabs gathered around, ready to commit pogrom. And suddenly a miracle happened. The boy stood up and silently pointed to his real killer. The Jews were saved. However, the Rabbi himself rendered a verdict for the violation of the Sabbath. He ordered that after his death, anyone who passed near his grave should throw a stone at it. But the grateful Jews in their own way fulfilled the instructions of the sage and his savior. Coming to the cemetery, they carefully put the stone on the pile of other stones that have accumulated on the tombstone. Thus arose the custom of laying a stone on a Jewish grave and was adopted by the entire diaspora.

A corner of the cemetery was used to hide holy books that had become unusable. Once a year or every two years, books were buried with certain prayers. A special place was allocated for the burial of women who died in childbirth. Such a death was considered the highest level of holiness, that is, a woman gave her life, but brought new life into this world. Dead rabbis were often buried in separate tombs. Men and women were buried separately, that is, there was a row for the burial of women and a row for the burial of men, which alternated, or separate quarters were allocated.

The Jews had made the traditional visit to the cemetery (Kever Avot – in Hebrew) during the month Elul before the start of Rosh ha-Shanah (new year). During this period, the Jews visited the graves of relatives, friends, tzadiks and asked for health, and good for themselves and their families in the new year. Favorable days for visiting the cemetery were considered Monday and Thursday. Headstones (matsevot) were with epitaphs in Hebrew. The Bar cemetery had burials from 16th -19th centuries.

While visiting Bar in 1671, Ulrich von Werdum wrote that in the town there is a separate Jewish cemetery, it is located to the North of Bar, opposite the castle. Here was part of the overthrown Jewish tombstones.

The cemetery's "highland" location had mystical powers: heavy climbing is thought to prevent the living from seeking to get to the cemetery of God-appointed time.

There is also a pragmatic aspect. The community bought a plot of land from the landowner under the cemetery at its own expense. "Mountain Land" that is unsuitable for building or farming was the cheapest.

Now there is nothing left of that cemetery: a multi-story house was built on that place during the Soviet times.

House built over ancient Jewish cemetery from 16th-19th centuries

Germans from the GDR, who built the international gas pipeline, refused to build a multi-story apartment building on the site of the cemetery. Regardless, it was built. The land, along with parts of bones, was taken out from the Jewish cemetery for filling of the square on Memory Square and for construction of the road on Kotsyubinsky street.

The Jews installed the commemorative plague on the house, it says: "The holy place. House of life (cemetery) of the holy community of Bar". In the center of the cemetery in the ohel buried tzadik David Ben Israel Leykes, a disciple of Baal Shem Tov, who died in 1791. Also buried here in 1746 Rabbi Zeev Wolf, near the grave of Rabbi David Leykes, a friend of the Rabbi Shmarel Verkhivker." And then the text of the memorial prayer – Hebrew translation.

Commemorative plaques remind us of the old Jewish cemetery

The venerable disciple of BESHT in Bar, David Leykes, in the community held the position of Chairman of the Beys-Din (rabbinical court), which spoke of his education, intelligence. He was called "muflag" – outstanding, excellent knowledge of the Torah and for such qualities as joy and hope in God.

Rabbi David Leykes was loved for his great cheerfulness, prayers brought him to euphoria and criticism he always turned into a song. He was survived by his wife, four sons and three daughters. In mourning of his wife and lonely, Rabbi David Leykes met his 74th anniversary. On this day he said: "To give praise to God, you must live, and to live, you must enjoy life, enjoy life in spite of life itself." Cried the Rabbi David Leykes only once: on the day of the death of his teacher the Baal Shem Tov.

He later married again to the landlady of the inn. She bore him three sons and a daughter.

Rabbi David Leykes was father-in-law of Rabbi Mordechai of Chernobyl, his grandchildren – the tzadiks of the Chernobyl dynasty of Tverskys from the towns

Makariv, Turiysk, Talne, Skvyra. He was already more than a hundred years old and, while lying on his deathbed, heard in a neighboring room judicial disputes and said: "Why did you leave me alone? All my life I have helped God in his work below. Has the time come to dismiss me?" And he listened to the witnesses, pointed out the contradictions in their testimony, and delivered a just verdict.

Later, with an enlightened face, he uttered his last words: "Behold, I leave one court to stand before another." He died on 21 Nisan (26 April) 1799 year, at the age of 113 years, as was born in 1686 year. Rabbi David bequeathed to his descendants that in the year when the end of the month of Elul falls on Wednesday, if one of his descendants comes to his grave, then everything that he will ask at the grave, he will receive it. And when you consider that only one of his children – his daughter Feiga, was the "mother" for the five Hasidic dynasties, it is difficult to count all his possible descendants.

Her childrens names are : Nahum Tversky, Sheindel Tverskaya, Yitzhak Tversky (Itzik Skvirer), Chana Khaya Tverskaya, Abraham Tversky, Johim Tversky (Khune of Rotmistrovka), David Tversky.

Meyer Leykes and Moshe Aryeh Leyb Leykes, sons of David Leykes, were rabbis.

I would like to recall the Jewish wisdom of D. Leykes: "*Sometimes the holiness is just an evil temptation.*" Once David Leykes asked Hasidim of his son-in-law, Rabbi Motel from Chernobyl, who went to meet him up, when he came into the town: "*Who are you?*". He was answered: "*We Hasidim of the Rabbi of Chernobyl Motel*". Then David asked: "*Is there a true faith in the teacher?*" Hasidim did not answer, because who dares to say that his faith is true. "*I will tell you,*" said the Rabbi, " *what faith is. One Saturday, as was often the case, the third meal at the Baal Shem Tov's house lasted until late in the evening. Afterwards, we blessed the meal standing up, immediately recited the evening prayer, made Havdalah for and sat down to the meal which ends Sabbath. All of us were poor and there was not a penny in us, especially on Saturday. But when after the meal the saint Baal Shem Tov said to me: "David, give me a honey drink!" and I put my hand in my pocket, though I knew it was nothing there, and found a gold coin, which I gave for the honey-drink.*" That's the story.

The followers of the rabbi want to build a chapel on the place where he was buried - it is such a small chapel. But for several years there have been contradictions between the local authorities, the Jewish community and the residents of the house where the ohel is to be built. And these contradictions are not solved yet.

The cemetery of the late 19th century and up to the 40s of the 20th century was destroyed during World War II. Its remains are still preserved until this day. Nearby is a modern cemetery where funerals take place. It is supported by the local community at its expense. After all, the local government does not want to take care of the cemetery, they believe that this cemetery is used for burial of non-residents of Bar, but God is their judge.

In the minds of people this or another shtetl is associated primarily with the name of the famous rabbi or tzadik who lived there, his tomb gave holiness to the town. In the mind of the people it was thought that graves of righteous people protect the town from various cataclysms. In this regard, it was thought that shtetl Medzhybizh survived from pogroms and epidemics.

The grave of Malkele Tzadekayte, dated in 1773, is located in Kopaihorod's old cemetery from 17th-19th century. This grave is visited by Hasidim from different countries, they consider Malkele a righteous woman. Malkele was a contemporary of the Baal Shem Tov and one of the late followers of the Rabbi. When there was a misfortune or sickness, the Jews came to the tomb of Malkele and asked her to help because they believed in its power.

Malkele's grave is well-groomed, the thickness of the stone is 21 cm and the top shape of the grave a triangle. It's a very rare occasion of such grave's form.

Malkele's grave, Kopaihorod

Tombstones (matzevot) were established a year after the burial. Almost all gravestones, since the 17th century, were made in the form of a portal (vertical plate) - a kind of gate to the other world. This compositional scheme survived until the early 20th century. The text on the matzevah was created by one of the children of the deceased. In this text it was mentioned where the deceased was from, his occupation, and sometimes - a historical event that took place when a person died, and the date of death; photos of the deceased person as were not installed. For many centuries, matzevot retained their original simplicity. Only later, during the Renaissance period, matzevah gains other features, becomes the object of artistic creation. Professional stone carvers created true works of art. The carved drawings expressed the features of the deceased, associated with his religious and ancestral affiliation, sex, age, reproduced biblical scenes, images of animals, which were associated with the name written on the stone. There were personal signs that determined the vocation of the deceased, profession, traits of his character.

In the 19th century, the technique of making pillars was influenced by the artisans called from Italy by the land owners of Podolia. These stonemasons worked in the village Dzyhivka (now a village of Yampolsky district) and together with local craftsmen made monuments, crosses, Church ornaments for the needs of the Catholic and Orthodox clergy, gentry, wealthy peasants. Also they carried out the orders of Jewish merchants for matzevot.

Different in size, thickness and quality, matsevot were decorated with a combination of symbolic composition and text. All the monuments had epitaphs.

Later matzevot were covered with images of animals, birds, plants, objects of the real world, attributes of craft and life. In some tombstones of the 16th -17th centuries there is an image of the two-headed eagle. Such an image is found on the graves of rabbis. The heads of the eagle, turned in different directions, signify the two qualities of the Creator, through which he rules the world. That idea is that opposite phenomena have a single beginning - the Almighty, who punishes and pardons. In general, matzevah were small, simple, with a Magen David (from Hebrew "Star of David"). Such burials were typical for poor communities of the 19th century and the first half of the 20th century. Matzevot of this period had a characteristic feature - the image of the star of David (Magen David) – a recognizable Jewish symbol. Sometimes Magen David also was on old matzevot, which meant such a talisman, which protected the soul of the deceased from evil spirits. In ancient times the symbol of the Jews was the menorah, its image was on most of the matzevot.

Magen David as a symbol, began to be used only in the late 19th century with the development of the Zionist movement.

Jewish stone carver

Star of David (Magen David)

From the 19th century the Star of David is considered a Jewish symbol. Even in ancient times, many people used a six-pointed star as a decorative element and perhaps, a mystical symbol. But most often it was used by the ancient Jews mainly on the household items. The oldest such known image was found in Sidon (city in Lebanon) - it was the seal dated from the 7th century BC, which belonged to Yehoshua Ben

Yeshayahu. During the Second Temple period, the hexagram, along with the five-pointed star, adorned a variety of objects and buildings, both Jewish and non-Jewish. An example is the synagogue in Kfar-Nahum, in the ornament of which pentagonal and hexagonal stars are alternated, as well as cross-shaped figures with broken ends (resembling a swastika). However, in the era of Hellenism, Magen David (from Hebrew "Shield of David") in Jewish symbolism was not used. A thousand years ago, the hexagonal star was an international sign. It was found on early Christian amulets and in Muslim ornaments called the Seal of Solomon. But already in the 13th-14th centuries Magen David appears on the pediments of German synagogues and on Jewish manuscripts, although this time it was only as a decorative element, without any symbolic meaning. In the same era they began to decorate amulets and mezuzot. And in the late middle ages Jewish texts in Kabbalah also were decorated with Magen David. The term "Magen David" refers to the Babylonian Gaon era. He is mentioned as legendary "the shield of King David" in the text on the magical "alphabet of the angel Metatron". This interpretation is widely accepted among Ashkenazi communities. The grandson of RaMBaN wrote about the hexagonal "Shield of David" in his work on Kabbalah (14th century). It was claimed that the shield of this form was used by the soldiers of the victorious army of King David. However, his personal seal contained the image, not stars, and a shepherd's staff and a bag. And the Royal seal of Shlomo (Solomon), son of David, had the form of a five-pointed star. In 14th-18th centuries Magen David was widely used by Jewish and non-Jewish printers and is often found on family coats. In 1354, Charles IV granted the Jews of Prague the right to have their own flag - a red flag with the image of a six-pointed star. Magen David also decorated the official seal of the community. During the 17th and 18th centuries, this sign was adopted by the Jews of Moravia and Austria, and then - Italy and the Netherlands. A little later it spread among the communities of Eastern Europe. In Kabalistic circles, the "Shield of David" was interpreted as the "shield of the son of David", that is, Mashiach (a literal translation from Hebrew, means "Messiah"). In the 19th century emancipated Jews chose the Magen David as a national symbol as opposed to the Christian cross. It was during this period that the six-pointed star was adopted by almost all communities of the Jewish world. It began to appear on the buildings of synagogues and Jewish institutions, on monuments and tombstones, on seals and forms of documents, on household and religious objects. Since 1799 Magen David was first used as a specific Jewish symbol in anti-Semitic cartoons. In 1822 the Rothschild family received a noble title and included Magen David in their family coat of arms. In 1840 poet Heinrich Heine began to put this sign instead of a signature under his articles in the German newspaper "Augsburger Algemeine Zeitung". The first Zionist Congress in 1897 adopted the six-pointed star as a symbol of the Jewish national movement, in the same year it graced the cover of the first issue of the magazine "Di Welt", published by Theodor Herzl. Over time, Magen David appeared on the state blue and white flag of Israel, though the more authentic and ancient Jewish emblem, Menorah, the image of temple light, was chosen as the coat of arms. For religious Jews Magen David also has a generalized meaning. There is a tradition to decorate with it a sukkah - a tent in which Jews live during the festival of Sukkot. The six ends of the star, which is hung in sukkah, correspond to the six exalted "guests" who visit each Jewish sukkah in the first six days of the feast of Sukkot: Abraham, Isaac, Jacob, Moses, Aaron and Josef. And unites them all the seventh "guest" - King David. Another detail is that Magen David has 12 Vav (a letter from Hebrew alphabet), which correspond to the 12 tribes of Israel over which David reigned. Kabbalists also say that the six ends of the star correspond to the six spatial directions - earth, sky, North, South, East, West - which means the omnipotence of God. A curious linguistic detail: in Hebrew, the words Magen David also consist of six letters. There are numerous interpretations of the symbolic meaning of the Star of David, both traditional and relatively new, including those proposed in the 20th century. Hexagram is interpreted as the Union and coincidence of male (triangle with "broad shoulders", directed top to bottom) and female (triangle, directed bottom to top) essence. In ancient times, it was believed that Magen David represents all four basic principles: a triangle pointing up symbolizes fire and air, while another triangle pointing down symbolizes water and earth. According to another version, the upper corner of the triangle, directed upwards, symbolizes fire, the other two (left and right) - water and air. The angles of the other triangle, which are directed to the bottom, respectively: mercy, peace (tranquility), grace. According to another interpretation, the six-pointed star symbolizes the Divine control of the whole world: the earth, the sky and the four cardinal points. Magen David is also treated as a combination of the heavenly principle, which directed to the earth and the earthly principle, which is directed to the heavens. According to the interpretation of Rabbi Eliyahu Essas, this sign symbolizes the 6 days of creation and reflects the model of creation. Two triangles – two directions. A triangle pointed upwards: the top point indicates the Supreme and that he is the only one. Further branching of this point to the left and to the right indicates opposites-Good and Evil. The tip of the second triangle is directed downwards. From two remote from each other vertices of the lines converge to the bottom of the third. Essas considers the second triangle as a symbol of the purpose of human existence in uniting the ideas of the "right" and "left" sides of the created world.

As it turned out, this star contains all 24 letters of the Hebrew alphabet, there is no such thing in any other language.

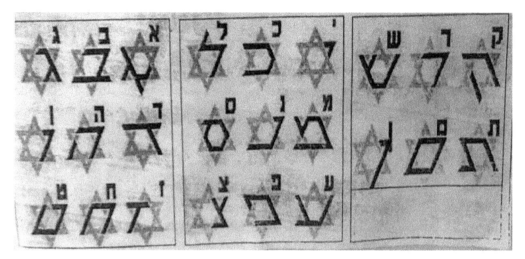

Display of Hebrew letters on the star of David

But back to the description of matzevah. As already noted, the image of a person on the matzevah is absent, but where its presence was assumed, the artist shows only the hand, or replaces the image of a person with a certain motif of an animal or a bird. Yes, there is a drawing on the stone: a lion pouring the water from the pitcher - symbolizes a person was from the tribe of Levi.

There are drawings on the matsevot showing the human virtues of the deceased. A stork pecking a viper indicates that the good of the deceased overcame his flaws, and a squirrel gnawing a nut - a sign of knowledge. Many other stories can be found on the matzevah.

In this regard, the most interesting in Podolia is the old Jewish cemetery in town Sataniv. Everyone should visit it. Because if Sataniv is a town-museum, the old necropolis is also a unique open-air art gallery. A lot to be said on the symbolism of Jewish graves of Sataniv, but this is a separate topic, which has been studied and is being studied by scientists from the St. Petersburg and Kiev institutes of Judaica.

There are burials from 16th- 18th centuries, which have survived to our times.

There is a matzevah in the center of which there is a pentagram, and it is located at the cemetery in the village Murovani Kurylivtsi in Vinnytsia region . In the same village's cemetery, next to it is another matzevah, but with the usual five-pointed star, and not far from that there is the traditional matzevah with the image of a hammer and sickle. These burials belong to the 1930s. This probably does not exist anywhere in the world. Perhaps the five-pointed star, hammer and sickle on matzevot played the role of a talisman. Only they had to protect not the dead, but the living. It was a period of repressions in the country. And this Communist symbolism on matzevah is a public display of loyalty and an attempt to distract possible repressions from themselves and their relatives. On the photo, a clearly visible matzevot with a five-pointed star, on the other photo - matzevah with the embossed hammer and sickle.

The epitaphs on matzevot deserve special attention. Short-spoken, usually consists of the name and the name of the father (without last name), one or two laudatory epithets, the literal date of death (according to the Jewish calendar) and the permanent five signs of the abbreviation of the posthumous wishes in Hebrew

"ת נ צ ב ה " which means "may his/her soul be bound by in the bond of eternal life".

Many grayer, time-laced and moss-covered matzevot await the study and writing of their history. In Bar no such burials of the 16th- 19th centuries have survived.

Matsevot in the Jewish cemetery in the village Murovani Kurylivtsi

MARKET

Markets and fairs periodically took place in the town of Bar. The market was the center of town's life. The market and shopping areas in Bar were located where the bus station is now. It was the organizing center of the town and near its houses, visiting yards were built. Here, to the shopping center of the town, approached the streets that began from the town gates. The presence of fortifications and market were the main difference between the town and the village. To confirm the status of the town, it was necessary to organize fairs. At first there were five such fairs a year in Bar. Permission for their conduct was issued by the Polish magistrate. Fairs were not necessarily held in the market square, because it could not accommodate everyone.

The fairground in Bar was where the stadium is now located, and the market square was a separate place. Trades were held every Friday and Sunday.

The market square in Bar was a striking example of classic style. There were one- and two-story purpose-built tenements (houses with internal courtyards inside), decorated with pediments, pilasters, cornices, rooms are covered with arches with tense arches.

Later, in Bar in 19th and in the early 20th centuries, were held twelve fairs per year, 26 market days were held on Thursdays, and 52 selling days were on Sundays. The duration of the fairs varied from a few days to a week.

Peasants from the surrounding villages, as well as from other cities, came here to the fair. Some wanted to buy, others to sell. The Jews prepared for market day in their own way. Tailors to this day prepared everything for fittings, ironed ready-made suits, trousers, shirts, blouses and other goods. Shoemakers were ready to display boots to prepare for new orders. All artisans and hand crafters waited on their clients to establish business relationships. The Jews knew how to trade, it was profitable for buyers to buy goods and products from them for the simple reason that no one could sell them cheaper than the Jews.

A classic of Jewish literature, Sholem Aleichem, traveling to Podolia, may have been in Bar. In the story "Motle, Peysi the Cantor's son" described a market day in the town:

"Today is market day in the town... Jews run to and fro like poisoned rats, make noise, get lost, pull peasants by the floors, beg, so they want to bargain something - just a theater with them! And the peasants have time, they move along, hats pulled down on their foreheads, examine, feel, itch, bargain, want to buy cheaper... The most interesting is the horse market. They buy and sell horses there. There you can see horses, Gypsies, whips, Jews, peasants and landowners. The noise here is inhuman - one can go deaf. The Gypsies swear, the Jews strike their hands, the gentlemen clap their whips, and the horses run to and fro like arrows.

Retail space in Bar, late 19th - early 20th centuries

Market lane

VILLAGE COMMUNITY LIFE

The essence of the Jewish community is best shown by societies or groups (chevrot). All positions here were elective, for members did not pay money, but everyone wanted to be elected in some commission because every resident wanted to take part in public life. Elections were held annually on the third day of Passover and in some communities - on Sukkot. Societies were of different types. Some were for helping the poor, others were engaged in burials, there were groups that were engaged in hospitals, shelters for the homeless and so on. A special group was engaged in the redemption of prisoners, in the 15-18th century redeemed them mainly from the Tatars. There were trade and sanitary departments, which monitored the observance of weights and measures, the cleanliness of streets and wells, the observance of the technology of production of products according to the Jewish laws on kashrut. These departments supervised the slaughter of animals, poultry and meat sales.

There also were societies that were organized for a professional basis. They were shoemakers, dressmakers, butchers, milkmen, etc. Each craft had their own society and engaged in the crafts of the Jews in the shtetl.

There were also special interest groups. Yes, there were groups who studied the Mishnah, or who recited the Tehilim. In every synagogue there was a "brotherhood of wise men", members of which after morning and evening prayers tutored others.

Regulation of each society was recorded in "pinkases" – a special book, where important events of the society were reflected in addition to the articles of the society.

In each shtetl the chief pinkas was, of course, the pinkas of the community. It recorded all the dates of birth and death of people, as well as all the historical events of the community. This book was very important for the Jews, it was considered the second holiest after the Torah. A usual custom: if a woman had a difficult delivery of her baby, then, a pinkas was laid under her head, so that what was written in this book, eased a woman to give birth to a child.

Book of the synagogue (pinkas community) of Bar was preserved for the period 1839-1848 and is located in the state archive of Khmelnitsky region.

But there are also pinkas of separate groups of the Jewish community of Bar, which is located in the National library of Ukraine of V. Vernadsky and they are written in Hebrew and partly Yiddish; pinkas of mohalim for 1775-1795; pinkas of reception for 1844-1883; pinkas of people studying the Mishnah for 1825-1849.

The study of the pinkas was conducted by the historian and archaeologist Ilya Galant and the result was published in 1929, "the pinkas of the chevra kadisha in the town of Bar" in proceedings of the Jewish historical-archaeological Commission of VUAN."

This material is very important in the historical plan of the modern understanding of the Jewish life in Bar in 19th century as even the graveyard of this period was destroyed.

The whole life of the community was led by kahal– it is such a special autonomous organization. Kahal was in every town where there was a presence of the Jewish community. It was responsible to the authorities and to the Christian population of all members of the Jewish community. The kahal paid taxes. So, in 1765 it was recorded that 579 Polish zlotys were collected from the Jews of Bar, and for equality of Jews with citizens 1000 zlotys for a year must be paid. Kahal presided over the litigation of Jew against Jew and regulated the entire internal life of the community. Kahal took care of everything: it controlled the synagogue, conserved and supplied the religious books, took care of sick people and of the cemetery. Every problem, every situation that needed to be solved, was solved by kahal.

At the head of each community stood foremen - from three to five people, that is, as the town council. They alone were responsible to the authorities and after the elections they swore a loyalty to the king and the Commonwealth. These elders alternated among themselves and each month one of them became the head of the community. It was called - parnassus, or parnassus ha-hodesh, that is, the director for a month.

Foreman of a kahal was the owner and leader of the community during his reign. He made the budget, paid kahal's taxes, approved the lists of families who were allowed to live in the town, and much more.

When taking office, the foreman swore that he would strictly adhere to the kahal charter and would not allow himself to cause losses to the society.

The spiritual leader of the community was a Rabbi. Assistant Rabbi was a public preacher, who on Saturdays read and explained the scriptures. At the synagogue there was a public cantor, there were butchers (shoichets), there was a scribe of the Jewish court, there were various officials who served the school, synagogue, cemetery, court and other institutions of the community.

All these people were paid. Doctors, apothecaries, community midwives, barbers, people who cared for the homeless in the shelter - received a certain income from the community.

The community had special authorized persons – shtadlans, who had a good command of the Polish language, were translators between members of the Jewish community and Christians and Catholics.

Having the right to settle only in certain places, deprived of the right to have land, Jews engaged in small trade, monetary transactions, rented estates, kept taverns and engaged in handicrafts. There were potters, tailors, shoemakers, coopers, millers, carpenters, weavers, furriers, blacksmiths, cart makers, bookbinders, jewelers, masons and people of other professions. In 1566 in Bar there were 13 Jewish shoemakers.

Jewish shoemakers at work

Before World War I, one of the most famous potters of Podolia and puppeteer was Jacob Batsutsa from the village of Adamivka from Vinkovtsy district. His spherical jars, painted with interesting ornaments, figures of people and animals, were bought even by merchants from Austria and France. His clay toys were in high demand. They even were sold in St.Petersburg, Moscow, Vienna and Paris. He did not forget about the local Podolia market.

One of the popular figures was a traditional goat from shtetl, which was in great demand among Jewish children.

If mainly Ukrainians were engaged in production of dishes in the 19th-20th centuries in Podolia, then in the 18th - first half of the 19th centuries "small" ceramic forms were made by Jews, such as tobacco pipes. After all, for such a workshop a craftsman did not need a large room – a table was enough. No specific skills were needed, it was enough to buy a few forms and a set of tools for carving decor. Of course, there were tobacco pipes, which were works of art. Besides, a tobacco pipe is a small object. A cupboard was used for drying, whereas a shed was needed for pots. In the narrow Jewish quarters, compactness was an important factor in the development of one's own business.

Toys made by Jacob Batsutsa

Most Jewish families did not own any wagons or horses. They carried on themselves heavy bags with goods and agricultural products, overcoming on foot kilometers between towns and villages, and their big bazaars. When a Jew was asked what he is carrying in the bag behind his back, he jokingly replied: "I carry the Torah!". There was a certain reason for this answer. It was believed that the Torah always helps the Jew.

The leadership of the society, which was called Kli-Kodesh, which literally meant "Holy vessels", lived near the synagogue. They were the Rabbi, shames, shoichet. I will focus on the profession shoichet - a butcher. Shoichet carried out an important ritual of butchering the poultry for the Jews. Usually the bird was cut on Thursday, so that it was already cooked on Shabbat. There was a shop near the shoichet's house where you could sit until the bird was slaughtered, the blood drained after the shhita, then the shoichet would pluck the bird in two tasks in the necessary places, although he could pluck the whole bird at the request. Then people took the bird, hid its head between the wings, wrapped it in a certain napkin and proudly carried it home.

In the pre-war period in the town, there worked as a butcher Sanya Moshe Shekhtman, and spiritual shoichet (butcher) was - Leyzer Goldman, who oversaw the observance of all necessary requirements.

JEWISH HOME

Old houses of the Jews were made of wood - chopped or dilovan. The walls on both sides were plastered with clay. The house was initially built for a family with 1-2 rooms. Because Jewish families were usually large with more than 10 children, new extensions were added as the family grew. The roof of the poor man's house was once covered with straw. After the 18th century, the roof was covered with shingles, which better protected the walls of the house from rain. Thus thanks to shingles some homes survived to this day. Usually the roof jutted out as a kind of canopy over the wall line for 1.5-2 meters and was supported externally by wooden props to form a gallery around the house. Roofs were hipped or gable with a crease. The entrance to the house was placed asymmetrically on the front facade. The entrance and interior doors were double doors. Sometimes there was a second way out. The windows were shuttered.

A mezuzah, attached to the entrance door jamb, was such a talisman. Lord says to Moshe: "Roll up a small piece of parchment paper with the text *Shma Yisrael* and attach it to the doorpost." (Deuteronomy 6:9). The parchment with the text was folded from left to right and put into a protective case. Then it was fastened in a certain order to the door jamb at shoulder level.

Mezuzas are written sequentially in order. This means that if the scribe wrote a word incorrectly, he can't just go back and correct the word. If he does, the corrected word will be written after the words that should follow it. So he has to erase everything that was written before the error and write it all over again. If one of the words to be erased is the name of G-d, the mezuzah cannot be corrected because the name of G-d cannot be erased. Mezuzah with an error that cannot be corrected, becomes psula, i.e. unfit for use and is sent in geniza - a special repository for holy objects (unfit tfilins and old battered sacred books). After that it must be buried in the Jewish cemetery.

Old houses were built in one and a half floors, but there were also two-story wooden ones. They had a low ground floor, sometimes half in the ground, thick walls of clay. The second floor had a very characteristic balcony along the end wall with access to the street. Wooden balcony with stairs, a canopy over the balcony – were an integral feature of the architecture of these houses. In the high basement of the first floor there was a utility room and a basement, the entrance to them was both from the street and from the kitchen of the house, for convenience. Such houses in Bar were not preserved, but they can be seen in the village of Kopaihorod, which is 25 km from Bar.

Brick houses began to appear only in the second half of the 19th century. But by that time many wooden houses were repaired and completed with bricks.

Individual houses had extensions with a removable roof, where a hut was held on the feast of Sukkot, and during the year this extension was used for other needs.

Mezuzah in a Jewish hut

The old house, the forgotten dream, the afternoon light... All as before in order, but nobody is there, the steps are not heard, Got lost footprint in that silence...

Stone building, entrance, Bar. Late 19th century

Jewish house, Bar. 19th century

Stories about life in the shtetl give us the opportunity to see, as through a magic crystal, this wonderful world of Jewish service, the world of devotion to the Almighty.

Waking up in the morning, the Jew glorified God. He wore and covered himself with talit, a white cover with blue stripes around the edges and dangling threads. Then he put a tfilin on his left hand and then a leather box with Holy texts from the Torah on his forehead. This is how the Jewish law was taught, so did the father, grandfather, great-grandfather, so did our ancestors thousands of years ago, and prayed.

To support such large families, it was necessary to work a lot and hard. The vast majority of Jews were artisans, they lived poorly.

World War II, as well as assimilation, virtually destroyed shtetls as a phenomenon. Despite all the hardships that led to the disappearance of shtetl, we have not forgotten about these Jewish towns. They are stored first of all in our memory, in thin lines of traditions which extend to modern Jews of Ukraine, Belarus, Russia - and these are the children, grandsons, great-grandsons of inhabitants of Jewish small towns.

Currently, Jews living according to Jewish laws continue to build synagogues and mikvahs. In large Jewish communities, in addition to the main synagogue there is a small synagogue - kloiz, for Hasidim.

Internally the modern synagogue is the same as it once was in shtet's synagogue, even the service has not changed. Similarly, women, although they are not required by law to do so, continue to find inspiration and comfort in prayer, taking their seats on the balcony of the synagogue – "With G-d's help". And melamed teaches children the same way as it was before, and students in the yeshiva all over the world study the Torah, the Jewish matchmaker still makes his shiduch, and young people, thanks to her, find each other.

Daily reading of the Torah

The Jews are no longer stupid and poor people who lived in shtetl.

We must know our history and culture, preserve and multiply everything that will lead to a thirst for knowledge of our culture.

JEWISH TRADITION

The Jews were distinguished by their peacefulness, sobriety, prudence and erudition. The Jewish tradition has deep spiritual, religious and moral roots. It is important to "define" and "legitimize" the good.

"Mitzvot" are commandments that formulate standards of morality in relation to God, people, even animals. The Tanakh (Bible) contains 613 basic commandments required of the Jews. In one form or another they have also entered into the teachings of Christianity and Islam.

The most important in the universal moral scale are the following commandments: honor the father and mother; do not kill; do not steal; do not cheat; do not envy; give 10% of the annual profits to charity (tzedakah); don't ask the price of the goods if you are not going to buy it (to not mislead the seller, do not give him false hopes); you can't say everything you think even it's true; to talk bad behind a person's back – is a sin; you need to feed all the animals before sitting down yourself at the table; you must rest on the Sabbath; not to hunt for sport (to kill only those animals needed for food and in a humane way); not to rejoice in the defeat of the enemy.

The old saying states: "More than the people of Israel cherish the Sabbath, the Sabbath cherishes the people of Israel."

Shabbat (Saturday) - is the main Jewish holiday, mentioned in the very beginning of the Bible, in the story of the creation of the world. Shabbat - time of peace of man with himself (it is necessary to use internal potential and abilities); with other people (Shabbat gathers a family; day of spiritual communication); with the nature (prohibition of intervention in the nature, ignition of fire, etc.); with God (a day entirely devoted to service to God, prayer, Torah reading, spiritual work).

Kashrut - laws of cleanliness in the household, in particular, rules of identifying usable products, their compatibility and certain features of their culinary processing. It is prohibited to eat blood, i.e.,"treif", in food (blood - is a symbol of life). It is necessary to bleed meat before eating; it is impossible to use the torn off or cut off part from live; milk and meat together ("not to cook a kid in milk of its mother"). It is a division connected with life and death, and milk is the source of life. Judaism proclaims the sanctity of life, (contrary to the cult of death in ancient Egypt). You cannot eat a wounded, dead animal ("do not eat any carrion..."), an animal killed by a blunt instrument (slowly, painfully for her), rodents, insects, reptiles, amphibians, eggs of non-kosher fish and birds.

It is allowed to eat kosher food: meat of animals of ungulates, fish with scales and fins, birds (except of carnivores and those who feed on carrion), bee honey.

I also want to talk about the clothes of the Jews. Jewish costume was formed under the influence of clothing of neighboring peoples, as well as religious norms. Universal features of traditional male costume: wool prayer shawls with tassels (tallit tails, etc.), long robes, cloaks, mandatory head covering on the street and indoors. The traditional Ashkenazi male costume contained a tunic-like shirt, black trousers, boots, a long-skirted kaftan (lapserdak), a black yarmulke bordered with fur (shtreimel).

Jewish holidays and commemorations can be divided into three groups. The first are the biblical holidays: Rosh Hashana - New year, Yom Kippur - judgment day, Sukkot - harvest festival, Simchat Torah - the joy of the Torah, Shabbat - Saturday (day of rest), Pesach or Passover - the holiday of liberation, Shavuot - the holiday of the gift of the Torah. The second group includes holidays with a historical basis: Hanukkah - the holiday of light, Tu BiShvat - the New Year of the Trees, Purim - a cheerful holiday of salvation, Tisha B'Av - a day of mourning. And in the third group — modern holidays and dates, such as Holocaust Remembrance Day and Independence Day of Israel.

Brit-Milah (from Hebrew "covenant of circumcision") is a circumcision ceremony performed on 8th day after birth of a male child. It symbolizes the union of God and Abraham (Abraham - the forefather of Israel, made a circumcision rite to commemorate the promise of God to the land of Canaan for the Jewish people).

Bat mitzvah (from Hebrew meaning *the daughter of commandment*) a Jewish coming of age ritual for girls (in 12 years girl becomes responsible before God for observance precepts).

Bar mitzvah (from Hebrew meaning *the son of commandment*) Jewish coming of age ritual for boys (13 years). It is a big and cheerful holiday. The boy becomes responsible for keeping the wills. He begins to put on tefillin, to make an ascent (aliyah) to the Torah while he reads it. From this moment he can marry (get engaged).

The symbols of traditional culture - lion, Capricorn, star, deer, fish.

What kind of Jewish wedding with klezmer music you could hear then! A variety of dishes: stuffed fish, fried chickens and other delicacies pleased everyone, and the sweet table was always served leykech (biscuit), fludn and strudel.

And what sanctity is given to the ceremony of the beginning of the wedding! The Rabbi, the bridegroom, the bride's representative and the witnesses make up the marriage certificate - ketubah. This is like a modern marriage contract, where the obligations of the groom to the bride are determined.

The ceremony itself is called chuppah. A portable canopy is held by the witnesses, symbolizing the home to be established by the newlyweds, where the bride is brought.

The bride's and groom's parents, the Rabbi and the newlyweds are standing under the chuppah. The ceremony begins with a blessing, then the groom puts the ring on the bride's finger and says: "Here you are dedicated to me with this ring according to the law of Moses and Israel." This is followed by readings from the ketubah, and then the distinguished guests recite the seven blessings. After each of them, the newlyweds drink wine from one glass. And at the end, the groom smashes an empty wine glass wrapped in a cloth. The breaking of the glass holds multiple meanings. First meaning - is the representation of the commitment to stand by one another even in hard times. But the second meaning represents a destruction of the Temple in the Jerusalem. These are the great Jewish weddings that took place in Bar.

The weddings were conducted the same way as they were carried out about 500 years ago, according to the laws of Judaism.

Weddings usually began in the evening and often finished in the morning. All this happened!

I want to tell about the Jewish folk tale. Jews not only told fairy tales, but also began to collect and record them. The oldest of these records was read by the whole world and retells them to this day. Others, such as the numerous Midrash, are less well known. Many magical Jewish fairy tales are devoid of national flavor. They have, as expected, kings and princes, princesses, wizards and even the wicked witch Baba Ha, an obvious relative of the well-known Baba Yaga. However, there are also a number of characters peculiar to Jewish folklore. For example, often in the role of magical assistants appeared not good fairies or grateful animals, but the patriarchs, the prophet Elijah, the secret righteous, sages and Hasidic tzadiks. The Jewish fairy tale is characterized by deduction and moralizing, which are not peculiar to fairy tale at all. So, the hero performs a feat, not seeking the hand of a princess or half a kingdom, but saving the Jewish community from trouble. Sometimes at the end of the tale, the king awards the hero the post of first minister and makes him "second after the king", but the hero also tries to use the royal favor for the benefit of the Jews. It is no secret that the Jews were inherent in those or other professions that put a certain imprint on their lives.

The greatest reflection of traditional Jewish professions found in the names of Jews. Up until the middle of the 19th century the Jews did not have surnames. And when the Russian government began issuing passports, it became a necessity to create surnames, which often were based on the profession.

And so appeared:

- Shoemaker, Sandler, Schuster and Schumacher - shoemaker in Hebrew and Yiddish respectively
- Takar and Toker (Yiddish *Toker*) - Turner
- Reznik, Reznikov, Reznikovich and Katsev (Hebrew *Katsav*) - butcher
- Bronfman, Bronfenmacher (Yiddish *Branfn* - vodka) - vodka producer
- Also, as an option: Vinokur, Guralnik (Ukrainian *guralnik*) - vinokur, also a producer of vodka
- Gamarnik (Yiddish *hamernik*) - in Ukrainian *hamarnia* is a metal smelter, forge, that is, the blacksmith
- Baker, Bekker, Beckerman (German *backer*) - baker
- Tkach, Weber (German *weber*) – weaver
- Mahler (German *maler*) - painter
- Kolesnikov, Kolesnik, Stelmakh (Polish *telmach*) - wheelwright
- Kapelyushnik - (Ukrainian *Kapelyuch*, hat) hat manufacturer
- Kravets, Kravtsov, Portnov, Portnikov, Schneider (Yiddish *Kravets*) – tailor

This is a small list of professions and corresponding surnames.

Surnames were also formed from the place of residence, from appearance, from the names of Jewish holidays, from the position of a person in the religious hierarchy and from other signs.

Jews were virtually excluded from the political life of the country and could not hold high positions in the state, as evidenced by a number of restrictive laws and regulations. Therefore, almost the only opportunity to realize yourself in public life was charity. Charity is one of the basic concepts in the Jewish tradition. Charity was obligatory not only for the believing Jew, but also for everyone who honors traditions and covenants of ancestors. Charity meant a lot in the life of Jewish communities. It became especially noticeable when Jewish industrialists, entrepreneurs and financiers were fully integrated into the social life of the countries of residence, and in Ukraine it became noticeable at the end of the 19th century. It was the time marked by the rapid development of Jewish charity, which had its own characteristics. The specific attitude of the state to the Jews caused a narrowing of the spheres of their self-realization in society. For Jewish charity a characteristic feature was its certain class-providing assistance mainly to representatives of their faith. But there were cases of assistance to non-Jews. Representatives of other nationalities and non-Jewish charitable societies also assisted Jews.

It should be noted that during the World War I, the Jewish community of Bar accepted Jewish refugees from the frontline.

A Bureau of Labor was also set up in Bar to help refugees find work, it was done with the initiative of the regional Bureau of Labor at the Kiev Jewish society of assistance to victims of the war. But local demand did not match supply. Mostly builders, joiners, tailors were looking for work, but the city needed bakers, workers in the sugar, wine factories, shoemakers, woodcutters. Therefore there was a proposal to create Jewish cooperatives to participate in the procurement of uniforms and linen for the needs of the army. These cooperatives worked successfully and provided all possible assistance to the military.

Unfortunately, the change of social order in Ukraine as a result of the victory of the Bolsheviks, who branded charity the definition of "bourgeois", put an end to this striking phenomenon of history. The era of military communism, and then – the victorious socialism, eradicated the very concepts of mercy and compassion.

Through the original religious and ethnic educational institutions - chederim, Talmud Torah, state and private schools, passed thousands and thousands of Jewish children who became famous rabbis, preachers, public figures, writers, artists, journalists, political leaders, many educated people. In Jewish primary schools, despite the assimilation policy of the Tsarist government, the traditions of national education were preserved, the Jewish language and rituals were studied. It should be emphasized that the majority of public initiatives came from the circle of Jewish teachers. It is significant in this regard that by 1910, thanks to the purposeful efforts of the Jewish teachers, almost all the towns of the Podolia province had branches of the "Society for the dissemination of education among the Jews". Particularly noteworthy is the fact that regular lectures of the society were held in specially equipped clubs. Such a branch existed in Bar, where lectures were conducted at full capacity.

The 1897 census provided the first opportunity to establish certain social characteristics of Jews. Thus, among the Jews of Podolia province literate was 124638 persons (33,7%), while among the Russians 44220 people (44,7%), among Ukrainians it was 261143 competent persons (10.7%).

This is only part of a large number of traditions, and commandments, which lived and should live in every Jew.

But there was a period, in the early 19th century, when Tsarist Russia began to restrict the Jews in their national traditions. Thus, in 1804, a Regulation was adopted that Jews must wear secular clothing in gymnasiums, schools, magistrates. The years 1835-1851 were a period of new assimilation of the Jews. Destroyed kahals (Board of the Jewish community); forbade men to wear a beard, side curls; forbade married women to shave their heads and wear a traditional wig. It was forbidden to wear Jewish clothing (Talit or Tales, kippah, fur hats) outside the synagogue.

In 1840, a committee was established to reform Jewish life.

Violators of the law had to pay a fine (tax for wearing traditional clothes). These taxes were paid in 1848 in Podolia: merchant 1st Guild - $ 250 rubles, 2nd Guild - $ 150 rubles, 3rd Guild - $ 100 rubles, commoners – from 50 rubles to 15 rubles depending on the class.

The first Jews who gave up wearing traditional clothes and their traditions were tax farmers. They were engaged in rent and income from estates of the Polish and Russian landowners. These people moved freely around the country and for a long time lived in cities outside the Pale of Settlement. This right was also granted to merchants of all guilds and their clerks since 1848.

The Jewish people are great, different, and their people live in places with different everyday reality, mentality, culture. But, despite all this, we always feel our unity, as if we intuitively perceive the joy and grief of our fellow tribesmen at a distance, and we try to support and help. We understand that thanks to this we will overcome everything, because there is no other option for us.

POGROMS

Everyone needed something…

The first mention of Jewish pogroms refers to the year 1113. From the book *The Tale of Bygone Years* it is known that during the uprising of 1113 the Jewish quarter was defeated. This happened after the death of Prince Svyatopolk. The reasons of revolt could be both political (Jews supported Svjatopolk, and rebels - Monomakh), and economic.

Then to mass murders the Church prompted: "Kiyans plundered Putyatinsky's yard, go on Jews and plunder them".

The famous historian, Professor V. Petrukhin believes that the Jewish pogrom could be the result of a religious conspiracy, allegedly Evstratiy Postnikov was killed by a Jewish employer for refusing to accept Judaism. It was such the legend of those times.

In 1124, there was a large fire in Kiev, which destroyed the Jewish quarter: "and the Jews burned."

In Podolia in the town of Tyvrov in the Jewish cemetery preserved from 1240 tombstone of Shmuel, probably the head of the community, on which the following words are engraved:

"Death follows death. Great is our grief. This monument is erected over the grave of our master; we are left as a flock without a shepherd, the wrath of God has overtaken us...".

This was the year of Batu Khan's invasion of Southwestern Russia, which probably caused pogroms and the death of Jews in those days.

Life in the town was divided into two parts: Jewish and Christian. Therefore, Bar was filled with social, cultural and, most importantly, religious contradictions, which means that they were the scene of bloody clashes, despite the fact that the religious buildings of Jews, Christians, Catholics were not far from each other.

The following fact testify on certain relationships between different faiths in the 17th-18th centuries.

After the turbulent times of the mid-17th century a significant part of the land, which was owned by the Uspenska church in the town, turned into a wasteland. And subsequently these lands were inhabited by Jews. Jewish butchers settled here. The owner of the town at that time Frantsishek Lyubomirsky obliged them to give each year to the rector of the church two stones (stone - a measure of weight about two pounds) of pure fat, which was then used in lamps of the church.

Timofey Latkovsky - the rector of the Uspensky church, according to the decision, transferred to the Jewish community of Bar (kahal) 4000 zlotyh with the obligation to pay annually a certain amount of interest, which were to be used for the repair of the church.

In 1719, the Bishop of the diocese of Kamenets S. Rupnevsky discovered that the land on which the synagogue, which was destroyed at the time, belonged to the church's parish. He demanded that the Jewish community move the synagogue to another location. The Bishop ordered the transfer of 100 zlotyh to the Jews, as if for the land and the transfer of the synagogue.

The Jews in Bar were tactful, tolerant, friendly, with a well-developed sense of humor and self-irony.

Although at different times all the communities in Bar: Jewish, Orthodox, and Catholic had a very difficult time, but the fate of the Jewish fell the most severe tests. Because they are Jews?!

Pogroms and brutality turned life into severe torture. And the only consolation suffering was faith in G-O-D.

After subsequent bloody events, life in the town was hard, but they slowly adjusted.

And again, everyone who entered the synagogue was looking for an answer to the only rhetorical question: "For what?".

In Bar were underground passages which were built, probably, in 14th-16th centuries.

These passages were at a depth of 5-6 meters in solid yellow clay. These dungeons were a shelter from attackers.

The town of Bar, like all Podolia, was the border between the Christian world and Muslim Turkey. The Tatars were constantly harassing residents of Podolia.

The existence of underground passages and exits was kept a great secret. But the system of underground passages was not very large, because in the town there was a fortress that protected from the attacks.

The individual cellars were under every Jewish house, it was then connected to the "underground street", from which may have paved the sidewalks to the castle, or to the river, wetland. And river, forest, wetland began on the settlement.

Whom did they save? We'll never know for sure. This topic has not been studied in the town, because the abyss is rarely manifested.

Experts do not exclude the cult version of the origin of the dungeons, their assumptions are based on the fact that the technology of digging underground passages and caves were the same in all places where they were needed.

This underground passage opened during the construction of the memorial complex on Memory square, 1980s

The entrance to the underground structures, formed near the store "Geese-Swans", Bar, 2012

In June 2012 near the store of the retail chain "Geese-Swans" (now "Grosh") in Memory square there appeared a large hole after heavy rains, collapsing part of the sidewalk.

Since the appearance of Jews in Bar and before the tragic events of August 19 and October 25, 1942, they went through all the circles of hell here. In the 15th-16th centuries, the town was burnt by the Tatars and the Turks who massacred Jews, Ukrainians, and Poles.

During the Cossack wars of the 17th century with the Poles, everyone blamed the Jews. The Cossacks, Haidamaks saw in Jews the offenders, the reason of the troubles.

The Jews were hired by the Poles as managers of their possessions, and they spent more time in Poland, and therefore all considered the Jews oppressors. As mentioned above, after the events of 1648 in Bar, after the census, only 20 Jewish homes remained.

In the spring of 1648, the former Chigirinsky centurion, Bogdan Khmelnitsky gathered around him Zaporozhye Cossacks, who proclaimed him Hetman. Troops under the leadership of Krivonos, Gonta, Morozenko killed Catholics and Jews, destroying both churches and synagogues.

Fearing to stay in villages and shtetls during this period, the Jews fled to the fortified cities, and there they fell into a trap. Thus, there were 600 families in Bar, and with the arrival of Jews there were 15 thousand people. Here were refugees from Mogilev, Verkhivka and other towns. Jewish community of Bar (together with a small detachment of German landsknechts) played an important role in its defense. Despite the desperate resistance of the Poles and Jews, the Cossacks made a tunnel and with the help of the local population captured the city. This happened on July 15, 1648. And the chieftain Krivonos, as it was written in the South-Russian chronicles: "he ripped off all the skin from the Jews".

Let us turn to the description of the battle of Bar in the *History of the Rus' people*: "From Korsun' was sent Khmelnitsky Scribe Krivonos (in summer) with his corps to the town of Bar, which, according to reports, gathered a lot of Poles and Jews, who coincided with Volhynia and Podolia. He, on reaching this town, found it in a defensive state, with a sufficient garrison. The first attempt of Krivonos on the town was repulsed by the garrison and burghers with a great loss of people on both sides. Krivonos, possessing under itself enough artillery, was able with these forces to do the brutal and unexpected attack with flank and with rear sides on citizens and garrison. They, after a short resistance, being shot down and scattered, fled - some with the garrison to the castle, and others took refuge in their homes. The infantry, pursuing the fugitives, followed them to the castle and took possession of it; and then a terrible massacre was committed in the town and the castle, especially over the Jews and their families, of whom not one remained in the town alive, and thrown from the town and buried in one of the reigns of the dead, there are about 15,000. There was Polish military killed and evil leaders of the people, the rest spared and released into Poland; the town was robbed and left under the rule of the local Russian residents with a Cossack garrison."

Here is how these events are described in the Chronicle of Grabianka: "And when Vishnevetsky came to shtetl Rossolivtsy, and heard that Krivonos took on Bar (and there with his army stood Andrew Pototsky, the Hetman's son), as if he and the Cossacks approached the town's gate and saw that it was open (as for Lyah, it was very heavy), stormed into the town, killed all the nobility, took the castle, kept alive only Pototsky, and all the others were run through with a sword, and more than fifteen thousand of the Jews of Bar were killed".

Take from the movie by Jerzy Hoffman "With Fire and Sword" (1999 release)

showing Bar's fortress burning

The chronicle of the "Calamity of the times" says: "the Jews were gathered in one place, tearing off their dresses and leaving them half-naked, they were beaten with sticks until they fell to the ground, then trampled under the hooves of horses and stabbed with spears to make sure that there were no survivors, and again beat those who could not refrain from shouting." According to the chronicle of Samuel Velichko, up to 14,000 people were killed in Bar.

 It was written in "Chronicles Samovidtsa": "Maxim Krivonos, Khmelnitsky close adviser and assistant, by taking town of Bar, cut down all Lyahov in it, except one Pototsky, by taking him alive, and more than 15,000 Jews were beaten."

There is a Cossack large earthen mound on the road Bar – Harmaky. This place is a monument to the events of the battle of Bar, and there is a special sign for the dead rebels.

It must have taken a long time to work together to locate the mass graves of Jews who were destroyed during the capture of Bar, and to erect a memorial on the site reminiscent of these tragic events. The prayers that were recited in synagogues, the prayer houses in Podolia and in other places annually on the day of 20 Sivan, that is, on the day when these tragic events took place, remained a miraculous monument to these bloody events.

These are the two prayers translated by A. Skalkovsky from Yiddish into Russian and published in 1845 in his work *Haidamak Raids on Western Ukraine in the 18th century*. The name of the rabbi from Bar, Moses Ben Ionovich, who was hanged in the town, was mentioned in one of the prayers. Below are photocopies of fragments of Skalkovsky's book with the texts of these prayers.

Молитва Евреевъ, въ память убіенныхъ гайдама-
ками въ Немировѣ и Барѣ ихъ братій.

1647.

———

Говоря о побіеніи Евреевъ гайдамаками, мы
долгомъ сочли присовокупить здѣсь еще одно об-
стоятельство. Несчастные Евреи уже не разъ испы-
тывали подобное пораженіе и подвергались не
разъ подобнымъ безчеловѣчнымъ жестокостямъ.
Всѣмъ извѣстны тиранства и мученія, которымъ
предавали ихъ козаки въ XVII столѣтіи, въ са-
момъ разгарѣ войны ихъ съ Польшею, за незави-
симость Украины. *Остапъ Павлюкъ*, *Морозенко*,
Кривоносъ, *Нечай* и *Пульянъ*, рыцари Запорожскіе
(въ 1640 годахъ), цѣлыя тысячи жертвъ, пре-
дали смерти и пыткамъ въ пылу ненависти своей
къ Полякамъ, Уніятамъ «и всякой нехристи». Въ
Барѣ (Подол. губ.) погибло ихъ до 15,000, въ
Немировѣ столько-же, безъ различія возраста,
пола и состоянія. Младенцы и взрослые, нищіе и
богатые, старцы и женщины — все было обре-
чено смерти. Памятникомъ этихъ кровавыхъ со-
бытій остались молитвы, до сихъ поръ произно-
симыя въ Синагогахъ. 20-ое число мѣсяца Сивоп
($^{17}/_{29}$ Мая), Евреи проводятъ въ строгомъ постѣ,

постъ помилованія, въ память убіенія козаками Немировскаго раввина *Эхіеля Михеля*, замученнаго съ многими тысячами Жидовъ въ 5408 (1647) году. Въ этотъ день во всѣхъ молитвенныхъ своихъ домахъ, Евреи съ воплемъ и завываніями, поютъ гимнъ на сей случай сочиненный въ XVII столѣтіи, котораго содержаніе слѣдующее: [1].

« Молитва за усопшихъ ».

«Господи всемилосердный, сущій въ небесахъ! пріими души мучениковъ, дай имъ насладиться миромъ хотя послѣ смерти! Это души праведныхъ, учителей и пастырей твоего избраннаго народа.

« И вотъ они теперь закланы какъ стадо звѣрей безсловесныхъ; орда проклятыхъ нападаетъ на нихъ, завладѣваетъ ими и заставляетъ ихъ испить всю чашу злополучія.

« Сердца наши раздрались отъ горести, узнавъ, что въ эти несчастные дни, въ эти злопамятныя ночи, погибли отъ меча убійцъ величайшіе изъ нашихъ книжниковъ, толкователей священнаго закона.

«Тѣ, которые день и ночь изучали священный завѣтъ твой, пролили ручьи своей крови; множество учащагося юношества и дѣтей пало отъ ударовъ истребителей. Ихъ стяжанія сдѣлались добычею пламени.

«Глава учителей (раввиновъ), мудрый *Эхіель* палъ, простирая руки свои съ молитвою къ единому Богу; мечь поразилъ главу его и его праведная душа отлетѣла къ Всевышнему.

«Преклонные лѣтами старцы, младенцы у грудей матерей своихъ, напрасными воплями наполняли воздухъ.

«Господь отмститъ за неправду! Священная книга (Библія), Божественный законъ, осквернены руками нечестивыхъ; о нѣтъ! они попраны ихъ ногами!

— «Гдѣ вашъ Богъ? — говорили эти варвары, эти страшилища, — «пусть защититъ онъ васъ». О Господи! взгляни на насъ горѣ и всѣ нечестивые разсѣятся и падутъ какъ плевела изъ колосьевъ.

«О заповѣди! о Святой Завѣтъ! (Библія) прикройтесь рубищемъ! посыпте главу вашу пепломъ! Кто теперь будетъ читать васъ, кто васъ истолкуетъ намъ?

«Излей Милосердный Отче, твои милости на этихъ мучениковъ, да пріютятся они подъ сѣнію твоихъ крыльевъ и да насладятся миромъ, хотя послѣ смерти»!

«Аминь».

Другая Еврейская молитва о томъ-же предметъ'.

1648.

―――――

«Господи милосердный! сущій въ небесахъ, успокой души мучениковъ Немирова, Бердичева, Погребищь, Тульчина, Пулинъ, Бара, Умани, Краснаго и 300 другихъ городовъ Руси (Черм-ной), Украины, Подоліи, Литвы и Волыни. Эти несчастныя жертвы были великіе учители (равви), писатели, просвѣщенные служители Божества, отличные проповѣдники, посвятившіе всю свою жизнь изученію закона. Раввины: *Эхіель Михель*, сынъ Эліазара, *Хаимъ*, сынъ Авраама, *Соломонъ*, сынъ Самуила, *Исаакъ* и *Элеезаръ*, сыновья Эки-зіеля, *Азріель*, сынъ Якова, *Моисей*, сынъ Іона-ѳина, а также раввины *Лазарь, Яковъ, Самсонъ* и другіе благородные мужи погибли! Мущины, жены, дѣвицы, младенцы, всѣ были умерщвлены. Ихъ кровь текла ручьями въ этомъ злосчастномъ 5,409 (1648 отъ Р. X.) году. Эти мученики не хотѣли измѣнить своему закону: «Богъ есть единъ!» восклицали они и пали подъ ножами убійцъ. Раз-бойники не пощадили ни пола, ни возраста, земля

―――――

была усѣяна убіенными; ихъ кровь дымилась какъ ѳиміамъ предъ олтаремъ Всемогущаго!

«О господи милосердый! упокой души му-чениковъ сихъ, награди ихъ за ихъ испытанныя добродѣтели!»

A folk song in Yiddish language was also composed about the Cossack massacre at Bar in 1648. This song was found in the notes of M. Litynsky's, who was the author of a book about the history of the Jews of Podolia. The song was recorded by him in Bar in 1894. It was sung by Jews in Yiddish with sadness and pain for those who died in this massacre. This indicates that even 250 years later the Jews did not forget those bloody events. It was then printed in Yiddish in historical collection *Experienced* under the title *The folk song about the Cossack massacre in Bar in 1648* in 1911, and the transcription of it was printed in German.

Briefly about this song in translation:

"Who of the Jewish children does not know about the Cossack wars, and each of us does not know about the Haidamak revenge? And in those hard times came Krivonos in Bar - Cossack hero, and with him and Lysenko with "good" guys. Setting up a cross at the place where the Jews were killed, among the people who were cut up, he brought more Jews here and said words to his boys and to them. You suffered from cold and hunger, from all sorts of troubles and thirst. Therefore, one must bow down and accept the faith. And the Jews answered Krivonos: "No! Our faith is as clear as the sun. You can cut us, burn us, kill us, and we won't take any other faith." All the Jews died with the name of the Allmighty on their lips. And the place remained empty and wild, though filled with the bones of Jewish victims."

The following are photocopies of the printed fragment "Experienced" with a song recorded by M. Litynsky in Bar.

Документы и сообщенія.

Народная пѣсня о казацкой рѣзнѣ въ Барѣ 1648 г.

Среди бумагъ покойнаго М. Н. Литинскаго (автора книги по исторіи евреевъ въ Подоліи—"קורית פאדאליא„), имѣющихся въ архивѣ „Пережитого“, находится записанная имъ въ гор. Барѣ, Подольской губ., народная пѣсня на разговорно-еврейскомъ языкѣ объ одномъ изъ кровавыхъ эпизодовъ еврейскаго мартиролога въ эпоху возстанія Хмельницкаго—о рѣзнѣ евреевъ въ Барѣ, учиненной въ 1648 г. казацкимъ отрядомъ подъ начальствомъ сподвижника Хмельницкаго, Кривоноса (именуемаго въ пѣснѣ—„Кривно“). Простота тона этой пѣсни и безыскусственность ея формы свидѣтельствуютъ о народномъ характерѣ ея. Записана она Литинскимъ въ 1894 г., съ указаніемъ, что въ то время она еще распѣвалась въ Барѣ. Публикуемъ эту цѣнную въ историческомъ отношеніи пѣсню:

ווער פֿון אונז, יודישע קינדער,
ווייסט נישט פֿון די קאזאקען-מלחמות?
ווער פֿון אונז אידער בעזונדער
ווייסט נישט פֿון די היידאמאקען נקמות?

דענסטמאל אין דער ביטערער צייט
שטעהט אין באר קריווגא דער קאזאקען-העלד,
נעבען איהם ליסענקא מיט די גוטע לייט,
און א צלם האבען זיי אנידערגעשטעלט.

פֿערהאשעכט, מיט צובראכענע גליעדער,
פֿון א וויסטען גרוב, א פֿינסטערע נעסט,
פֿיהרט מען צו אונזערע אונגליקליכע ברידער,
און קריווגא האט זיי מיט די דבורים געמרייסט:

Wer vun uns, jidische Kinder,
Weisst nischt vun die Kasaken - milchomes?
Wer vun uns ajeder besinder
Weisst nischt vun die Haidamaken Nkomes?

Denstmol in der biterer Zait
Steiht in Bar Kriwno der Kasaken-held,
Neben ihm Lissenko mit die gute Lait,
Un a Zeilom hoben sei anidergestelt.

Vercheischecht, mit zubrochene Glieder,
Vun a wisten Grub, a finstere Nest,
Fihrt men zu unsere unglikliche Brider,
Un Kriwno hot sei mit die Dibirim getreist:

„כ'האב שוין געשמועסט מיט אייערע ראשים און גבירים,
רופֿט ער זיך אָן און טהוט דערבײ א לאך,
אצינדערט זאג איך אייך מיינע לעצטע דבורים
פֿאר מיינע לייט און פֿאר אייך:

נעגוג האט איהר און אייער ווייב און קינד
געליטען פֿיעל צרות, הונגער, דאָרשט און קעלט,—
בוקט זיך צום צלם און זייט נישט בלינד,
וועט איהר לעבען גליקליך אויף דער וועלט!"

„שטום דו, רשע, און רעד נישט מעהר א ווארט!
האבען אלע יודען געענטפֿערט אזוי,
טויט אונז בעסער דא אויפֿ'ן אָרט,
אָבער בייטען אונזער אמונה--לא, לא!

אונזער אמונה שיינט ווי די זון,
ס'וועט דיר, רשע, גאָר נישט געראָטען,
קיין אנדער אמונה נעהמען מיר נישט אין זין,
מעגסט אונז האקען און ברענען און בראָטען!"

באלד האט מען געזעהען א שרעקליך בילד,
אויף קידוש השם זענען זיי אלע געשטארבען.
ראָס ארט איז געבליבען פֿוסט און ווילד,
פֿול מיט ביינער פֿונ'ם יודישען קרבן.

„Ch'hob schoin geschmuesst mit aiere Roschim un Gwirim,
Ruft er sich on un thut derbai a Lach,
Azindert sog ich aich maine letzte Dibirim
Var maine Lait un var aich:

Genug hot ihr un aier Waib un Kind
Gelitten viel Zores, Hunger, Dorscht un Kält,
Bukt sich zum Zeilom un sait nischt blind,
Wet ihr leben gliklich auf der Welt!"

„Stumm du, Roscho, un red nischt mehr a Wort!
Hoben alle Juden geentfert asoi,
Teit uns besser do auf'n Ort,
Ober baiten unser Emuno—loi, loi!

Unser Emuno schaint wie die Sünn,
S'wet dir, Roscho, gor nischt geroten,
Kein ander Emuno nehmen mir nischt in Sinn,
Megst uns haken un brenen un broten!"

Bald hot men gesehen a schreklich Bild,
Auf Kidusch Haschem senen sei alle gestorben.
Dos Ort is geblieben pust un wild,
Vull mit Beiner vun'm jidischen Korbon.

Nathan Hanover thus describes the capture of Bar by the troops of Hetman Khmelnytsky:

"The Tartars and the Orthodox completely ruined the camp left by the Poles, seized in it a lot of silver, gold, carts and beautiful horses. And Khmel' went with all his army to seize the fortified towns located in Poland, and some of his men he sent to capture the holy community of Bar, because in this fortified town there was a large concentration of Jews and gentlemen. As the rioters approached the town, the men on the walls began to shoot at them, and the Cossacks were unable to approach the walls; for many days the siege of the city continued. What did the Orthodox citizens do? They made a tunnel, through which the robbers entered the city at night, and began to kill. The Jews and the gentiles fled to the citadel within the town and fortified themselves there; there were no

Orthodox among them. The siege of the citadel lasted many days. Ramparts and towers were erected, and the enemy fired large cannons, called in German Raderbuchsen, until the citadel fell. All the Jews and gentiles who were in the citadel were killed by all the existing forms of killing described above, and their property was plundered. In total, about two thousand souls of Jews were killed in the holy community of Bar. And the robber Khmel' went with his army to the holy community of the capital city of Ostrog."

Very often rich Jews – usurers, escaped from the town just before the pogroms started, and the Jewish peasants paid with their own life for their sins. Women and children became their victims.

According to various chroniclers, the number of Jewish victims in Ukraine in the period 1648-1658 was from 200,000 to 500,000 (at that time the Jewish population in the world was one and a half million).

In fact, B. Khmelnitsky was three centuries ahead of Hitler, physically destroying a fifth of world Jewry.

In the summer of 1649 Khmelnytsky signed with Poland the Zborowski Treaty. According to this treaty, the Polish Kingdom gave back to Cossack Ukraine the territories of Kiev, Chernigov and Bratslav Voivodeships. The agreement stated that Jews could be "neither authorities nor residents in Ukrainian towns where Cossacks have their regiments... And if Jews appear beyond the Dnieper, then Zaporozhye army is allowed to plunder them and send them back to the Dnieper". According to this agreement, town of Bar returns to Poland; the Jewish population gradually returns to the Podolia towns.

According to the register of the Polish census of houses in 1654 - Bar had 64 Jewish households and 81 houses were rented.

In 1662 according to the data, the number of Jews paying tax poll in the town was 16.

In 1667, two Jewish taverns and about ten ordinary houses were exempted from the tax. In 1672, Bar, like other Podolia towns, fell into the Turkish captivity.

During the reign of the Ottoman Empire in Podolia, the number of Jewish populations decreased dramatically. Thus, in 1681 there were no Jews in Bar. According to the description in Bar's district (eyalet) by the Turkish authorities, there were 4 Jewish households: three in Zinkiv (which is currently located in Kamenets-Podolski region) and one in village Popovtsy.

The reason is that the Turks resettled Jews in Turkish towns, and in addition, the Jews fled to other towns and cities.

In the spring of 1686 the Turks left Bar.

In 1700, the main headman of Bar appealed to all subjects who had fled during the war to return to Bar to establish life in the town.

In 1712, the number of Jewish households numbered 16.

With a total of 355 houses in 1736, there were 155 Jewish houses. In 1754, 526 and 218 respectively. Until 1765, more than 1,000 Jews lived in Bar.

This attitude to the Jews was at the time when Ukraine was part of the Russian Empire. Jewish pogroms took place under various far-fetched pretexts, without any reason.

There were Cossacks in Bar, Denikin's troops, white Poles, Petliura's troops, mismatched and diverse gangs, Kotovsky and his cavalry – and everyone wanted something from the Jews.

In February 1768, under the pressure from the Russian government, Polish King Stanislaw Poniatowski signed a treatise on the formal equation of rights with Catholics of Orthodox and Protestant believers. A significant part of the Polish nobility was not satisfied with this treatise. Under the slogan of protecting Catholicism, gentry rights and the liberation of Poland from the influence of the Russian Empire in the town of Podolia, gentry created a Bar Confederation in 1768. The confederates began to torture and plunder the Ukrainian population and Jews.

The conversion of Orthodox Ukrainians into a Catholic faith began.

In 1820's appeared detachments Haydamak (this is a Turkish word - free), also they were called levintsy, opryshky, koliyi (koliyi or ruts, it is the person who carried out the slaughter of animals), hence the name Koliyivshchina.

In Bar the nobles took up arms on 29 February 1768. They called for help from French military advisers, led by General Dumouriez. The pursuit of the Orthodox and Jews turned into open terror.

The impetus for the uprising Koliyivschiny, was the decision of Catherine II to enter on the right bank of the troops to suppress Bar's confederates.

Former Cossack-Zaporozhets M. Zheleznyak called for an uprising against the gentry. Thus began Koliyivshchina, which covered Kiev, Bratslav, Uman, Podolia. The Haidamaks did not spare their enemies: Poles, Jews. Jew who were the governors of lord's estates, money changers and others were killed. They had a hatred of all the rich. In two weeks after the beginning of the revolt, groups of Zheleznyak reached 40,000 rebels.

June 19, 1768 the rebels captured Uman, there was the residence of count Pototski.

Here the haydamaks organized a great pogrom. About 5,000 Poles were killed. The rebels massacred the entire 30,000-strong Jewish population in the town. Rivers of blood flooded the city. The massacre in the town lasted eight days and nights. Haydamaki hung on one branch together a nobleman, a Polish priest and a Jew and made a signature (Pole, Jew and dog - the same faith). By the way, Bar's confederates did the same thing: hung a priest and a Jew on the same tree with similar words.

Fighters for the Christian faith, as the historian Karamzin narrated, cut the stomachs of women, mocked the corpses. This event is known as the "Uman massacre". After the capture of Uman, Zheleznyak sent troops to various regions, including Bar, where the scenes of bloody events also happened.

In May 2018, Ukraine celebrated one of the anniversaries in its history — 250 years since the Cossack-peasant uprising in right-Bank Ukraine. In history, it was called *Koliyivshchyna*, its movers were haydamaks, who opposed the national, social, religious oppression of Ukrainians by the then Polish authorities. As a result of bloody clashes, according to historians, they killed up to 20,000 people: Roman Catholic Poles, Jews and Ukrainian Greek Catholics. In Ukraine, this period is called one of the episodes of the national liberation struggle, and the leaders of koliyivshchina Maxim Zheleznyak and Ivan Gonta - heroes. Opponents abroad have a different opinion. Some Polish historical researchers consider of Zheleznyak and Gonta as "robbers", "traitors", and Jewish scientists - "rioters" and "murderers." Koliyivshchina is referred to as "Uman massacre".

Events of the Koliyivshchina gave a brutal lesson: blood is calling for a new blood, brutality breeds a new brutality. And regardless of whether the blood was fairly shed or not – there is no excuse for cruelty.

After these events, Bar was devastated, the fortress was destroyed and was no longer restored. Therefore, the Polish Sejm in 1774 allowed not to pay crown taxes, the so-called "quarts" and the Jewish poll tax. This circumstance allowed to develop the Jewish population of the town of Bar. According to the Polish record of 1784, the number of Jews in Bar was 596.

Since 1793, Bar was part of the Russian Empire. According to the 1848 revision, the Jewish community of Bar numbered 4,442 people (2,176 men and 2,266 women).

Map of Bar's surrounding villages, 1861-1867

Speaking about the pogroms, it is necessary to recall the term "anti-Semitism". It originated in 1879 in Germany, there was also an "anti-Semitic League" to save from Jewish invasion. Modern anti-Semitism was different in relation to the classical Judaism of past centuries. His thesis: "the Jews - our trouble" began to spread throughout Europe, then reached Russia.

On 27 June 2016, members of The International Alliance (IHRA) gave a working definition of anti-Semitism.

Anti-Semitism is a special attitude towards Jews, which can manifest itself in hatred of them in the form of expressions, or in use of physical violence against Jews or non-Jews, their property, as well as against organizations of Jewish communities and religious sites.

The purpose of this definition, as stated by the Chairman of one of the NATO committees M. Weizmann, the following:

to begin to solve the problem of anti-Semitism, there must be clarity in the terminology. And the adopted working definition contributes to this. It is essential that it becomes another tool in the fight against anti-Semitism.

In June 2017, the European Parliament adopted this definition and recommended that all EU members put this definition of anti-Semitism into practice in order to strengthen the efforts of the judicial and law enforcement agencies to identify it and file lawsuits. It has already been implemented in England, Germany, Austria, Romania, Lithuania,

Bulgaria, and Israel.

By 1880, about 4 million Jews lived in the Russian Empire. In relation to the Jews new laws, circulars, explanations of the Senate, which dictated where to live, how to live and much more. That is, for the citizen of Russia everything was allowed, except that the law forbade, and for the Jew everything was forbidden, except if the law allowed it.

According to the law, Jews had to live in a ghetto called "the trait of permanent Jewish settlement." Podolia province and respectively Bar were included in these borders.

There is a history of the word *gheto*. On March 29, 1516, the Senate of the Republic of Venice announced that the 700 Jews who lived there at the time must move to a clearly restricted part of the city. It will be guarded and closed at night. This quarter was called *gheto*. The word originated from the name of the nearby smelting workshops that were nearby – in Venetian dialect.

The sign at the entrance to the former Jewish ghetto in Venice

The new jetto was the first religious segregation site in history. And also became an example for all other ghettos, until the mid-20th century.

Ashkenazi Jews transformed the Italian word *'jetto* to their guttural *ghetto*.

On March 1, 1881 Tsar Alexander II was killed. During the investigation, it was found out that the organizer of the murder was a peasant A. Zhelyabov, a noblewoman S. Perovskaya directed the operation, the bomb was prepared by the son of the priest M. Kibalchich, and a petty bourgeoise G. Gelfman, a Jew, kept a safe house. That is, the assassins of the Tsar were representatives of Russian society, which has always been considered a pillar of the throne and the state, but it did not explain why the incitements of the masses against the Jews began. In the spring of 1881, pogroms of Jews began in the South and South-West of the Russian Empire. The pogroms of 1881-1882 lasted fourteen months. They covered 152 settlements. In the Jewish magazine *Voskhod* it was written:

the ruins are already demolished, the dying are already dead and long buried. The authorities directly declared that we will not be beaten any more. How not to calm down, how not to rejoice? Even the festival should be established, like Purim, and enter into the book of memory of the sacred words: now no longer beat. Zion Rejoice!

During this period, thousands of Jewish homes and shops were destroyed, many people were killed, and women were raped. This wave of pogroms has come to Podolia. There were pogroms in Balta, Zhmerinka and Bar.

Painting "Jewish family after the pogrom",

by Wilhelm Wachtel (c. 1905)

Here is how the pogroms took place in Balta, Podolia province. They took place on the second day of Christian Easter on March 29, 1882. The Jewish Newspapers of those times wrote about the events in Balta: "Not a single shop survived... taverns and wine cellars are ruined..."; "In all Jewish houses windows, doors, shutters are broken, inside everything is broken, destroyed...Released from feather beds and pillows was down"; "Seven synagogues were looted, the crowd was looking for Torah scrolls, but the Jews had previously hidden them..."; "Attacked the women and raped them in the streets, in barns, in the stalls. The drunken beasts did not discriminate between the old and the young..."; "At one old Jewish woman who tried to resist, a furious man tore off a piece of a breast, ran out on the street and with pleasure shouted: "A Jewish boob!" The breast was thrown up in the universal jubilation of the disgusting clique of frantic people;

"The morning after the pogrom, the whole neighboring village Cossatskoe came to

Balta to take away Jewish property. There were hunched old women, pregnant women, young women, girls, children, old men and boys, all hurrying with empty bags. But the soldiers did not let them into the town, and they were perplexed about it and even felt offended."

The troops began to restore order in the robbed town. The local authorities became the defender of the Jews. The Tsar Alexander III at one of the reports said: "*This is what is sad in all these Jewish riots.*" After Balta there were pogroms in other towns of Podolia, including Bar. As one resident of Bar wrote to the newspaper:

"*we are surrounded on all sides by horror and despair... All night long we are awake, waiting for a sudden attack of robbers. We are openly told that your days are numbered...*"

After the pogroms of 1881, the government did not allocate any money to the Jews affected by the pogroms, although it always helped others.

The year 1881 was a turning point in the history of the Jews of Russia. There a fear came to all, fear for their lives and loved ones. A spontaneous emigration from European countries to America began.

Emigration then becomes mass, but not everyone understood and did not consider that the new situation has developed in the Russian Empire.

Various groups were created in cities and towns which were going solve one problem: where to go? Some shouted "to America," some - "to Palestine", some - "to Australia", some - "to Algeria". But while the groups were deciding where to go, tens of thousands of Jewish refugees were already at the border.

700,000 Jews left from 1884 to 1903, and, in general, by 1913 about 2 million Jews left the country. It is such a sad statistic.

Several hundred Jews from Bar emmigrated to America, Palestine, Argentina, England, Australia and other countries. Some of their descendants maintain contact with relatives in Ukraine and Russia.

The names of Jews who went abroad in the late 19th- early 20th centuries from Bar:

Leyker, Waysman, Wayner, Schnayder, Edison, Katz, Bresler, Ambinder, Moreynis, Zaydman, Brubeyn, Feldberg, Perselin, Peretz, Gornbein, Khazin, Pfeffer, Zalitrinik, Gilko, Fleyscher, Zilberman, Levin, Berenshteyn, Gelman, Rizhyi, Zusman, Faterman, Krakhmalnik, Reyzer, Fishov, Bar, Kodner, Gak, Lerer, Yastremets, Traktman, Gluts, Fleyschman, Spirt, Zakman, Shatken, Sheynbach, Fishev, Barondess (Brandes), Marantz, Lizin, Belfer, Shlafer, Mazur, Tabachnik, Elstershamis, Koyfman, Zalzberg,

Gershenzon, Kozak, Rozen, Oistrakh, Zeydman, Valkovich, Zilberman, Kodler, Zelvedman, Sheinbuch, Chajkowski, Zon, Saligorsky,, Dresin, Segal, Shiman, Erhardt, Gvozdev, Tsvek, Wasserman, Chazan, Drayzin, Melikes, Maroor, Kalorit, Rapoport, Felberg, Krase, Maydman, Bereta, Frenkel, Tsoen, Bredkay, Brodsky, Seifer, Perelos, Heifer, Vilsker, Kenavska, Umedman, Fritzman, Valoviti, Susman, Virman, Shapiro, Polyak, Garber, Tkach, Luk, Kasher, Katzenelenson, Shtock.

But they always remembered where they came from and passed on memories of Podolia to their descendants. All of them contributed to the development of the country where they settled. And one example, Joseph Barondess can be cited.

Barondes (Brandes), was born July 3, 1867 in Bar. He was a Union leader, politician. Dad – Juda Shmuel Brandes, the Rabbi. Mother – Feiga (Goldman) Brandes (1851 - 1928). Brandes arrived in New York in 1885. When asked by an immigration official: "Name?" He replied: "Brandes, Odessa." The official wrote it down as he heard it: "Barondess". He dreamed of becoming an artist, but began to work, like many immigrants of this time, in the garment industry. He also studied law for a time at New York University (following an example of his relative, Judge Brandeis), but he did not complete the course.

He was a fine orator with a flamboyant appearance and, thanks to his charisma, found himself in no time at all in a leading role in America's labor movement, which was mostly Jewish. In 1891, during a strike he organized, he was convicted on false charges and went into hiding in Canada for some time. By the early 20th century Barondess received an unofficial title "King of the Sewers".

In 1900, Joseph Barondess presided over the conference that founded the later famous International Union of Women's Clothing Manufacturers, and helped create the Union of Jewish Actors. In 1904, he ran unsuccessfully for Congress from the Socialist party, then served for a time on the New York Committee on Education. He was friends with Woodrow Wilson long before he became the President. Barondess later became an active Zionist and one of the founders of the American Jewish Congress. In 1919, he was part of the congressional delegation to the Paris Peace Conference at which the Treaty of Versailles was signed.

It is also worth mentioning about another resident of Bar, whose name was Tsalek Shimon Davidovich Loshak, born in 1894, who after graduating from elementary school in the town, went with his parents to Latin America. Until 1929 he worked as an artist in Havana, the capital of Cuba. After listening to Communist propaganda, he decided to come back to the USSR, home, to describe the peaks of communism here. But he barely managed to get a job as an artist in Vinnytsia medical school. He was arrested on September 15, 1938 on denunciation, as a member of the anti-Soviet group in the medical institute. Distrust of him caused the fact that his wife's brother and two sisters of his mother lived in America. He was sentenced to 10 years in prison under the verdict of the Military Tribunal. By decision of the Supreme Court of the USSR, on September 23, 1939, his sentence was overturned. According to the decision of the NKVD of Vinnytsia region on December 1st 1939, he was released from custody and rehabilitated, and the case was dismissed. He continued to work as an artist at the medical institute before the war. This is the story of real patriots of their country.

Pogroms were periodically repeated. In 1890 there were pogroms in Chernihiv, Kherson, Cherkasy provinces.

In 1905, after active revolutionary events, Tsar Nicholas II "gave" the Manifesto on 17 October to citizens of the Russian Empire, namely – freedom of speech, conscience, press and assembly. Immediately rallies and demonstrations were held throughout the Empire in support of the freedoms declared in the Manifesto. Not apart from these events was the population of the city of Bar, which staged a mass procession of up to 500 people. The participants of the rally were mainly Jewish youth and representatives of various political parties.

After the rallies, pogroms against the Jewish population swept across the Russian Empire. They had in common: a period (18-29 October), slogans (protection of the autocracy), the object of the attack (the Jews).

Two weeks of pogroms killed about 2000 people, mostly Jews. In Vinnytsia 10 people were killed, only material losses were done in Bar.

During the revolution of 1905-1907, pogroms continued for three days in Zhytomyr, 20 Jews were killed there. 660 settlements were involved in these pogroms in the South-Western provinces of Russian Empire.

And so the pogroms continued until almost the end of 1920. From December 1918 to August 1919 50,000 Jews were killed in Ukraine by the Petlyura's troops (data from the International Red Cross).

One of those killed by officers of the Volunteer army in October 1919 was the assistant controller of the Committee for Assistance to Victims of Pogroms R.T. Red Cross in Kiev, a resident of Bar, I. G. Bichuch.

From M.'s report. I. Levenson, Secretary of the Committee:

"On Monday, October 7, when it seemed that the bloody passions had subsided a little, and the Jews, reluctantly and fearfully looking around, began to appear in the street, I. G. Bichuch went to work in the office of the Committee, located on the Theater square, building No. 18-a, apartment No. 3. There was a lot of work in the office, the great

misfortune that happened over the garden, required intense, strenuous work. Bichuch worked until 3 o'clock, and, taking with him a pack of paperwork, went home. Before that, the vice-chairman suggested that he tell his brother, a doctor in the service of the Committee, to go to the Committee room the next day at 10 o'clock in the morning. Bichuch hesitated, explained that he was afraid to walk the streets. But he lived two steps away, on Pushkin street. But Bichuch still requested his release from this assignment. The fact is that two days before he had been robbed and nearly killed in the apartment, and therefore he was particularly frightened. Order to his brother-the doctor took head of the children's department N. L. Beer, who was on her way.

He left the office with his bride, a young girl. On Reitarskaya street, not far from the house, they were overtaken by a cab with three military officers, judging by the serviceability and even some elegance of uniforms, officers. One of them said by looking into Bichuch's face: "Jew, come here". Bichuch approached them, they got in the cab with him and drove off. In vain the bride ran after them, hysterically sobbing and grieving, in vain she appealed for help and protection to passers-by - gentiles. Many indifferently passed by, and those who were interested in this extraordinary spectacle, learned that he was a Jew, simply spat or angrily assented: "So it should be."

At about 6 PM a car with 8 military men, among those who took Bichuch on Reitarska street, pulled up with "drastically altered" Bichuch to the house, where his brother, a doctor, lived on Pushkin street. The gate was locked, they called and asked for Dr. Bichuch. Stating they arrested his brother Bichuch, they said they could release him for a ransom of 30,000 rubles. Bichuch's brother rushed to the apartment to raise money from the neighbors, but was able to collect 17,000 rubles, which were handed to the bandits through the latissse at the gate. But they said little. Then he ran and brought a watch, wedding rings and jewelry. They took away and again repeated that it is not enough. The doctor brought silverware. The bandits scornfully rejected this, got into the car and drove away with the prisoner. The Chairman of the House Committee, a Russian man, interceded for the unfortunate Bichuch and some residents who were Christians, among them a doctor of the Red Cross at the Volunteer army, who happened to be visiting in this house. But the military men dismissed them in disgust, angry: "How do you stand up for a lousy Jew at a time like this? You know about the order." All the trouble and pains taken in the town to liberate him came to nothing. His trail was gone. On October 10, his corpse was found in the anatomical theater. His skull had been split in two by a point-blank shot.

Bichuch did not belong to political parties, he was not interested in political issues at all, he was not in the Soviet service. In the document, except for the report on the death of I. G. Bichuch, there is data on his admission to work in the Department of Victim

Assistance, as well as a statement addressed to the Chairman of the Commissioner of the RKKK in Ukraine I. Heifetz of June 19, 1919 on his admission to the position of accountant, as well as a questionnaire:

<u>Questionnaire (must be completed and signed)</u>

1. **First name, middle name, last name - Bichuch Iosif Gershovich**

2. **Date of birth (year, date, month) - 32 years old in December 1887**

3. **Place of residence (city, county, province) - town Bar Mogilev county, Podolia province**

4. **Education - 3 classes of technical school**

5. **Marital status (family composition) - I support my father and mother who are not able to work**

6. **Attitude to military service - not served**

7. **Previous activity before entering the Red Cross - for 9 years I worked in the bank and in the office of the sugar factory**

8. **Working anywhere at the same time as serving in the Red Cross. If it works, then where exactly, at what time and for what remuneration – no**

9. **Address – Pushkinskaya street building No. 39-a, apartment 8. I. Bichuch.**

On February 15, 1919, there was a great pogrom in the town of Proskurov (now Khmelnitsky) by Petlyura's troops. There, in four hours, 1650 Jews were massacred by order of ataman Semesenko, without being allowed to plunder.

Victims of Petliura pogrom in Proskurov, February 1919

The reason for this was that the Jews took part in the work of the Bolshevik government. In 1919, various gangs played a role in the Ukrainian civil war. Their leaders Grigoriev, Struk, Zeleny, Tyutyunik, Sokolovsky and others hated the Jews and started the pogroms at every opportunity. Often the leaders of the gangs demanded from the Jews "indemnity", and at the same time organized a massacre. It happened that one gang started the pogrom, and another gang ended it.

During the summer-autumn of 1919, several forces operated simultaneously in Ukraine: the troops of the Directorate (Petlyura), the Volunteer Army of A. Denikin, peasant gangs, the Red Army and the anarchists led by N. Makhno. All of them to a greater or lesser extent took part in the Jewish pogroms.

I want to focus on the personality of Simon Petlyura. He was not an inveterate anti-Semite, it is a known fact. However, he had to retain troops, so he gave them the right to arbitrariness in relation to the Jewish population. That is, he paid his soldiers Jewish lives for loyalty. And this does not justify him for such criminal activity. In general, he lost everything, as well as his posthumous lawsuit. So was it necessary to erect a monument to such a figure in Vinnytsia especially in an area where his troops were killing UNR citizens for their Jewish origins.

It should also be said that for celebration of the 100th anniversary of the Ukrainian revolution and on the occasion of the 120th anniversary of the birth of the centurion of the army of the UNR Semyon Yakerson, at the corner of Sobornaya and Ivan Shipovich streets in Vinnytsia a memorial plaque in his honor was installed. This commemorative plaque was positioned in December 2017 to centurion S. Yakerson on the house where his mother lived. The plaque has information in Ukrainian language and in Yiddish language. I think it was a gesture to the reaction of the Jewish community on the establishment of the monument to S. Petlura.

Semyon Yakerson was born in Vinnytsia in 1897. He joined the UNR army because of his faith in Ukraine, at that time many Jews served in this army. His military rank was Cornet. From 1920 he lived in Poland, then in Czechoslovakia, where during World War II his whereabouts were lost. The name of S. Yakerson was not on the deportation list, nor in the German documents of the time, nor in the *The register of the dead in Prague over the years 1940-1949*. However, the researcher Shimon Briman, who with the help of the activist of the Jewish community of Prague Irina Lashmanova, managed to find three granddaughters of S. Yakerson, and the following information became known. After graduating from the Ukrainian Academy in Podebrady, S. Yakerson worked as an engineer on the construction of bridges and roads in Transcarpathia, which was part of Czechoslovakia in the 1920-1930s.

Semyon's gentile wife saved him from death. Anna showed heroism and hid her husband in Prague until May 1945. After the war, Yakerson continued to work as an engineer on the construction of roads and bridges. He died C. Yakerson on March 27, 1951 at the age of 53.

The name of S. Yakerson is not found in the memoirs of famous figures of the Directorate and emigration. Nor is there any evidence of his acquaintance with S. Petlyura. His views can only be read from one sentence in the memoirs of inspector of army UNR M. Skidan, an acquaintance of Yakerson, with whom he met in Berdichev, but the sincerity of the words of the latter is doubtful, given the high rank of Skidan.

It is also interesting that the "associate of Petliura", as indicated by the media, was not at the trial of Schwarzbard in Paris, where he could be an important witness, and did not speak in the press in defense of the Chief ataman.

Whether he was really a hero, or just a Jew who wanted to survive in those hard times - there is no answer. However, there are many who want to make Yakerson the "right figure" of those times.

During the civil war in the Podolia province, pogroms against Jews were more than in other areas. In 1918-1920 there were 164 pogroms in 52 settlements of Podillya, 125 of them were organized by Ukrainian nationalists, 30 - White Troops, 9 - Poles. The number of victims of pogroms was approximately 3700 people.

In the message of the Commissioner in the Central Committee of the help to the victims of pogroms to Jews of August 16, 1919 it is specified that the Ukrainian military divisions entered Bar for the first time at the end of May, 1919. There were rampant murders and robbery. The following people were killed: Nukem Leiderman (age - 35), Shkolnik (age - 70), Melakhzuber (age - 70), three children of Malamud, Hersh Janov (age - 25), 10 Jews were taken hostage.

In Bar in June 1919, the Directory troops committed a Jewish pogrom during which 20 Jews were killed. This number of Jews killed is indicated in the Commission's findings "Jewish public Committee for assistance to victims of pogroms", which operated in the period 1920-1924.

Houses of Jews after the pogrom in 1919

Mayhem in Bar may have been committed by the troops of ataman A. Volynets, but he acted in Haisyn and Uman district, according to other sources – it could be the chieftain of Ya. Shepel or Ya. Galchevsky, they acted in Letichevsky district, and around all the Podolia region. By the way, there was a battle between ataman Galchevsky's detachments and self-defense detachments under the leadership of the chief of Bar's militia Zh. V. Bleck in 1919 (1895-1919), the latter in this battle died and was buried in Bar in a mass grave.

The Jews of Bar paid their indemnity in money, food and fodder. But, despite this, Jewish homes, shops, and a synagogue were robbed. In the synagogue the bandits kept horses. There were maimed people.

"Beat the Jews" - the slogan under which the pogroms occurred inertly, and the question was never raised, and why beat? This was probably the last pogrom in the town before World War II.

Although still the team S. Khmary (57 people), who crossed the border and entered the compound of Ya. Galchevsky, on the night of August 5, 1922, made an attack on Bar. Thus the buildings of party Committee, Executive Committee, mail, militia, Prosecutor's office was crushed. Those killed were the commander of the detachment Khon, a duty guard from militia and one soldier. The same attack happened in the village Yaltushkiv on the night of August 7, 1922.

Many workers and the intelligentsia opposed the pogroms, together with the Jews they created a self-defense unit in towns, which gave a definite rebuff.

From the end of 1917, and especially in the period of 1918-1920, Jewish self-defense detachments began to be created in the towns of Podolia province. Such a detachment existed in Bar. It patrolled the streets and guarded houses and shops. It served during the bazaars and fairs. This detachment successfully defended the Jewish population from the pogroms, but could not withstand the regular troops. Its activities were directed not against any political force, but against the manifestation of any violence in the town.

The activity of the Jewish self-defense units are related to one of the tragic and heroic pages of the history of Ukraine. With the final coming to power, the Bolsheviks began a campaign to disarm these detachments.

The details of the Jewish pogroms in Ukraine 1919-1920, is described in the *Crimson Book* by S.I. Gusev-Orenburzhsky, published in 1922 in Harbin.

All the massacres in Ukraine ended in 1921 after the complete defeat of all the gangs. After the end of the civil war, the life of Jews in Ukraine was relatively quiet, although anti-Semitism at the state and domestic levels remained. And despite all this, the Jews made a great contribution to the development of the national economy of the Soviet Union in the prewar period.

Since the beginning of World War II, a new wave of pogroms began - the Holocaust.

"Not all victims of Nazism were Jews, but all Jews were victims of Nazism". (Elie Wiesel).

The Holocaust is a terrible tragedy of the Jewish people, which has long been suppressed, although the facts were known. It was a closed topic.

The word "Holocaust" is taken from the Latin Bible, which means "sacrifice of burning". The term was first used in 1910 in reference to the Armenian genocide in the Ottoman Empire, and in its modern meaning in 1942, when the mass extermination of Jews by the Nazis began. This word has acquired its widespread use since 1950, thanks to the books of Elie Wiesel.

In the Hebrew language the Jews use the term Shoah, which means disaster, catastrophe. This term replaces the less correct one - "Holocaust". In the Yiddish language in this case, the term is used - "driter Hurban" (the third destruction, after the destruction of the First and Second temples of Jerusalem).

The Nazis came to power in Germany on January 30, 1933. Together with the first measures to strengthen its power, the new regime organized a large-scale anti-Jewish campaign. Jews were removed from public posts, Jews were persecuted, a boycott was declared for the Jewish shops and businesses. Aggravation of the repressions began at the end of 1936 together with preparation for World War II. Jewish organizations and institutions were deprived of public status.

In 1938, the expulsion of Polish Jews from Germany began. Poland did not let them back into the country and they were on a border strip in serious condition. Among these Jews were the parents of Hershel Grinshpan, who had studied in Paris. In order to draw the world's attention to the situation of these Polish Jews, Grinshpan made an attempt on the life of the German Embassy adviser von Rath. This shot was the reason for the Jewish pogrom in Germany.

On the night of November 10, 1938, an all-German Jewish pogrom, the infamous "Kristallnacht", took place. 92 Jews were killed, hundreds maimed, synagogues were set on fire, more than 7,000 shops were destroyed. About 30,000 Jews were arrested, and in general all Jews in Germany were fined in the amount of 1 billion marks. Thus began the genocide, which became one of the main goals of Hitler's aggression in other countries.

Starting with the Nazi occupation of Poland in September 1939, a wave of arrests and pogroms began. Thousands of Jews were sent to forced labor, where they were subjected to humiliation and mockery.

In October 1939, the head of the General Directorate of Imperial Security of Germany, R. Heydrich ordered the creation of special areas of compact settlement for the Jews of Poland in large cities – ghettos, where they relocated Jews from the countryside, as well as from Germany itself.

An order was issued to form Judenrat - "Jewish council" - from the local Jewish population, through which the Nazis conveyed their orders and orders to the Jews of the ghetto. The Jews were ordered to wear a yellow armband "Star of David" (Magen David, six-pointed star).

In 1940, the largest Nazi concentration camp, Auschwitz, was established in Poland on the orders of Himmler, which had eight cremation furnaces. The first transports with the doomed arrived in Auschwitz in March-April 1942 from Slovakia, then from France.

In the Auschwitz death camp, according to the Nuremberg trials, 1,613,000 people were killed, including 1,100,000 Jews, about 140,000 Poles, 100,000 Ukrainians, and 23,000 Roma. Other people also were among the victims.

On the eve of World War II by the number of Jewish populations of Ukraine, which was home to 2.7 million Jews, ranked first in Europe and second in the world.

After Germany's invasion of the Soviet Union on June 22, 1941, a planned and consistent extermination of Jews began.

As early as in 1924, Hitler in his book *Mein Kampf*, substantiated his "concept" of exterminating the Jews.

The Nazis created special groups (Einsatzgruppen), whose task was the destruction of "commissars, Jews, Gypsies". Activities of these detachments was organized on a certain scheme: after the capture of the settlement, they immediately established with the help locals, the names of the rabbis and the most famous members of the Jewish community. Then they were required to gather all the Jewish population to register and sent to the "Jewish district", that is, to the ghetto. The Jews had no idea of the true intentions of the Nazis, so they obeyed the orders of the occupiers. Jewish civilians were destroyed directly in the places of residence.

Mass killings of the Jewish population occurred in Kiev, Kharkiv, Lviv, Berdychiv, Odessa, Vinnytsia, and in many other large and small Jewish towns of Ukraine. The Nazis and their servants killed 1.5 million Jews in Ukraine, including about 200,000 Jews in Vinnytsia region. More than 1,500 mass graves of Jews burned in the Holocaust are known in Ukraine today. Around 400 of such graves are on the territory of Vinnytsia region; 141,825 Jews lived in Vinnytsia region in 1939, it was 6% of the total population of the region.

From 14 to 29 July 1941, Vinnytsia region was occupied by German-Romanian troops. In July-August 1941 Vinnytsia region was under the control of the German military administration, and in September 1941 transferred to the control of the civil authorities. The structure of the German General district of Zhytomyr included gebiti (districts): Vinnytsia, Haysin, Illintsy, Kazatin, Kalinovka, Lipovets, Monastyrische, Nemirov.

Areas of Bar, Yaryshev and Murovani Kurilovtsy were included in the gebit "Bar" of the general district Volhynia-Podolia.

Areas South of the southern Bug and Rov rivers entered the governorship of Transnistria ("across the Dniester"). On 30 August 1941 an agreement was signed in the town of Tighina (now Bendery), according to which the territory between the Dniester and the Southern Bug was given to Romania for temporary economic exploitation. Mogilev, Tulchin, Zhugastrov (Yampol), Balta counties were created. About 100,000 Jews were deported here from Bessarabia and Bukovina. Several thousand Jews were deported from Romania.

The first execution of Jews in the Vinnytsia region was carried out by the Nazis on July 14, 1941 in the village Tereshpil (Khmelnitsky region). The peasants were called to the square and 31 local Jewish collective farmers were shot in front of them. Rozenblit Haim Gelowicz, a musician, was hanged by the Nazis on July 20, 1941 in Bar for alleged links with the guerrillas. This happened four days after German troops entered Bar. In 1941 alone, more than 35,000 Jews were killed in the region.

For the purpose of isolation and the subsequent destruction of Jews, invaders created 126 ghettos - original concentration camps in the territory of Vinnytsia region for their temporary forced maintenance, including 35 ghettos in the German zone of occupation. The Nazis also created about 20 labor camps for the construction of the strategic highway (Vinnytsia-Taganrog), in which 10,000 Jews, including those from Transnistria, died.

The prisoners of the camps and ghettos were tens of thousands of Jews, both local Jews and those forcibly driven from Bessarabia and Bukovina. There are known cases where Ukrainians were also kept in the ghetto, mainly those who had a mixed marriage.

The ghettos located in the German occupation zone the least amount of time had existed due to the accelerated, complete elimination of their prisoners. Transnistria's Jews were more likely to live, where the occupation regime was to some extent, not marked with such cruelty. Until March 1944, more than 70,000 Jews died here, mainly from hunger, disease, various epidemics, as a result of the terrible unsanitary conditions of prisoners, extreme cold, and the exhaustion from backbreaking labor. In total, about 200,000 Jews, including about 50,000 deportees, died in the Vinnytsia region during the years of occupation.

In the ghetto, mainly in the Romanian zone of occupation, operated a clandestine group (the largest in Bershad' and Sochi). A clandestine group under the guidance of Filberg was in Bar.

The act of proclamation of the Ukrainian state, with recognition of close cooperation with the national socialist greater Germany to fight against the Moscow occupation to establish a new order in the whole world. July 1941

OCCUPATION OF THE TOWN

At the time of the Nazi occupation on July 16, 1941, more than 4,000 Jews remained in the town. Along with the enterprises that were evacuated, 360 Jews, the workers of these enterprises, left the town. The Germans entered Bar around 11 o'clock on July 16, 1941 from different sides without a fight, because the Red Army troops left Bar and retreated as it was away from the main attack of the Germans.

And before that, on July 1, the Hungarian Air Force bombed Bar to prepare the offensive of their troops. A number of houses were destroyed in the town.

At the same time, the military commandant's office and the field gendarmerie office appeared. A former teacher of singing and drawing, Koliveprik became the Chairman of the Council in Bar.

Evacuation of the population looked like this: a cart drove up and in 20-30 minutes it was necessary to collect all the necessary belongings, which was almost unreal. The refusal to evacuate the population was also influenced by the policy of the authorities during the recent agitation: "the Germans are a cultured civilized nation; they will not hurt anyone". Representatives from among the residents, dissatisfied with the Soviet power, decided to meet "liberators" with bread and salt, flowers and welcome banners. The meeting took place at the intersection of the current Ostrovsky street and Frunze. The delegation was headed by Vladimir Andreevich Koliveprik (later the Germans appointed him as a Head of the District Council). The teacher of the German language Efim Minkin was a translator, also Antonina Yurievna Mack (a teacher of German language, who worked with the Germans as translation secretary in the German commandant's office, which was on the premises of the police at that time). After the occupation of Bar, there were almost no major changes in the life of the town. Businesses, stores, hospitals (there were two) continued to work, also, the Germans launched a military hospital in the building of the present school №4. A hole was in the yard of the hospital where they buried bio-material, mixing it with chlorine. According to unconfirmed reports, the German war grave was located on the territory of the current school No. 1, and after the war it was destroyed. Two cinemas (one only for Germans) and a bakery also operated there. In August 1941, a group of people from Western Ukraine, about 700 people who called themselves nationalists of the Melnik's direction, arrived at Bar. On arrival in Bar with help of the Chairman of the Council, Kolibeprik and the Chief of Police Andrusev organized a meeting at the end of the concert. Some of these people were the main staff of the police (in the future, they became the perpetrators of mass shootings of Jews in Bar). Others joined the ranks of the police in other districts of Podolia. The chief of police Andrusev traveled around the town and district on the cart, without additional protection, accompanied by sheepdogs. For the entertainment he had to whip disobedient residents or violators of discipline. There were cases when he warned some residents about sending them to work in Germany, so they had time to hide. But the attitude towards the Jewish population was very cruel. Several times he gathered a group of Jews on the market square (now called the Square of Memory), kept them for a long time, threatening to shoot and requiring the Jewish community to pay ransom in gold. Once he received the ransom, after some time he repeated such action until the mass killings were started on August 18-19 and October 14-15, 1942.

In the town there were two newspapers for the population: *Barsky Vestnik* and *Weekly review of Bar's district*. The editor of the last was the teacher of school No. 2, Alexander Yakovlevich Kolodchenko. The editorial office was located in Bar on Bohdan Khmelnytsky square building No. 5, and the circulation of the newspaper was printed in the town's printing house.

The mayors of Bar at the time were Vladimir Koliveprik, Alexander Kuznetsov, and Maksymchuk. Also other officials collaborators: chief physician of Gebitskomisariat Vikenty Pavlovich Maliy, senior agronomist Ostap Ivanovich Bondarenko, director of Bar's sugar factory Levkovich, director of Bar's school of agriculture Severin Mikhailovich Polishchuk, chairman of Bar's Catholic religious community Prukhnitsky, a resident of the village Verkhivka Kulik (wrote poems with anti-Soviet content, a kind of journalist-correspondent), the secretary of the district Council Chepurnyuk and many others. Social life was quite intense: there was a drama club, football matches and concerts (dedicated to various events like Hitler's birthday). But, of course, the main task was the production of food for the fascist army. Here the workers of the sugar factory distinguished themselves. Under the leadership of their traitorous director they were able to reach the prewar level of output and even exceed it in some respects. For all the occupation, the fascist power in Bar has been represented the longest time by gebitkommissar hauptmann Shteffen.

In the early days of the occupation an appeal to "Jews of the town" was issued. It stated that the Jews are those who have been Jewish for two generations and who profess Judaism. It was forbidden to greet gentiles, to visit public places, to be treated by a gentile and to treat gentiles. It was required to wear a special white bandage with the Star of David, and later this bandage was replaced by a yellow cloth flap with a hexagonal star sewn on the right breast and on the left shoulder behind. It was necessary to register in the town's Council and much more. Execution was performed if somebody failed these rules.

In August-October of 1941 and at the beginning of 1942 there were Jewish pogroms in the town and district. It was not possible to establish origin of each pogrom which killed about 3,690 people.

On August 5, 1941 the Germans demanded from the Jews a contribution in the amount of 10,000 gold. In order for this amount to be paid, the Nazis took 10 people hostage. They were shot, despite the fact that the necessary amount was collected. In the town, the Nazis launched Jews in action production. They worked sugar, mechanical, alcohol factories, weaving factory, Jewish collective farms. Jews were driven here to work. From September 1941, Bar became the center of gebet "Bar" general district Volyn-Podoliya.

Soon the Germans organized the Judenrat. Judenrat allocated people for work, and carried out distribution of things and values. Some people worked in factories, in the former Jewish collective farm, on the repair of roads, receiving 300 grams of bread per person.

On December 15 1941 an order of the Chairman of Bar District Administration No. 21 to create a ghetto for Jews in their places of residence, where the Jews of Bar and surrounding villages were to move. Until mid-December, Jews of Bar lived in their homes. From December 20, 1941 Jews were to be relocated to ghetto of Bar and Yaltushkiv.

Three ghettos were created in Bar within the compact residence of the Jewish population ("the Jewish quarters"). The first was on the former street Sholem Aleichem near the old synagogue, and the second - on the former street 8th March, Komsomolskaya and Cooperativnaya, third - on the former street 8th March near the stadium. The last ghetto was inhabited exclusively by artisans according to the lists of names drawn up by the Jewish Council (Judenrat).

*8th Street March, a Jewish ghetto that was
inhabited by artisans. Bar 1941*

НАКАЗ № 21
По Барській Районній Управі
від 15 грудня 1941 року
§ I.
Жидівське населення Барського району з 20 грудня ц. р. розміщується в ізольованих місцях (ГЕТТО) м.м. Бару та Ялтушкова.
§ II.
Жидівське населення населених пунктів району повинно до 20 грудня пересилитися до м. Бару, або Ялтушкова (куди буде зручніше) і теж з 20 грудня розміститись в (ГЕТТО).
§ 3.
Жидівське населення м. Бару розміщується у таких частинах міста: ГЕТТО № 1—бувша вулиця Шолом-Алейхема місцевість бувшої старої сінагоги, ГЕТТО № 2—бувша вулиця 8 березня, Комсомольська, Кооперативна та ГЕТТО № 3 частина бувшої вулиці 8 березня, що прилягає до стадіона.
ПРИМІТКА: ГЕТТО № 3 заселюють виключно ремісники за списком, який оголошується через жидівську раду.
§ 4.
ГЕТТО для жидівського населення м. Ялтушкова визначає сільська Управа м. Ялтушкова.
§ 5.
Всьому жидівському населенню району в зв'язку з переходом у ГЕТТО, забороняється руйнування житлових та не жилих приміщень, які вони залишають.
§ 6
Українському населенню, що живе в місцях, які відведені під ГЕТТО звільнити свої приміщення і з'явитися до житлового відділу Районної Управи для одержання іншого приміщення.
§ 7.
Житловому відділу наказую взяти на облік всі приміщення, які будуть звільнені жидівським населенням.
§ 8.
На органи безпеки м. Бару та в районі покладено відповідальність за організацію вищезгаданого міропремства та застереження від грабунків.

The order of Bar district Council on the establishment in the towns of Bar and Yaltushkiv ghetto for Jews.

The circulars before this order stated that the resettlement of Jews in the ghetto must take place in 5 days. None of the Jews had the right to evade this order. It was also forbidden to accept Jews from other areas and many other restrictions. Execution was performed if someone failed the orders. The Germans appointed a former locksmith as a first Chairman of the Judenrat, whom the Jews in the ghetto nicknamed Petlyura for his cruelty to people. Later, the Germans replaced him with Joseph Krokhmalnik, who knew German language. He was a somewhat violent man, but more intelligent.

The village administration was responsible for the creation of the ghetto in Yaltushkiv. During the vacancy of residential and non-residential premises, their destruction by the owners was prohibited and they fell under the account of the housing department of the district administration. If somebody robbed Jewish apartments, this person would be killed. The population living on the ghetto streets were moved to a different location by the housing department. However, this decision was more likely to work on paper, since most of Bar's Jews continued to live in their homes near the stadium and the bridges across the Rov river, in the so-called "open ghetto". Enclosed with barbed wire, the ghetto appeared after the first mass shooting of Jews in August 1942. 11 ghettos and 6 settlements were created on the territory of the present Bar's district. About 10 thousand Jews lived here before World War II.

Jews were forbidden to leave the ghetto under threat of death. Citizens who sympathized with the Jews and who approached the fence to pass a potato or a piece of bread were severely beaten by the policemen.

On July 18,1941 the town Kopaihorod, which is 25 kilometers from Bar, was occupied by German invaders. In late September, the Germans drove all the Jews to the camp at the railway station Kopay, located 6 kilometers from the town. There was a plot of forest, enclosed with barbed wire, watchtowers with machine guns.

People in the camp were kept in the open. For 2 months it was a nightmare for old, young and kids. What kind of bullying they could not stand! But in the camp people read prayers, they were wearing prayer shawls and tefillin and hoping for salvation.

Only the transfer of this territory to the Romanian occupation authorities saved the Jews from imminent death (my grandmother, her sister, my mother and a dozen other relatives were in the camp).

To search for food at night, people crawled under the wire and went to the nearby villages Kosharintsy, Shipinki, station Kopay to exchange things and hidden valuables for food. Often these searches ended in the death of people.

Toward the end of November 1941, all those who remained alive were driven back to Kopaihorod in the created ghetto, in devastated and robbed houses. In mid-August 1942, rumors began to spread about the extermination of the Jews. On the morning of August 19, the Sonderkommando, which had arrived at Bar from Kamenetz-Podolsky, with the support of the schutzmans, drove the Jews out of two ghettos into a stadium, surrounded by German gendarmes and policemen. On 19 August, 1942 the largest action to execute the Jews of Bar took place. It all started in the morning after two Jewish neighborhoods were surrounded. Residents were kicked out on the streets with their things and lined up in columns, driven to the stadium, where there were other residents from surrounding villages. The stadium was surrounded by policemen and German gendarmerie. In the center of the stadium were the leaders of the gendarmerie and the local police, Gebitskomisar, three SS men with the emblem "dead head". The selection began: in one direction they drove the disabled - the elderly, the sick, young children, women with children. In the other direction - young and middle-aged Jews.

Fascists lead the Jews from Kopaihorod to a concentration camp, located about 700 m from the railway station Kopay, September 1941. Among them is my mother, Anyuta Koyfman, 20 years old

The day before, in the tract by the road to village Garmaky, locals from the nearest villages dug up 5 holes. According to other sources, these pits were dug by prisoners of war on the evening of August 18, 1942.

The Nazis took away about 3,000 old, sick, and women with children. They were told they were moving to another place. There was a terrible yell and crying. The prisoners were escorted and transported to the place of shooting though the streets of the town. This was the last road of Bar's Jews, the road of death.

Groups of 40-50 Jews were stripped naked and brought to the pit. Planks were thrown across the pits, on which people walked before being shot: the Axelrods..., Barsky..., Wisemans..., Goldmans..., Lerners..., Oxman... and other names in alphabetical order.

Gunshots, cries and yells of the doomed could be heard far from the scene of the murder. For 10 hours, Germans and policemen fired machine guns at the victims in the back of the head, people fell face down. Very young children were banged on the car which stood next to the pit. The local police chief G. Andrusev ordered babies to be thrown into the grave alive and then he shot them with a pistol.

According to the documents of the Extraordinary State Commission for the investigation of Nazi crimes and in the materials of O. Kruglov, more than 3000 people were killed, according to German data and the directory "Tkumi" – 1742. During August 20-21, 1942 the former Jewish hospital was destroyed along with patients and doctors, another 100 people died.

Andrusev came to Bar in 1939 from Western Ukraine and worked as head of security at a sugar factory. G. Andrusev first became a deputy, and then the head of the district police in Bar, which was subordinated to the police apparatus of Bar, Murovani Kurilovtsy, Yaryshev, Nova Ushitsya.

With direct participation and under the leadership of Andrusev, more than 8,000 innocent people were murdered. After the mass shootings, he liked to walk on human bodies and finish off survivors with his pistol.

In addition to the executions of Jews in Bar, he organized the executions of thousands of Jews in Murovani Kurilovtsya, Nova Ushitsya, Yaryshev, Yaltushkiv.

No wonder the fascists appreciated his service to them. They awarded him the order and conferred the rank of officer. During the interrogation of the SS officer Richard Schultz, who was captured in the area of Bar in 1944, he called Andrusev the most devoted assistant.

For 22 years, the state security authorities did not stop searching for Andrusev. He was hiding in different countries, constantly changing his name. But eventually his time came and the government of Yugoslavia transferred Andrusev to the Soviet justice.

On October 18, 1966 the field session of Vinnytsia regional court started in Bar's center for the culture. It was a trial of Andrusev - for his misdeeds during the war against the people. One of the witnesses at the trial was a resident of Bar, Polina Shterenberg. During a confrontation with Andrusev, the latter didn't recognize her, then asked: *"Polya, is that you?"* He must have thought there could be no living witnesses among the Jews.

Not everyone could get into the courtroom. The entire square in front of the center for culture was packed with people. The trial was broadcast outside.

A short message went around all the central publications:

> *For grievous crimes in front of the Motherland, the field session of Vinnytsia's regional court which sat for four days in the town of Bar, condemned Andrusev G. V. to the highest measure of punishment - shooting.*

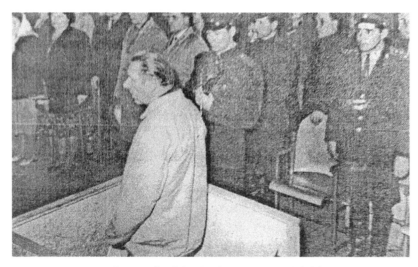

The trial of G. Andrusev, Bar, 1966

Deputy of Andrusev – Alexiy Keba, fled to Brazil. The Soviet authorities could not get to him there because there was no Soviet-Brazilian Treaty on extradition of criminals.

The shooting of the last Rabbi of Bar, D. Zaidman is described in the collection of memories "For the rest of his life" of L. Kleban, who was Bar's resident at that time. When the undressed rabbi began to pray, he asked the naked Jews who stood nearby to go obediently to execution because this execution was sent to them by G-d. The words which were said by the Rabbi were translated to the German who directed execution. Then a fascist suggested to leave the Rabbi alive, but he refused, the Rabbi only asked to wear a prayer shawl to go into the pit in it.

I would like to offer you a letter written by Vadim Slutsky from Petrozavodsk about his great-grandfather D. Zaidman, and his correspondence with S. Dodik, which was published last in the essay "Echoes of the Holocaust":

My great-grandfather, David Zaydman, was born in Poland, into a large, wealthy and deeply religious Jewish family. His father was a "forest king": a very successful merchant, engaged mainly in cutting and selling timber. As is often the case with the Jews, he was at once extremely businesslike (and in the modern sense of the word, and in its present meaning too), and highly moral, and religious. He was engaged in charity and helped, as far as I know, both Jews and Christians. He also was an educated man, meaning not only Jewish, but also European education. At the same time, he was no stranger to ambition and self-esteem, his daughters danced at balls at some of the Royal courts of Europe. He had several children; I don't know how many. But, as is often the case, his children grew up to be people with non-practical mind. At least, that's true of my great-grandfather. Up to the end of his life he remained an extremely naive man in all so-called practical affairs. The children of the "forest king" did not need to become practical, they were given everything, they were waiting for a rich inheritance, they received a great education, again, not only Jewish.

At the same time, this man, internally quite vulnerable, very kind, more than anything in the world appreciated and loved conversations on religious topics, had a representative appearance. Unfortunately, none of his photos or letters were preserved in our family.

When David Zaydman became an adult and married, he received as a wedding gift a factory, it seems a match factory, which was somewhere in Belarus, it seems in Vitebsk, or somewhere else, I do not remember. It is known for certain that he was not engaged in his factory at all, was not interested in it, had a factory manager, and all his interests were the Torah, the Talmud, religious disputes, the family and Jewish charity, to which he was more committed than his father, because he did not count money, did not appreciate them, and at the same time he had a pity and loved people, especially those who needed help.

He had 8 children, including 5 daughters, one of whom (the third in a row) - my grandmother, Nina Zaydman (Neha, completely Nehama) Davydovna. It was said of her that she also resembled her father in appearance. So, her pictures are in us – she was an incredible beauty, but very Jewish: extremely serious, concentrated, a little pale face, look dreamy-detached – her appearance was almost ethereal - absolutely some exotic beauty, not a sensual beauty.

Before the revolution, the family of David Zaydman had nothing to do with Bar. They moved to Bar in 1920s, why there I do not know. The factory, of course, was requisitioned. At Bar my grandfather soon became a respected man, and there he was the head of the Jewish community. At least until the moment when we could talk about the real state of the Jewish community, it was still the 1920-1930s. All his children, including my grandmother, had an extremely difficult fate. My grandmother grew up in the love and care, among people who loved her dearly, she received a magnificent education, something like a noble (she was taught foreign languages, she had a teacher who taught my grandmother music), finally, she was, by nature, not of this world. She was not adapted to the life she had to live. But my story is not about her.

When the Nazis occupied Ukraine, and a ghetto in Bar was created, then there was my great-grandfather, I do not know, which of his family members also were with him in ghetto. He was one of those who believed in salvation and they would not be destroyed. As far as I know, he believed that it was impossible to resist the Germans, this is madness, and apparently in this sense he spoke to people, as the Germans probably knew. He was considered a useful man, and when the time came for the "action", it was David Zaydman who was put at the head of the column, as he had a calming influence on people. He, of course, thought that they were being relocated or something, of course, the Germans, as usual, had lied.

But when they were brought in, they saw the ditches, the guards, and so on, and it was all clear to everybody, then this soft man showed himself. The fact is that the Germans considered it useful for themselves and, apparently, hoped to use more. So they said to him, "and you, old man, stand aside". He was then 56 years old, but he looked, apparently, already like an old man.

How is this episode known? The fact is that, as often happened, someone from the executed then got out of the mass grave and survived. After the war, one of the sons of David Zaydman (he was also called Semyon, now he is long gone in the world) went to Bar and found this "live shot", and she told him everything.

On November 23, 2005, after receiving my book, Vadim again sent me a letter, where he writes:

"...Thank you so much for the book. I already read it, now my mother, who is only 2 years younger than you, is reading it, and she remembers her grandfather. The episode you described on page 26 (cited by me above with reference to the book of L. Kleban S. D.), is legendary - and you write so yourself – and the legend most likely originated on the basis of the real episode that I described. True, my great-grandfather was not a Rabbi, but he was a deeply religious man, was at one time the chairman of the Jewish community, observed all the commandments – and could "turn" in someone's mind into a Rabbi..."

On 5 December 2005 I again received a letter from Vadim, where he writes:

"...I spoke this week on the phone with my aunt Iva (my mother's older sister, she is the same year as you and lives in Israel). I told about your book, and she remembered that after the war, my grandmother sent an official letter to the Executive Committee of Bar with a request to inform about the fate of her father. The answer was received, where the story that I told you (that my great-grandfather was offered to save his life, but he refused) is confirmed officially. She couldn't remember how it became known to the Executive Committee, but apparently there were witnesses...".

On 12 December 2005 Vadim writes in addition:

"...Unfortunately, the letter from the Executive Committee could not be found. The only thing that I can still report: my mother and her sister remembered that there was definitely said about cheating by the Germans (which I wrote supposedly) - they said

that they were driving people to work. My grandfather was put at the head of the column, because people believed him...".

That's the story of the living legend, one of the participants of moral resistance to fascism.

Not everyone who fell into the pit was dead. For a long time the earth stirred above these terrible pits. Only a few managed to get out of the grave at night.

In the letter of the employee of office of SD Kamenets-Podolsky of August 18, 1942 there was a message that for the road works Lviv-Proskurov-Vinnytsia-Rostov it was necessary to reserve 800 Jews from Bar. But by the time the letter arrived, most of the Jews had been shot.

Only a few hundred young Jews were deported to labor camps near Yakushentsy for the construction of these roads. They were housed there in a school, which was fenced with several rows of barbed wire. Jews were forced to work on the construction of the road in very difficult conditions. They almost all died there.

On October 15, 1942, the second execution of Jews of Bar was carried out. It was conducted by the SD team from Kamenets-Podolsky with the support of the gendarmerie and the Ukrainian police. In October 1942, on Yom Kippur, the policemen went around the houses and drove the residents to the streets, giving no time to gather their stuff. They said to bring warm clothes. They started to form a column of 6 people in a row. A fictional legend was created that they will be sent to the Kherson region to create agricultural settlements for the cultivation of lands that are abandoned. Along the movement of the column they put a cordon of local policemen, which was removed outside the city.

About 2,000 people moved in the column. When the column began to withdraw to the Ivanovo road, people realized that they were going to die. Teenagers organized the escape. Among 30-40 fugitives, a significant number were killed or wounded, only a few managed to reach the garden and hide. The Germans did not pursue the fugitives, because it was necessary to escort the rest of the victims. In the morning, the schutzmans combed the ghetto and shot those who were hiding.

The rest of the ghetto prisoners - artisans, were driven to the place of execution near village Ivanovtsy. About 2,000 Jews died on that day. In total, about 5,000 Jews were killed in Bar, this is the data of the experiment, which was carried out by the authorities in 1944 after the liberation of Bar from the invaders. This figure is obviously understated, but may not have been counted correctly because there were also deported people from Bessarabia, Bukovina, Romania, and other Jews from the surrounding villages.

First page of the list of executed citizens (actually only Jews)
Bar, 1942.

Counterintelligence "SMERSH" arrested and shot the head of the district council Koliveprik, arrested and convicted some members of the council, many former policemen. Two schutzmans who shot two Jews near the ghetto wire were also executed. The others were sentenced to 8-12 years in prison, of which they served 5-6 years. Policemen Gurshal and were sentenced to 10 years of imprisonment each, of which Gurshal served 4 years.

The Ukrainian chief of police Andrusev went along with the Germans and lived in Yugoslavia. He changed his name and appearance; however, he was still recognized by one of the former inhabitants of Bar's ghetto, Mezhman. In 1965, the Yugoslav side transferred him to the USSR. In 2001 the collection "The book of Sorrow of Ukraine Vinnytsia Region" was published. The historical and memorial edition includes the names of civilians who died at the hands of the Nazis fighting during World War II during the temporary occupation. The first volume of this book contains information about the victims in Bar and Bar area - here the surname, a name and a patronymic, year of birth, a nationality, a profession and where and when they were executed is specified.

At the expense of relatives of the dead Jews, as well as with the help of all other Jews who lived in Bar, monuments were erected near the villages of Gayev and Ivanovtsy at the place of execution.

There is also a mass grave in the Jewish cemetery. There are two graves in the Eastern part, where 10 people are buried, and one grave in which 7 people are buried. They were later joined by a closed concrete headstone into a single grave. Four obelisks were erected with corresponding memorial inscriptions on them.

Several mass graves of victims of fascism are located in village Kopaihorod (in the Jewish cemetery), on railroad station Kopay (near the edge of the railroad tracks), in village Primoschany (burial in trenches in the woods), in village Popovtsy (the Jewish cemetery), in village Yaltushkiv (4 km from the village towards village Myhalivtsi 1 km from the village Myhalivtsi, village Mateikiv (near the forest), the rest of the graves in Bar's district are still waiting for their time to install memorials.

А К Т. №

1945 года апреля 16 дня председатель Барского горсовета Винницкой области т. Ткачук, секретарь горсовета т.Кремень, составили настоящий акт в том,что за время оккупации г. Бар немецкими войсками расстреляно 5138 граждан.

В отношении 2784 чел нами установлены фамилия, имя и отчество, а над 2354 чел фамилии установить нет возможности, но сколько это количество граждан являлись не местными жителями, т.е. приезжими из западных областей укрытыми во время эвакуации.

Расстрелу подверглись главным образом еврейское население. Первый массовый расстрел произведен 19 августа 1942 года на поле городского колхоза им Фрунзе в двух километрах от города по направлению к селу Гормаки в лощине с правой стороны дороги.

Второй расстрел произведен 15 октября 1942 года на поле колхоза им Петровского с. хутор Майдановецкий,Ширецкого с/совета, около лес урочище "Зеленьки", в трех километрах от города.

Кроме того расстрелы производились группами до 40 человек в более на городском еврейском кладбище, периодически на протяжении 1942-43 года.

Организаторами и руководителями расстрелов являлись немцы: гебит-комиссар Шварц, его заместитель Геслер,начальник жандармерии Шульц, его заместитель Деринг, обер-лейтенант член лично производили расстрелы, расстрелы производились путем укладывания людей группами в могилы,затем строчили их с автоматов и закапывали, не считаясь с тем,что многие были живыми. Малолетних детей перебрасывали по полям бросали в могилы и закапывали.

О изложенном и составлен настоящий акт.

Председатель Барского горсовета _____ /ТКАЧУК/.

секретарь горсовета _____ /КРЕМЕНЬ/.

Факты расстрелов, граждан мы жители города Бар подтверждаем своими подписями.

№ п/п	Фамилия имя и отчество	Домашний адрес	Личная подпись
1.	Чаган Петр Соломонов.	ул.Ленина - 42	
2.	Штеренберг Полина Евна	ул.8 марта - 12	Штеренберг П.Э.
3.	Шустер Венцион Абрам.	ул. ___ - 8	
4.	Воскобойник Давид Хаим.	ул. ___ - 11	
5.	Дунаевич Абрам Эмер.	ул. ___ - 20	

The act of April 16, 1945 on the executions of Jews in Bar,
drawn up in the city council

The place of Jewish execution. Near village Ivanovtsy, 1950s

Representatives of the Vinnytsia Jewish community visit a Jewish execution site in commemoration of its 60th anniversary. Bar, 19 August 2002

Honoring the memory of the executed Jews by the representatives of the Jewish community and the public. Bar, May 9, 2008

Village Gaevoye, monument to the fallen Jews in 1942. Rabbi Shaul Horowitz of Vinnytsia region and chairman of the Jewish community of Bar Grigory Ryzhy read a memorial prayer

Prayer read by the Rabbi of Vinnytsia region Shaul Horowitz at the mass graves. Near village Ivanovtsy, 2017

Monument to 150 unknown Jews from Bessarabia, Bukovina, Romania who were burned in the Holocaust. Village Mateikiv, 2017

Former young prisoners of the German concentration camp near the grave of the executed Jews. Kopay, 2007

The restored monument in memory of those who died in a concentration camp on railroad station Kopay, 2016

On the 75th anniversary of the shooting of Jews in village Yaltushkiv, 2017. Pictured are representatives of the Jewish community of Bar, Vinnytsia district, the Ambassador of Israel in Ukraine, representatives of rural communities and villages Yaltushkiv and Myhailivtsi

*On the 75th anniversary of the shooting of Jews in village Yaltushkiv, 2017. The speech
is read by Svetlana Kupershtein, whose grandparents were among those killed*

At the mass grave of the Jewish residents of the village Khotyn, Chernivtsi district. A former juvenile prisoner of the ghetto in village Popovtsy, where he was deported with his family from Khotyn, Bukovina. 2017

Every year, since August 19, 1945, residents of Bar come here from different cities and countries to this traditional meeting near the memorials - graves of the innocent people shot by the Nazis. In the valley near village Haiove and on the lawn of the forest, near village Ivanovka, where these witnesses of the brutal massacre of more than 5,000 Jews are, Bar's residents perform requiems, light the candles, and each of those representatives ask silently with pain in their hearts: for what did these people suffer, for what?

According to the act drawn up and signed by the Chairman of Bar district commission for the consideration of the atrocities of the Nazi invaders K. Gres, member of the commission M.I. Meshchuk, authorized by the regional committee of the Communist party Yu. Koshevy established that during the occupation of the area 7,500 civilians, about 6,000 residents of Bar, 4,700 prisoners of war and 96 underground and guerrillas were murdered. According to the updated data of the Book of Memory, in World War II in Bar district 8,500 inhabitants died, and these were mainly Jews.

Then along came local barbarians and dug up the mass grave hoping to find something. But they did not understand that all of these victims were naked when they came to the ditches and then were shot by Nazis.

A Jewish cemetery in Bar was destroyed in World War II by fascists and the local population in late 19th century through 1940s. Image taken 2009

Mass grave of Jews who died during World War II. Kopaihorod, 2010

In 1941-1942 about 100 Jews from Bar managed to move to the village Kopaihorod, which belonged to the Romanian zone of occupation. There were no executions, although the life of the Jews in Kopaihorod was hard. Almost all of them managed to survive thanks to the support of the local Jewish community and they returned home after liberation of Bar from the Nazis. I will name only a few surnames of these people: F. Krasnianskaya, N. Mints, Zh. Kelman, G. Shterenberg, I. Anshin with their parents. When I met with these people, they always sincerely and with great gratitude told what invaluable support they received from the Jewish community of Kopaihorod. They were sheltered, despite the prohibition of the invaders not to accept strangers.

Many Jews did die from diseases, epidemics and famine in the village Kopaihorod during the period of 1941-1944.

Monument near the village Ivanovka dedicated to the Jews executed there in October 1942. It was installed at the expense of local Jews. Bar inhabitants: (top row left to right) B. Greenshtein, I. Anshin, S. Kutz; (bottom row left to right) surname not known, P. Greenshtein, S. Greenshtein, G. Kutz.

A poem that was written by resident of Bar, Alla Krentsina (maiden surname Kupershtein) is dedicated to the memory of Jews murdered in 1942:

On the same day, year after year,
Our memory is calling us to you, to our people.
We remember the innocents when we come here.
Without the past, we will never have a future.
The whole ocean of Jewish tears is wept out here,
And there are thousands of scars here from unhealed wounds.
And it seems that still the earth beneath us breathes,
A silent cry there is for help as if heard.
Here dreams are buried,
Which never will come true,
And children that could not be born.
There are thousands of unfulfilled desires,
And thousands of unspoken declarations of love.
There is a whole world and a whole era,
And loyalty, dying only with the last breath.
So many lives and destinies are broken here.
But our memory will remember this forever.
We will remember and ask God,
To have only happiness in life, but not fear and anxiety.
So that the horror of war we did not even dream in dreams,
And so that a terrible day will never happen again.
And no matter how our people's life was thrown around the world,
And wherever we meet the sun gentle sunrise,
Let not even one Jewish grave be forgotten!
A huge price has been paid now for our lives.

THE MEMORIES OF WITNESSES

Memories of eyewitnesses who survived an unprecedented tragedy in history (Holocaust, Shoah) is a documentary about the fate of Ukrainian Jewry during the Nazi genocide. They show the lives of people doomed to death, who fought for their existence; preserved humanity and conquered death; they show the relationship between Jews and non-Jewish collaborators, and those brave - Righteous peoples of the world, thanks to which the authors of the memoirs of the Holocaust survived.

These human documents are part of the peoples' memory, the triumph of memory over oblivion; they have great scientific, educational and humanitarian significance.

Before the Holocaust, no one thought that this could exist, many did not believe that this might happen. After it took place, many do not believe that this was and can happen again.

Therefore, we need strong evidence and, foremost, the memories of eyewitnesses and participants of those events. "Only the one who was there knows," said Auschwitz prisoner, Nobel laureate Elie Wiesel.

Reading the memoirs of Holocaust survivors, one can come to the conclusion that the essence of history is not only historical documents, but also living people and their enthusiasm. The participants of the events themselves become the subject and object of history.

From the memoirs of Lisa Brush (Moschel), born in 1925:

I was born on June 25, 1925 in Bar, Vinnytsia region. My parents were my father, Froyko Moschel, a tinsmith by profession, my mother, Rebekah Moschel, a housewife. I also had a younger sister Manya, 12 years old. When the war broke out, we lived in Bar, near the second school, near the apartments of our teachers: Molchanovsky, Lerner, Kuperman. In our house lived two families of our relatives - blacksmith Koumanov (my mother's brother). I was in my 16th year and I clearly remember the entry of the Germans. The Germans entered Bar around 11 a.m. from four sides without a fight.

I saw them marching down the main street in formation of 4 people, in shorts and blue ties on the naked torso, without shirts, with guns in their hands, without hats, blond, tall, slender. We quickly ran away to hide in the cellar, where we stayed with all the relatives for a day, until a neighbor came and told us to go out, that the Germans did not touch anyone. When we came out of the cellar, we saw that there were many Germans in our yard, and we decided that they would kill us after all. But they did not touch us, they said that they are veterans and will soon leave. I was hired to clean floors, carry stones, carry water. All the timeI worked as a convict, in the yard, I avoided going into the building. This continued until we were forced into the ghetto.

There were three large ghettos in Bar surrounded by wire. We found ourselves in a ghetto behind the monastery, not far from the church. When we were driven into the ghetto, we were allowed to take our things with us with which to live. It was forbidden to go outside the ghetto, but my little sister Manya was not afraid to get under the wire and brought us something from friends. Ukrainians themselves sometimes approached the wire behind which we lived, and brought us potatoes, peas, beans, whatever they had. It was a terrible time. I was escorted to work every day with everyone else, each time to a new place. When we left, we did not hope to return, because every day someone was beaten, killed, shot for no reason.

On Sunday August 19, 1942, we were all kicked out of the house at 4 am and told to take our most valuable possessions with us. We had nothing at all. The Nazis ordered all valuables to be handed over, pointing to the stool that had been placed, and said that whoever faithfully performed this would survive. I began to cry and asked my Dad to give me everything he had, and then I felt in his pockets and asked him to fulfill their request. My mother immediately lost consciousness, and the neighbors covered her, knowing that she would immediately be shot.

Fears were not in vain, because one local schutzman began to accost the harvester Janover - where are his three sons? He said he didn't know. This was reported to Gebietskommissar, and he immediately ordered to kill the harvester. But worst of all was the shooting of Sofia Fiereshtein, a 16-year-old girl of amazing beauty. Gebietskommissar spotted her and ordered to shoot, saying that with such beauty people do not last long. The horror was unimaginable.

The sun beat down relentlessly. Nazis began to select young girls and guys for work. An unimaginable cry arose. All of them died in the Yakushintsy labor camp in 1942.

Most of the people in our ghetto were still alive. However, everyone understood that this delay would not last long. Every day they waited for a pogrom, and every day they marched to work. One day Dad comes and says that priest told him that tomorrow the Germans decided to do something bad with the Jews. At this time Avrum Kravets (the husband of my father's elder sister) came to us with the same message. And my parents decided to take me to my mother's older brother, Benzion Kauman, who stayed outside the ghetto because his forge was at home.

Further memories from Lisa Brush:

It was already the month of October, it was cold in the morning, and I went lightly dressed barefoot. I was very cold, it was foggy, and I was walking in fog. Suddenly Podlisotskaya, a young woman who lived near the field, where she was grazing a cow, calls out to me: "Lisa, where are you going?" I answer that in the field. And she told me – that I'm not supposed to go into the field, and advised me to hide in a pit. Podlisotskaya said that I must not go home, that there is no one there.

Before meeting her, I noticed that the Germans and schutzmans were running in the distance, and I knew that I should hide, but I was in a kind of stupor. Her advice, and the fact that she'd pointed out where to hide, gave me a jolt. I jumped into one hole, and there was Ida Pinelis, my friend.

How long we sat in the pit I do not remember. I remember only that we heard heavy firing, single and machine-gun, but did not feel any cold, no hunger, no moisture.

In darkness I went to Ivanovetsky forest, where I heard the shootings, I hid in pits. I heard cries alive buried people, saw their naked bodies, blood and drunken Germans and I fainted. I don't know what happened later. I don't know either how did I wake up. I just remember I couldn't get out from the pit. But when I reached the plank on which the poor naked people walked before they were shot and fell into the hole, I got out and went back to the fields. Again Podlisotskaya grazed her cow and called to me: "Lisa, where are you going, you're naked," I didn't know that. She led me into a stable and brought me an old coat and a handkerchief. She began to explain to me how and where I should go in order to cross over to the Romanian territory, but nothing came to my mind - one thought was spinning in my head: "I was lying in the pits with the dead, blood stained, I was stripped, like everyone else, and killed, and I'm alive...

After a while, Lisa moved to Romanian territory and ended up in Kopaihorod, where her relatives lived. On 27 March 1944, she returned to Bar after the liberation of the town from the Nazis. 106 of her relatives died in the period 1941-1945 in the ghetto, and in the war - 38.

Another witness to the tragedy in Bar Semyon Dodik in the book "The Boy From the Ghetto, Which Was Shot" also describes these events.

By the time it happened he was 15 years old. On August 19, 1942, when all the Jews were herded to the stadium and selected in different columns, Dodik was in the team, which was sent to a labor camp near Yakushintsy. From this camp he managed to escape, and reappeared in Bar. Many of his relatives were killed.

Later he managed to move to the Romanian territory and in these difficult conditions remained alive, and also managed to fight with fascists.

About all of this S. Dodik wrote in a historical paper that was published in 2004. S. Dodik died in 2014 in Moscow, where he had been living. May he rest in peace.

At the conference of the Association of former prisoners of camps and ghettos, Tanya Kuperman, a former resident of Bar who now lives in Israel, gave a speech in which she mentioned that her parents were killed in Bar ghetto. Before the shootings she managed with the help of Alexei Tkachuk to cross into the territory occupied by the Romanians in the Zhmerinka district, that's why she remained alive. After liberation of Bar from fascists Tanya returned to the town and saw that on a place of execution there was a flat surface of the earth and cattle were grazed. She said that over time a fundraising began for a monument to the people killed in Bar. She and her sister took an active part in this work.

Evdokia Estis, who was born in 1926 in Bar, recalls:

The Germans entered the town of Bar in Vinnytsia region three weeks after the beginning of the war. A month later, all the Jews were resettled in the ghetto, where I got in with my family (father Solomon Moiseevich, teacher of the high school in Bar, mother Rosa Pinkhusovna, sister Zhenya and I). We immediately were ordered to sew on clothes two six-pointed stars, one on the chest and the other on the back. And then the dark days began - the hunger, cold and the worst of all - humiliation. We lived in constant fear, raids were often carried out.

On the night of August 19, 1942, the ghetto was cordoned off by soldiers and all the residents were taken to the stadium in "organized" way. The German soldiers put the ghetto residents on their knees and began to "sort": young - in one column, the elderly and children - in the other. I was 16 at that time. When a German with a whip came up to my older sister and shouted "Schnell!" and showed her where to escape, my mother suddenly a force pushed me to my sister and shouted: "Take her, Zhenya!" How had she reacted then? I don't know. But, as it turned out, she saved my life.

We have not seen our relatives since. We were taken to a camp outside the town. And after a while we were taken to work - to collect tobacco in the fields. From the same as we, other miserables, we learned that the place of execution of all "sorted" in the stadium was very close to the field where we worked. Once my sister and I managed to get to the place of execution. What we saw shocked us. I don't know how many innocent people were executed, but there were several graves (cracked plots of land). Children's toys and documents were scattered everywhere.

Around October, there were disturbing rumors that the pogroms had started again, and my sister and I decided to flee. We decided to go to the front line and headed to Vinnytsia. In the town of Lityn, a policeman approached my sister and began to inquire: who was she and from where? We were rescued by a strange elderly woman who, pretending that Zhenya was her daughter, grabbed her by the hand and began to scold her: where is she hanging around? The woman took us to her home, where she lived with two of her sisters. We stayed awhile with these good women. Every morning they were forced out to work and we hid in the cellar. At any moment we might be discovered, and then the Jews of Lityn would be severely punished.

For two interminable years my sister and I wandered. From Lityn we went back to Bar, but in the village of Luka Barskaya we were warned that there were no Jews left in Bar. We went to Romania. Then, again crossed the border, heading to relatives in Kryzhopil. We can say that we were lucky, all the time we met good people who helped us in any way they could. We returned home after the Red Army liberated Bar from Nazis. It was necessary to start life anew.

Tsilya Hoda recalls:

I, Tsilya Fedorovna Hoda (maiden name Schneider), was born on September 17, 1918 in the town of Matseev, Volyn region (until 1939 it belonged to Poland. Now - town Lukov Volyn region). Family: father - Schneider Fedor Abramovich, mother - Schneider Zlata Meerovna, brother - Semyon born in 1912, myself - Tsilya born in 1918, sister - Sonya born in 1926, sister - Dora born in 1930. In 1939, Soviet troops entered Poland. In 1940 I married the political instructor Mikhail Izrailevich Libman. In January 1941 I arrived with my husband in Kiev, where he was sent to work as a teacher in the Kiev military-political school. In May, after the end of the classes, the entire staff of the school went to study in the special camps. My husband sent me to his sister in Mogilev-Podolsky district of Vinnytsia region. The war caught me in Mogilev-Podolsky district. It was not possible to evacuate. I went on foot in the direction of Bar Vinnytsia region, I was told that perhaps I might be able to leave with the employees of the military enlistment office, but I did not have time.

I got into the ghetto of the town of Bar, Vinnytsia region during the round-up in July 1941. I was unloading brick, about 30-40 people lived in one room. All of us were dirty and hungry. Then they sent me to work in a sugar factory. Here I got acquainted with Grigory Gavrilovich Hoda. He was one of the first Komsomol members in the city of Bar. And during the war he created an underground organization. When he learned that the Jews would be shot, he offered me to run away with them, but I refused. It was uncomfortable to be alone with strange men.

On August 19, 1942 the Jews of Bar were led to the execution. Nazis forced us to strip naked in front of the pit. I decided to run away from the scene of the shooting. I thought if they will shoot me in the back it will not be as scary as in the face. When escaping, I was wounded in the leg, and was hiding in a haystack in a field for a while. My leg was swollen and sore. I decided to knock on the house, which was next to the river. The woman (I can't remember her name) hid me at home and treated the leg. And when in September they began to dig potatoes, she dressed me in her clothes, we took shovels and went like to a field.

So I came to Bar. That's where Gregory Hoda hid me in his attic. Again it was round up and again I was in ghetto. In October, 1942 Gregory Hoda organized the escape. We went together to his relatives in the village Kotyuzhany.

We got a job on a collective farm, which the Germans did not dissolve, established a connection with the partisans. I washed bandages, carried products to guerrillas. I was there until Soviet troops liberated the area in March 1944. After the war I was looking for relatives and wrote in all sorts of places. Residents of Matseev and neighbors testified that our entire family was shot by the Germans as soon as they entered the town. My husband M. S. Liebman went missing in 1942.

After the war, I married my savior, G.G. Hoda. We raised three children. The eldest son, Yevgeny Hoda, is a chief engineer of the machine-building plant in Bar, academician of the Ukrainian Technological Academy, laureate of the State prize. Daughter, Zinaida Predko (maiden name Hoda), graduated from the Kiev Institute of Food Industry. Now she is retired. She is raising my grandchildren and taking care of me right now. Son, Valery Hoda, is a captain of a long-distance vessel.

In the collection of B. Zabarka "We wanted to live...Evidences and documents" there are the memoirs of Bar's resident of Michael Blekhman (he was born in 1929). He says that he was in the ghetto with his parents, where there were artisans. He worked in the stables. When the execution was to take place in October 1942, he was warned by Slava, who carried the gebitskomissar on a phaeton and knew a lot. Blekhmann told his parents about this, and they in turn told about it to the Head of the Judenrat I. Krakhmalnik. But Krakhmalnik didn't believe in the shooting and did not warn anyone, thus betrayed them. However, with Slava's help M. Blekhman hid and later moved to the Romanian territory - railroad station Bar. Later he went to town Kopaihorod, where he had relatives. His parents and younger brother were shot on October 15, 1942. The full text of M. Blekhman's memoirs is presented in the following photocopies.

Город Бар[1] Винницкой области, где я родился и жил, был оккупирован немецкими войсками уже в июле 1941 года. А примерно в августе в разных местах города были организованы четыре гетто. Каждое было огорожено забором из колючей проволоки. В гетто согнали около 5000 евреев, и вход в него круглые сутки охранялся немцами и полицаями.

Сразу же после оккупации в городе были закрыты все магазины, и для обмена вещей на продукты один раз в месяц евреев под конвоем вели на базар.

Вскоре же был издан приказ, в котором предписывалось всем евреям носить на руке белую повязку со звездой Давида. Затем повязку сменили желтыми кругами с шестиконечной звездой, которые нужно было носить на правой стороне груди и левой стороне спины.

Another resident of Bar, a retired Colonel E. Tarlov, in his memoirs published in 2001, *The Holocaust: eyewitness' testimony*, describes the period of his stay in the ghetto, where there were artisans.

I. Gursal, Zaika, Tsetsyursky, Lutsak - some of his school friends enrolled in schutzman, and they created the "closed ghetto". They monitored the residents, accompanied (escorted) able-bodied people to and from work, kept watch at the gates, took part in night and day inspections in the ghetto, announced the orders of the occupation authorities. Usually the name check of people was done on the parade ground. At the same time, the policemen went around the room and brought out those who were hiding. They were beaten in front of everyone, and then shot at the command of the SS warden. Tarlov remembers cases when the Germans executed those who were late for check in or failed to step out from the row of people. The bodies of the dead lay on the parade ground for several hours and it was forbidden to remove them.

According to the order of the Gebitskommissar, in the early summer of 1942, some Jews, including 16-year-old Efrem Tarlov, were brought to temporary work in the labor camp near Lityn, which was subordinated to the military construction organization "Todt" and was guarded by Lithuanians. Prisoners of war lived in separate barracks of the camp. The site was located in a granite quarry near the river Zdor. The rate of production - 1 cubic meter of crushed stone per day, which was used for the construction of the bunker and Hitler's headquarters near Vinnytsia. For failure to comply with the rules of the camp were waiting for the beating and deprivation of food (of soup). Usually, in the camp the Lithuanian guards were beating the prisoners. To save the Jews of Bar from the death in the quarry, the Jewish community headed by Krakhmalnik collected money and jewelry for the bribes to Gebietskommissar through translator K. Waldeck and Jews were sent back to the ghetto. The labor camp near Lityn was liquidated in the autumn of 1943.

During the liquidation of Bar's ghetto in October 1942, Efrem Tarlov hid in the Jewish cemetery, and then temporarily hid in the ghetto in village Luchyntsi, on the Romanian territory. In November 1942, Efrem Tarlov went to village Mlynivka, Kopaihorod district of Vinnytsia region. There he was granted asylum by the Ukrainian family, Kravchuk, in whose house he hid until March 1944. Ivan Semyonovich Kravchuk passed him off as his distant relative, an orphan from the village Man'kivtsi. After the liberation of Mlynivka by the Red Army, Tarlov returned to Bar.

Here is the story about Inna Voskoboynik:

Inna was a young girl when the German occupiers drove all the Jews to the stadium in Bar for "registration". Those who had a work card "A" (from the German "arbeiter") were told to stand in one line, the rest – in another. Jewish families, in which the father was arbeiter and the mother was not, were separated forever. The arbeiters were sent to work, and the rest were promised to be taken to the Promised Land. Inna had a card "A", but her mother began to call her into their ranks, as she thought the girl will not survive in the hard work. A few hours later, those who lacked an "A" card were told to strip naked; Germans began to shoot them. When she realized her mistake, the Jewish mother said "don't kill her! She can work!" The scrupulous German asked to confirm her statement card. The naked woman in despair rushed together with the daughter to look for a jacket in which pocket there was a card. Finding it in a pile of clothes was like finding a needle in a haystack. The German stared at them with genuine curiosity, waiting to see if they would find it. "Found it!" The German shouted to the girl: "Weg!"(away), and the mother, covering her nakedness with her hands, went to the mournful Calvary. Is it possible to forget?

2001: testimony of Margarita Oistrakh, Yad Vashem Institute:

Grisha Ferman - one of the few survivors of the war in Bar. He was fifteen. Someone close to him, as the column was being led to the firing squad, whispered to him: "Run!" and he shielded the boy. Grisha disappeared into the forest, and behind him for a long time there were shots, shouts, groans. The ground shook for several days... G. Ferman, with his modest income has erected an obelisk, on which appear the names of his fallen classmates. G. Ferman died 14 years ago.

In 2005-2006, Steven Spielberg and Viktor Pinchuk produced the documentary *Spell Your Name* about the Ukraine's Holocaust. Directed by Sergei Bukovsky, the film is based on Holocaust survivors testimony. In 2006, with Foundation support, it premiered in Kiev with Steven Spielberg. It was shown in many cinemas and schools in Ukraine.

One of the film's heroes, Michael Felberg - a prisoner of the ghetto, was born in Bar in 1928. Mikhail lost his mother and 4 year old sister in 1942 at the first execution of Jews committed by the Nazis in the ghetto. Then 14 year old Mikhail was selected for forced labor and continued to live in the ghetto. Luckily, he escaped before it was liquidated by the Nazis in October 1942. Then off to Kopaihorod, where he was again forced to live in a ghetto. Later, he was sent for some time to mine peat in the concentration camp in Nestervarka, and then to the demolition of the synagogue in Tulchin concentration camp. In the spring of 1944, Mikhail, along with other prisoners of the Kopaihorod ghetto, was released by the Red Army.

The Nazi genocide was hardly possible without the help of "indigenous nations" and the state's anti-Semitism atmosphere created by Stalin's power. Taking into account everything, after all participants in Babi Yar in Kiev, in Drobitsky Yar in Kharkov, in hundreds of other similar places in Ukraine, there were the Ukrainian policemen...

The shooting of the Jews. Bar, August 19, 1942

Righteous Among the Nations

After the final solution of the Jewish people in Bar, the fascists called it *Juden Frie*, that is, a city free of Jews. During this period in Bar and villages that were part of the German occupation zone, the Gebitskommissar's announcements about the ban on giving refuge to Jews were placed. Each burgamaster (village headman) was obliged to arrest the Jews found and send them to the police in Bar. For failure to comply with this order and for harboring Jews - execution.

But, despite this, there were people who risked their lives to help the Jews by saving them.

Those people who helped to save the Jews, were given the name by the State of Israel - the Righteous Among the Nations. In total, about 25,000 citizens of different countries have become the Righteous of the world. In Ukraine, hiding Jews was much more dangerous than in the West. This honorary title has been granted since 1953. Later that year by the Knesset's decision, Yad Vashem was founded to honor the memory of the victims and heroes of the Holocaust. One of the provisions was the decision to honor the "Righteous Among the Nations". The righteous, according to the decision, recognized gentiles who risked their lives to save the Jews during the Holocaust. In 1953, a Commission was established under the jurisdiction of the Supreme Court of Israel, which is responsible for granting the honorary title of "Righteous Among the Nations". In its work, the Commission is guided by certain criteria, carefully examining all documents, testimonies of those who survived, and other eyewitnesses, it assesses the historical circumstances and the risk to the rescuer, on the basis of which decides whether a particular case meets the necessary criteria. To receive the "Righteous Among the Nations" award, a person must meet several requirements:

- only the Jewish community can nominate a candidate
- not taken into account are those who helped their family, or Jews who converted to Christianity
- help should be repeated and/or significant
- assistance should be provided without the expectation of any financial compensation (although the cost of food and accommodation is considered acceptable)

A person who risked their life to save Jews during the Holocaust and is recognized as a Righteous among the Nations receives a nominal medal, an honorary certificate and the right to add her name to the Wall of Honor in the garden of the Righteous in Yad Vashem in Jerusalem (the latter instead of planting trees, which was abandoned due to lack of space). Rescuers or their next of kin receive the award during a ceremony in

Israel or in their home countries on the premises of Israeli diplomatic missions. These ceremonies are held in the presence of local government representatives and are widely covered in the media.

According to the law, Yad Vashem has a right "to grant honorary Israeli citizenship to the "Righteous Among the Nations" in recognition of their actions, and if they have died, commemorative citizenship of the state of Israel." Everyone recognized as a "Righteous Among the Nations" is entitled to a certificate from Yad Vashem. In the event of his death, his next of kin is granted the right to recognition of permanent citizenship instead of his late relative. Recipients who choose to live in Israel receive a pension in the amount of the average salary, free medical care, as well as assistance in housekeeping.

Memorial wall in the Garden of the Righteous with the immortalized names of the Righteous and their country of residence

Ukraine ranks second (after Poland) among European countries in the number of Jews who died during the war at the hands of the Nazis and their accomplices, and in the number of Righteous people, Ukraine takes fourth place after Poland, the Netherlands and France. This statistic of course does not reflect the true number of the Righteous because it is not always submitted the necessary documents to obtain this title for various reasons. In addition, out of 2573 Ukrainian Righteous people of the world, only 61 people were awarded this title in 1991. That's the math.

Consequently, state anti-Semitism in the USSR hit not only the Jews, but also those who helped them in the terrible times of persecution. And today we have no way of knowing the names of all these heroes, who for decades were hushed up by the Soviet authorities.

In Yad Vashem there is a monument to the "Unknown righteous person" and I think that there, near the monument, invisibly stay all those people who during the war managed to save at least one human soul!

There are several Righteous of the Nations who lived in Bar. G. I. Stasenko (1876-1963), who was hiding a family of Jews by surname of Schuster. The award went to her granddaughter T. I. Mishchenko on July 3, 2012.

Stepan and Lukerya Gritsenko and their son Leonid received the honorary title "Righteous Among the Nations" for saving the life of 14-year-old Sophie Kuperman. The award was received on September 7, 1997.

Fedor Miller (1900-1945) rescued 13-year-old Sofa Kremin, Faina and Fira Krasnyansky. After the liberation of Bar, Miller went to fight with the enemy, he died in Berlin. The award was received by his relatives on November 16, 2009.

Alexey Tkachuk (1904-1963) from village Antonovka, near Bar, saved the lives of Tanya and Bronya Kuperman, 12 and 7 years old. His relatives received the honorary title on November 27, 2009.

Tsitsyurskiy Stanislav, his wife Elena and daughter Valentina saved Michael and Nuta Masenzhnik (they were from Snitkov, but they were led under escort to Letychev through Bar, where they escaped), giving them shelter. On January 11, 1993, Kletz (Tsitsyursky) was awarded the honorary title "Righteous Among the Nations".

Anton Novak, Czech by nationality (1888-1952), hid Jews Peter Segal and Raisa Borovska from 15 October, 1942 until the liberation of Bar from occupiers. Novak was a joiner and sold various wood products, and with the money he earned he fed his family and Segal's family. A. Novak received the title of "Righteous Among the Nations" on September 23, 2001 posthumously.

Gregory Ruzansky (1899-1964) was hiding the family of Jacob Felberg, and then moved Felberg's family to the village Balki, where the Romanians were, later he also helped this family survive. G. Ruzhansky was given this honorary title " Righteous Among the Nations " on December 9, 2009 posthumously.

Certificate of Merit of the "Righteous Among the Nations"
of G. Ruzhansky

Kravchuk Ivan Semyonovich (1910-1963) from village Mlinovka of Murovy Kurilovtsy district of Vinnytsia region, saved the life of a 15-year-old resident of the town Bar E.Tarlov, who appeared in his village. Kravchuk passed him off as his orphaned relative. He hid Tarlov until 19 March 1944. The honorary title "Righteous Among the Nations" was given to the relatives of the deceased on February 1, 2001.

Here is another episode. Paul Hetman saved from execution Huma Kremin, a Jewish girl from Bar who he was in love with. He served in the auxiliary police department and guarded the bank. At night P. Hetman led the girl out of Bar ghetto. Huma hid in the Hetman's house until the liberation of the city from the Nazis in March 1944. During the occupation, she had her first child - a son, who was named in honor of his father Paul. She gave a birth in the cellar of the house where she was hiding. The baby's father Paul Hetman, together with his stepmother assisted her during the labor.

After the war, the Secretary of the town council of Bar Huma Moiseevna Hetman managed to prove to the local NKVD that Paul, her husband, is not a traitor and did not kill anyone.

She waited for his return to his home throughout the sentence (5 years of labor at the Donbass mines) for cooperation with the occupiers.

The salvation of Huma Kremin is one of the examples of assistance to victims of the Holocaust. However, P. Hetman was not presented the title "The Righteous Among the Nations", that's the story.

The local population seriously risked their lives, saving citizens of Jewish nationality. Here is how a Jew, a prisoner of the ghetto in Bar, Arkady Sobol recalls it.

"At the end of September 1942, a friend of our family Vasyukovsky, a Ukrainian man, made his way to our ghetto at night. He decided to warn us, that there should be mayhem. He told us to get out of here as soon as possible. The next evening, Vasyukovsky came again and offered to take us to the Romanian territory. He gave each of us a piece of bread, and we went. There were about 20 of us. He transferred us, said goodbye and left. We went to the village of Paliivka. My father had a friend there with whom he had once served in the army. His name was Pyotr Slobodyanyuk, He had a wife, Anna, and a son, Victor. We got there about two o'clock in the morning. Our father hid us in the barn and went into the house to Slobodyanyk. Peter was glad that we were saved. He and his wife gave us shelter and food. If someone reported us, they would have all be shot."

The first thousand Ukrainian rescuers were found thanks to the search work of the Jewish Council of Ukraine. They received the honorary title of "Righteous Among the Nations".

In addition, for humanitarian reasons, the Jewish Council of Ukraine has created its own awards: "Righteous of Ukraine", "The Righteous of Babi Yar".

It is our sacred duty to preserve the names of the saviors and the people they have saved. This must be done for the sake of future generations.

Six million Jews worldwide were the victims of fascism during World War II. This figure was named at the Nuremberg trials and it seems to suit everyone. According to other sources, the actual number of victims of Nazism is approximately 10 million Jews. After all, there is no complete list of dead Jews by name. Of the 70 Jewish centers in Ukraine, 43 were destroyed in 1941, and the rest before the end of 1942.

It is written in some publications that 485,000 Jews died in Ukraine during the occupation, in others - from 850,000 to 900,000. It is indicated in Yad Vashem that on

June 22, 1941 2.6-2.7 million Jews remained in the Soviet Union under Nazi occupation. No more than 100,000-120,000 Jews remained alive after the war. 88 Jews remained alive in 1944 according to the list of the town council of Bar.

One of the causes of the tragedy of the Jewish population during the war is the concealment of danger in the first months of the war. The Soviet government fought the panic during the German Blitzkrieg in only two ways known to it: executions and silencing. By the time the Nazis invaded Ukrainian territory (1941), the war had lasted two years. There were already Jewish ghettos in Warsaw, Jews were persecuted and killed in other occupied territories of Europe. Most people simply could not know about the horrors of the brown plague, after all the Soviet authorities hid from its citizens the facts of the murdering of Jews.

In addition, after the Molotov-Ribbentrop Pact, when the USSR became an ally of Nazi Germany, the phrase "German fascism" disappeared from the Soviet press. They no longer wrote about the gangs of thugs who carried out anti-Jewish pogroms in Germany in 1938.

It should also be taken into account that on the right bank of the river old Jews cherished the good memory of the Austrians and Germans during the existence of the Ukrainian state, headed by Pavel Skoropadsky. A small example: when the marauders tried to organize pogroms of Jewish towns, the German army and Austrian troops acted as a stabilizer that stopped it and restored public order. They were very friendly to Jews, as there were a lot of Jews in the ranks of the German army. And the memory of the good Germans remained in people for a long time. Besides, people well remembered the Soviet repressions, Holodomor... People thought, whether it is necessary to be afraid of arrival of the new power? Perhaps it will be no worse than the Soviet... However, some Jews did not think so and understood that it was necessary to evacuate. But it was only a small part of Jews. There are several examples from the Jewish life in Bar.

From the memories of Margarita Oistrakh:

"My father, Grigory Abramovich Oistrakh, born in 1920, all his life he reproached himself for not saving his family. Shortly before the Germans entered Bar, he, already in the army, came to the town (or rather, came on a horse) and begged his parents and brother to leave Bar with him. He could take care of them by sending them to the rear in one of the trains with the wounded. But my parents said that they remember the good Germans in the World War I, and flatly refused to leave Bar. All of them were shot by fascists in Bar in 1942".

Another example from the family of A. Mook. Being already mobilized, Mook ordered his wife to gather for evacuation. Several times she refused to go. But when he took a gun to shoot himself if she didn't go, his wife packed up the kids (they had three), and hit the road. All of her relatives who refused to evacuate were killed in Yaltushkiv in 1942.

The main causes of the tragedy of the Jewish population can be attributed to the complete concealment from the Jews of the facts of genocide against them by the Germans in the cities of Western Ukraine (having been captured by the Third Reich), and the lack of centralized evacuation of people who were in mortal danger. Not a single document has been revealed. There is no evidence that the Soviet government took measures to save those of its citizens, who in the conditions of occupation were not waiting for a hard, joyless, hungry, but still life, and cruel and imminent death. Until mid-August, Soviet propaganda reported nothing at all about mass shootings of the Jewish population. And when it began to recognize such facts, it presented them exclusively from such an angle that, they say, executions of Komsomol and Communist activists take place.

The bloody pogroms of the Jews ceased with the end of World War II. There was a period of "quiet" genocide in the Soviet Union, in particular, in Ukraine.

In Poland, in 1945-1946, Jewish pogroms took place as a result of the inaction of the Polish government. This led to the mass departure of Jews from Poland to other countries.

Ukrainian Anti-Semitism existed at both a state and domestic levels. In 1953, the deportation of Jews was to be provoked by the "case of doctors". With Stalin's death, all these things fell apart.

Despite this genocide, Jews were successful in various areas and spheres of activity, thereby confirming that they are also full citizens of their country. After the collapse of the USSR and Ukraine's declaration of independence, public anti-Semitism emerged sharply, as manifested in the media, which represented a particular reactionary group.

All these conditions contributed to the fact that during the years of Ukraine's independence, Jews began to leave Ukraine en-masse, mostly, of course, to Israel. They also began to leave Bar for permanent residence in other countries. This has resulted in the Jewish community of Bar now numbering only around 40 people.

THE FRONTLINES OF WORLD WAR II

Ilya Ehrenburg spoke in 1942 at the Plenum of the Jewish Anti-Fascist Committee with these words:

We must talk about how the Jews are fighting at the front. Not to boast, but in the interests of our common cause - as soon as possible to destroy fascism.

The first who started to implement this idea was our countryman from Vinnytsia region Efim Raize. In 1943 he began work on the collection "Jews - Heroes of the Great Patriotic War". He compiled and published in the newspaper *Einikayt* (May 1946) a list of the names of 101 Jewish heroes of the Soviet Union. According to incomplete data, in the ranks of the coalition against the Wehrmacht fought 1.685 million Jews. Of these, 500,000 Jews were citizens of the USSR, who honorably fulfilled their duty to defend the Fatherland.

About 10,000 Jews from Vinnytsia region were drafted into the army during the war. Since the beginning of the Great Patriotic War, for the period from June 23 to June 30, 1941, more than 500 Jews from Bar joined the ranks of the Red Army. During the years of war on the battlefields, 6079 residents of Vinnytsia went missing or died of wounds in the medical battalions, sanitary trains and hospitals, and of those, 1982 of them were Jews. Jews of Bar fought on all front lines during the Great Patriotic War.

Since 1982, the exact dates of death and burial places of 875 people have been established. According to the data of the General Staff of the Armed Forces of the USSR and the Central Archive, irretrievable losses among Jewish servicemen amounted to 40%, of which 77.6% were privates and sergeants and 22.4% were lieutenants.

148 Jewish soldiers were awarded honorary titles of Hero of the Soviet Union for valor, bravery and heroism on the fronts during the Great Patriotic War. Five of them are natives of Vinnytsia region. 15 Jewish soldiers were posthumously awarded the honorary title of Hero of the Soviet Union for personal valor and courage. 12 Jewish soldiers were awarded the order of Glory of the 3rd, 2nd and 1st degrees. Eight Jewish soldiers died by repeating Nikolai Gastello's feat, directing their burning planes and burning tanks at the enemy troop and transport cluster. Four Jewish warriors repeated Alexander Matrosov's feat, covering the foxhole of the bunkers from which the enemy fired with their bodies.

During the Great Patriotic War, 305 Jews served as generals and admirals, and at the beginning of the war there were only 23 of them. Jewish generals led the military industry, developed and supplied the army with tanks and aircraft, artillery equipment, machine guns and other weapons.

Generals A. Bykhovsky, L. Gonor, E. Rubinchik, I. Salzmann (he was a native of Tomashpil, Vinnytsia region) worked as directors of large military factories. About 50,000 Jews fought in partisan detachments and underground groups in Ukraine, Russia, Belarus. 4000 people were in 70 purely Jewish guerrilla groups.

Jewish regiments were in the partisan formations of A. Saburov and S. Kovpak. At the same time, 27% of Jews volunteered to the front lines.

During the war an unusual division, Jewish, as it was called, was in the Red Army. On May 22, 1942, the 16th Lithuanian rifle division had 12,398 personnel, including Lithuanians - 36.1%, Russians - 29.9%, Jews - 29%. In terms of the number of Heroes of the Soviet Union, first place in this division were Jews - 4 people, among the Heroes of the Soviet Union of Russian origin were only 3. In the division, commands were sometimes given in Yiddish.

Here is another example of the heroism of the Jews. 33 days before the execution of Zoya Kosmodemyanskaya, on October 26, 1941 in Minsk 17-year-old underground resistance fighter Masha Bruskina, a Jew, was hanged by fascists. She was the first underground resistance woman publicly executed by the Nazis in the occupied territories of the USSR.

Here is another an example of the courage and bravery of the Jews. On March 22, the Red Army entered Zhmerynka and tried to capture the station, which was well fortified by the Germans. But they failed. Then a group of Jews from the Zhmerynka's ghetto, using an underground passage, went to the Germans in the rear and at the cost of heavy losses helped to capture the station. Many Jews from the ghetto joined the Red Army and went to the front lines. The Jewish soldiers, sons and daughters, husbands and fathers, brothers and sisters of those who remained in the occupied territories fought hard. And they were martyred by Nazi executioners and their henchmen.

The memory of all the soldiers who died, went missing, died of wounds, and were shot and died in concentration camps will always be sacred. Jews fought, like everybody else at that time, together with others and they also contributed to the victory over the enemy. This is very well depicted in the three-volume book of S. Averbukh *Essays of Jewish Heroism* which was published in 1994.

I want to tell you about the brothers Mook from Bar and about the other heroes who were residents of Bar. Three brothers fought on the fronts of the Great Patriotic war. About one of them is written in the Jewish military encyclopedia. Alexander Moiseevich Mook, national hero of Czechoslovakia.

Alexander Mook

He was born in 1917 in Bar, Vinnytsia district to the family of a sugar factory worker. There were 14 children in the family. In 1935 he joined the Red Army, took part in the Battle of Lake Khasan, and was a participant in the war with Finland as a tank gunner. In 1942 he graduated from tank school in Ulyanovsk. He participated in the Battle for Rostov, Stalingrad and Kursk Battles, in the liberation of Ukraine, Belarus, and in the capture of Berlin.

During the battles near Kiev he crossed the river Dnieper, and connected a broken cable under the water and restored communication, for which he was awarded the order of the Red Star. On May 9, 1945 in battles for Prague the commander of the tank regiment Alexander Mook first rushed in to the capital of Czechoslovakia, destroying groups of the enemy and their destroying their weapons. He was badly wounded. His tank No. 23 was installed on Wroclaw square in Prague, but it has since been removed. Alexander Mook is an Honorary citizen of the town P'yatihatky in Dniepr district and of the city of Prague.

The second brother, Abram Mook, went through the entire war from July 1941 to May 1945. He met the Victory day in Berlin with the rank of Senior Lieutenant. He participated in the Battles for Stalingrad, Kursk, Kiev, liberated the countries of Europe. He was awarded the order of the "Red Star" and numerous medals.

Abram Mook

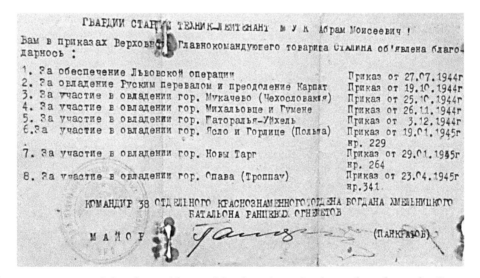

Announcement of thanks to Abram Mook written in the orders from the Supreme Commander. Issued for participation in the liberation of the cities of Western Ukraine, Poland and Czechoslovakia

НАГРАДНОЙ ЛИСТ

1. Фамилия, имя и отчество   МУК Абрам Моисеевич.

2. Звание. старший техник-лейтенант. 3. должность и часть. Начальник артснаб-
жения 38 отдельного Краснознаменного ордена Богдана Хмельницкого баталь-
на ранцевых огнеметов, 15 Штурмовой инженерно саперной Винницкой Краснозн
менной ордена Богдана Хмельницкого бригады НГК.

Представляется к награждению орденом КРАСНАЯ ЗВЕЗДА.

4. Год рождения 1902. 5. Национальность.. Еврей. 6. Партийность.. член ВКП/б/

7. Участие в гражданской войне, последующих боевых действиях по защите СССР
и Отечественной войне. 1.Ю-западный фронт с 5.41 по 6.42. 2.донецкий фронт
с 6.42 по 2.43 г. 3.Степной фр.с 2.43 по 8.43 г. 4.1-й Украинский фронт
с 7.44 г. и 5.4-й Украинский фронт с 8.44 года.

8. Имеет ли ранения и контузии в Отечественной войне. Легко ранен 15.3.43 г
9. С какого времени в Красной Армии с июня 1941 года. годен к строевой службе.

10. Каким РВК призван Барским РВК Винницкой области.

11. Чем ранее награжден. 1.Медаль За боевые заслуги-приказ 226 стрелковой ди
визии № 018/н от 8.2.43 года. 2.Медаль За оборону Сталинграда -Указом
Президиума Верховного Совета СССР от 22.12.42 года.

12. Постоянный домашний адрес представляемого к награждению и адрес семьи.

КРАТКОЕ, КОНКРЕТНОЕ ИЗЛОЖЕНИЕ ЛИЧНОГО БОЕВОГО ПОДВИГА или ЗАСЛУГ.

  Гв. старший техник-лейтенант Мук в дни боевых действий батальона
следовал за боевыми порядками рот, своевременно обеспечивал боеприпасами
и вооружением.

  При наступлении батальона на выс. 471 отказали в работе два пуле-
мета. Гв. старший техник лейтенант Мук в боевых порядках отремонтировал, чем
обеспечил боевые действия подразделений.

  В боях за с.Руске под огнем противника ночью лично доставлял сна-
ряженные РОКС в действующие подразделения.

  Работая по совместительству начальником похоронной команды, во время боя своевременно эвакуирует убитых и организовывает похороны в полном
соответствии приказа НКО № 023-44 г.

  Гв. ст.техник-лейтенант Мук исключительно заботится об исправности
специального и стрелкового оружия батальона. Лично отремонтировал и восста-
новил автоматов- 25 шт., пулеметов-1 шт., ПТР-1, РОКС-18 штук.

  Все вооружение содержит в полной боевой готовности.

  Достоин награждения орденом КРАСНАЯ ЗВЕЗДА.

   Командир 38 отдельного Краснознаменного ордена
   Богдана Хмельницкого батальона ранцевых огнеметов
   майор   /ЛАНФРАТОВ/

20 апреля 1945 года.

*Award list of Abram Mook on his presentation
to the order of the Red Star*

The third brother, Iosif Mook, was drafted into the Red Army on July 21, 1941 from city of Gorky, with the rank of Private. He went missing in November 1941 per Central Archives of the Russian Ministry of Defense (fond 58/ list 18/ file 41).

In June 2010 the search team "End the War" performed field search operations in the area of fighting near the village Baryshevske. The remains of Soviet soldiers at battle near Kyiv were found there. On the lid of the pot was scrawled: "Mook I." So was found another Soviet warrior and his name. His son A. Mook and his grandson attended the burial, which took place at the military cemetery on June 26, 2010. Mooke I. was buried in a mass grave at the memorial chapel of St. Archangel Michael in the village Brytsy in Kyiv-Svyatoshin region of Kyiv district.

Iosif Mook

Gregory Abramovich Mook, who was born in 1911, another warrior from this large family. From 1942 to 1945 he was in the Red Army and was awarded the medal "For Military Merit".

Luk Grigory Samoilovich, was born in 1907, Captain, operatives of SMERSH during the war in 1941-1945, awarded medals "For Defense of Stalingrad" and "For Fighting Merit", the Order of the Red Star and the Order of the Patriotic War - the second extent.

Mints Mikhail Shlomovich, was born in 1911, a Sergeant in the army since 1941, awarded the medals "For Defense of Stalingrad" and "For Military Merit", and the Order of the Red Star.

Altukher Mikhail Abramovich, was born in 1921, Private, military doctor, he was awarded the medals "For the Defense of Moscow" and "For Courage", and two Orders of the Red Star.

Tarnopolsky Peter Leonidovich, was born in 1922, drafted into the army after the liberation of Bar, petty officer, aviation scout. He was awarded the medal "For the Liberation of Budapest".

I. G. Gampel went to war in 1943 after graduating from medical school. He was the commander of the sanitary regiment. He finished the war in the Austrian Alps, then continued to serve in the army. After demobilization, Major of Medical Service I. Gampel began to work in town of Bar since 1952. At the time, he was the only dentist in the area.

I want to tell you about another famous resident of Bar. This is Boris Abramovich London, born in 1924.

Boris and London

When the war began, he, as part of another 500 pre-conscripts born in 1924-1926, from Bar district was sent to the East as a mobilization reserve. B. London reached its destination, though many had fled, he said. He studied at a military school, but did not finish it, and went on to fight with the enemy. During the whole war Boris was in the intelligence unit of his regiment, he was wounded and awarded orders and medals. He did not receive the rank of officer but remained a private.

*Award letter of B. London, his introduction to become
a recipient of the Order of the Red Star*

In 1997 B. London published a book in Israel *Gone To Eternity* about Bar, his parents, about himself and his life.

The cover of the book by B. London

In 1975 Marshal Chuykov in the book *Battle of the Century* (memories of the heroic defense of Stalingrad) wrote as follows:

To defeat the enemy's stronghold in the main office of the plant "Red October", the soldiers of the assault group of Sokolov's division were forced to build a capital wall. They broke through the wall with a 122-millimeter howitzer, which was disassembled in parts, dragged into the occupied part of the building. There they collected her and put into action. After several direct-fire shots, a gap was formed in the wall, and this ended the existence of the fascist garrison here. This operation with a 122-millimeter howitzer was done by the commander of the 6th battery of the 178th artillery regiment comrade V. R. Belfer, who reached Berlin, survived and now teaches in the Vinnytsia region.

Back in 1943, the front-line correspondent Kozyakin published a book *In Memory By Name*, which mentions the Senior Lieutenant (at that time) Belfer.

V. R. Belfer from the book of G. Kozyakin about
the actions of the 45th artillery regiment in
Stalingrad "In Memory By Name", 1943

Among the awards of Belfer: two Orders of the Red Banner, Order of Alexander Nevsky, two Orders of the Patriotic War second degree, Order of the Patriotic War first degree, Order of the Red Star, Order of the Badge of Honor, medals "For the Defense of Moscow", "For the Defense of Stalingrad" and many other medals. Victor Belfer reached Berlin and on the wall of the Reichstag building left his autograph with the inscription that there was a Jew from town of Bar.

Jewish residents of Bar, who also fought on different fronts: G. Kesler, A. Gontmacher, M. Altucher (was in partisan group), S. Dodik, B. Poteshman, E. Tarlov, N. Shpun, M. Kremin', D. Fishelevich, E. Freidzon, M. Gulko, A.Weisfeld, L. Weinberg, Sh. Vinokur, I. Vuldman, Sh. Kuts, M. Elyukim and many others.

I also want to tell you about the foreign language teacher David Isaevich Gerzenshtein. He was born in 1923 in Kryzhopil Vinnytsia district. From the first days of the war he was on the front, then captured, where he was from the summer 1942 until April 1, 1945. He was in different camps, including Sachsenhausen. David changed his name so he managed to survive. On April 1, 1945, he was liberated by American troops. After inspections, he continued to serve in the Red Army. In 1952 after graduation from the pedagogical institute, he began to work in Bar. He was a German language teacher at school # 1, and his wife taught English at school #3. Gerzenshtein was a talented teacher, who was loved by school children. He was a versatile person: he played musical instruments, sang, enjoyed painting and taking pictures. He died in 1991.

Victor Belfer

Thanks to such examples, it is with confident to say that all Jews from Bar, who could hold the machine gun, fought the enemy. Some on the war fronts, some in partisan detachments, some in underground groups, and some on the labor front fought for victory over fascism.

The horrors of the Nazi regime did not break the will of the Jewish people to resist and fight for life. It should be noted that during World War II, unlike in World War I, only one nation, the Jews, served and fought only on one side, in one camp. They saw in the struggle against Nazism not only the duty of the citizens of the anti-Hitler coalition, but also the national liberation mission of the sons of the Jewish people.

The participation of Podolia's Jews in the resistance movement to fascism can be the subject of a separate book. Here is some general data on Vinnytsia region. The guerrilla groups were attended by several hundreds of Jews. Only in the first regiment of the partisan brigade Kondratyuk, operating on the territory of the Vinnytsia region, according to October 1, 1943, 422 Jews fought with the Nazis. 135 Jews took part in the anti-Nazi underground movement in Vinnytsia region.

In February 1942 the underground group of Filberg and Mezhman had been set up in Bar. They died at the hands of the Nazis. The active members of this group were A. K.

Feldberg and M. L. Altukher, who later went to the partisan brigade. By the way, Mezhman's wife recognized in the face the former police chief of Andrusev in Yugoslavia and reported him to the Soviet authorities.

Beginning in 1943, underground and guerrilla groups became more active. In the newspaper *Barsky Vestnik*, which was issued by the occupiers, on February 25, the following order was printed:

"Recently, Soviet bandits appeared in the district and the local population provides them with shelter, food, transport. All the elders are immediately ordered to inform Gebietskommissar about the appearance of the bandits, the one who assists the criminals will be hanged, their houses burned and property confiscated. The ones who will betray the criminals will be awarded".

And this has led to certain results. After the attack on the Romanian border detachment, the leader of the underground group Filberg was arrested on denunciation, who was shot on 11 January 1944 after being severely tortured.

The organizer of the underground guerrilla resistance to the Nazis in Bar district was Secretary of the District Committee of the party A. F. Manyak, who was helped in this work by the Chairman of Bar's district Executive Committee M. I. Golbert and a resident of Bar Kosherev. On July 16, 1941 when fascists came into Bar, this group of 15 men had left Bar. The squad of A. F. Manyak in the first battle with the enemy was defeated. Manyak himself managed to cross the front line and joined the ranks of the Red Army. Subsequently, he was summoned to Moscow and appointed as a Chief of Staff of the Vinnytsia partisan unit, which was at that time in the Belarusian forests. In May 1943, Captain A. Manyak, having reached the location of his compound and jumped from his plane, died as his parachute did not open.

M. I. Golbert fought at the front, was seriously wounded and was commissioned. In 1944, after the liberation of Bar, he returned to the town, where he continued to work as Chairman of the Executive Committee from 1947.

The town of Bar was liberated by the 38th army of the 1st Ukrainian front. It was assisted by 18th and 40th armies. The enemy suffered significant losses here: 30,000 were killed and 5,000 were taken prisoner. Both highways in the direction of Vinnytsia and in the direction of Kamyanets-Podolsky were clogged with mutilated Nazi equipment. On March 25, 1944 at 6 p.m. soldiers of 305th division of 38th army entered the town of Bar.

The commander of the 1st Ukrainian front G.K. Zhukov praised the actions of the 38th army when he was passing through Bar and said to the commander of this army K. S. Moskalenko: "You did a good job here in Bar!"

The scheme of military operations of the former 38th army on liberation of Bar and nearby villages. 20 to 25 March 1944

After restoration of the Soviet power in the town, in each regional organization there were some German cars, various equipment, and machine-building plant used this scrap metal for the foundry.

The military Commissariat of Bar district called 14,405 people for the entire period of the war in the ranks of the Red Army, including about 2,000 Jews, but not all of them returned home alive from the battlefields. On the Square of Memory on the grieving granite 424 names of the inhabitants of Bar who died in this war are stamped on the plates, although it is known that 535 inhabitants of the town died on military fronts. On these plates, as in life, are intertwined names of Ukrainians, Jews, Poles, and Russians. The entire list of called up is available in digital version on the website www.pogvignaroda.ru (translated as "the feat of the people in the Great Patriotic War of 1941-1945").

Thousands of soldiers' letters in the form of a triangle from the terrible 1941 are currently located in the Kiev memorial complex "The National Museum of History of World War II 1941-1944". There they came back to Ukraine in 2010 after long negotiations with museums of Vienna where they were the past 70 years. These letters were written in Kamyanets-Podolsky from the mobilized military units, but were not sent due to the rapid retreat of the Soviet troops and the occupation of the city. Among the triangles is a letter addressed to Arkady Berdichevsky, who was working at the sugar factory of Bar at that time. It was impossible to read the sender's name, probably it was a close relative.

List of Jews from Bar who died or died of wounds on the fronts during World War II:

Altukher, Shmul Zelmanovich (1910)

Anshin, Abram Isakovich (1917)

Aranovich, Abram Srulevich (1906)

Averbukh, Moses Isakovich (1902)

Ayzenberg, Yakov Izraylovich (1921)

Banduryansky, Izya Lvovich (1921)

Baron, Chaim Shulimovich (1911)

Baron, Efim Abramovich (1918)

Baron, Pinya Shulimovich (1907)

Basyuk, Boris Froymovich (1913)

Bey, Mikhail Shlomovich (1905)

Bey, Moses Shlomovich (1906)

Bintel, Samuel Moiseevich (1910)

Brum, Boris Yakovlevich (1898)

Burda, Aron Kosovich (1913)

Chuck, Ian Shapsovich (1906)

Dumer, Dmitri Izraylovich (1918)

Dumer, Shmul Berkovich (1903)

Dunaevich, Fishel Abramovich (1912)

Elkis, Isak Naumovich (1900)

Engel, Ivan Grigoryevich (1912)

Engel, Naum Aronovich (1912)

Etingeym, Agnes Aronovna (died 1941, Major of the medical service)

Factor, Mikhail Semenovich (1925)

Fishman, Boris Itskovich (1907)

Fishman, Zus Lvovich (1914)

Freilikh, David Itskovich (1898)

Freilikh, Joseph Leibovich (1896)

Freilikh, Samuel Shimanovich (1902)

Friedman, Nikolai Efimovich (1898)

Gelman, Marcus Iosifovich (1925)

Gelman, Naum Yakovlevich (1910)

Gershenzon, Joseph Naumovich (1920)

Gershenzon, Mikhail Naumovich (1920)

Gluzman, Mikhail Pavlovich (1909)

Goikhberg, Abram Borisovich (1919)

Goldman, Benzion Lazarevich (1910)

Goltzer, Arkady Moiseevich(1919)

Gormand, Yul'gerd Antonovich (1910)

Greenshtein, Abram Davidovich (1917)

Greenshtein, Yankel Kopelevich (1906)

Grum, Boris Yakovlevich (1908)

Gruzman, Leontiy Efimovich (1912)

Gulkis, Mikhail Davydovich (1912)

Kai, Moses Davidovich (1909)

Kan, Isai Filippovich (1907)

Kantselmakher, Marco Shomowich (1905)

Kantselmakher, Mihayo Solomonovich (1909)

Kasha, Yankel Shmulevich (1901)

Khaim, Neisa Abramovich (1905)

Khaylo, Rodion Lazarevich (1920)

Kheyfits, Mikhail Alexandrovich (1904)

Kleban, Joseph Abramovich (1908)

Kleban, Kisel Yankelovich (1912)

Kleiman, Boris Lazarovich (1912)

Kleiman, David Yakovlevich (1920)

Knirel, Gregory Isaakovich (1921)

Knopman, Simko Itskovich (1911)

Krasner, Joseph Alexandrovich (1913)

Kraytman, Yakov Volkovich (1920)

Kryts, Naum Iosifovich (1922)

Lakhterman, Moses Gershovich (1916)

Leyfer, Grigory Zakharovich (1922)

Leyfer, Isaac Sukherovich (1915)

Leyvant, Shlema Khaimovich (1900)

Litynsky, Liukin Srulovich (1916)

Ludker, Joseph Lazarevich (1910)

Luk, Abram Saulovich (1920)

Maidman, Moses Lvovich (1904)

Mordkovich, Shmul Bentsionovich (1906)
Moshel, Dmitry Mikhaylovich (1918)
Moshel, Efim Shlomovich (1909)
Moshel, Mikhail Isaakovich (1921)
Moshel, Motya Moiseevich (1917)
Naftulinshen, Joseph Moiseevich (1815)
Nakinzon, David Shmulevich (1898)
Oistrakh, Boris Iosifovich (1917)
Oksman, Isaac Isakovich (1904)
Pitkus, Aron Ilyich (1900)
Pivenshtein, Gershko Lvovich (1900)
Rapoport, Yakov Emyupimovich (1903)
Raykhinshteyn, Ilya Isayevich (1903)
Rendel, Samuel Grogoryevich (1915)
Revchuk, Samuel Lvovich (1896)
Reznick, Naum Nukhimovich (1910)
Segal, Michael Petrovich (1920)
Shapiro, Shmul Anshelovich (1910)
Shapiro, Leizer Nigenovich (1904)
Shapiro, Isaak Shlemovich (1908)
Shmukler, Boris Markovich (1896)
Shmukler, Pinya Abramovich (1924)
Shor, Yakov Davydovich (1916)
Shor, Yulik Lazarovich (1904)
Shpiegelman, Grigory Naftulovich (1906)
Shtarkman, Isaac Abramovich (1921)
Shuster, Khaim Isakovich (1912)
Shuster, Naum Isakovich (1914)
Shuster, Semyon Lvovich (1921)
Shuster, Yakov Isakovich (1915)
Shvets, Naum Shmulevich (1904)
Shvets, Srul Abramovich (1915)
Sirota, Isaac Nukhimovich (1903)
Sternik, Grigory Isaakovich (1921)
Tabachnik, David Efimovich (1921)
Tarasovsky, Lazar Davidovich (1914)
Task, Yankel Abramovich (1908)
Tkach, Gersh Aronovich (1914)
Udler, Khaim Khaskelevich (1908)
Udler, Marcus Abramovich (1905)

Vasserman, Moses Chunovich (1920)
Vaynbrand, Yefim Naumovich (1903)
Vayner, Zalman Kelmanovich (1904)
Velgosh, Idel Shlomovich (1926)
Voskoboynik, Joseph Yakovlevich (1912)
Yanshtein, Anatoly Yakovlevich (1911)
Zaydman, Ber Kalmanovich (1906)
Zektser, Simon Naumovich (1899)
Zeltser, Gedal Shmulevich (died 1941)
Zilberman, Mendel Iosifovich (1922)
Zutler, Marcus Abramovich (1905)

In the Book of Memory of Jewish Soldiers there are names of people originally from Bar who died or went missing in the battles against fascism. Their names are not inscribed on the plates on the Square of Memory. They are:

Abram, Itskovich
David, Abramovich
Averbukh, Abram Itskovich
Azrilyevich, Pinya Moiseevich Bekker
Blyakh, Abram Borisovich
Burd, Aron Kosovich
Genadinich (Genadinik)
Gulkis, Mendel Elyevich
Katz, Abram Naumovich
Kodner, Joseph Yakovlevich
Krasilovsky, Lev Konstantinovich
Marakhovsky, Abram Leibovich
Mishuris, Joseph Yakovlevich
Moses, Vulfovich
Naidorf, Wolf Leibovich
Vainberg, Naum Srulevich
Zakman, Abram Shmulevich

This is an incomplete list of the dead, the search still continues, but, once again, it confirms that the Jews, like all other nations, defended their homeland from the enemy.

Many Jews took part in battles in the World War I. In the nominal lists of dead, missing and wounded, among the lower ranks on the fronts of this war was known about 61 soldiers from the town of Bar, 31 of them were Jews, that is, 50 percent. These are ordinary people:

Barenboym, Leib Srulovich, was wounded on 08/12/1914

Beregras, Vol Moshkovich, died 11/08/1914

Berenzon, Vol Shmulevich, died 10/07/1914

Blyakh, Itsko Abramovich, missing 11/14/1941

Bolinzon, Khaskell Shmulevich, died 09/24/1914

Bryl, Mendel Khaimovich, missing 02/12/1915

Firer, Ovsey Abramovich, shooter, missing 11/11/1914

Fix, Usher, private, wounded 10/01/1914

Glubar, Lev, private, missing 08/26/1914

Gordon, Abram Mordkovich, private, missing 10/12/1914

Goykher, Yankel Kiselevich, private, wounded 09/05/1914

Greenshtein, David Putovich, corporal, missing 10/17/1914

Khayt, Shalom Mendelevich, private, wounded 08/17/1914

Kisenzon, Boruch Srulevich, private, was captured 01/15/1915

Lieberman, Leyzor, private, missing 10/05/1914

Pivnik, Bendekh, private, wounded 08/17/1914

Popovsky, Moshko Shulimovich, private, missing 08/08/1914

Rapoport, Yudko Yudkovich, shooter, missing 11/11/1914

Rozenshteyn, Kissel, private, missing 11/27/1914

Sanuler, Leyzor Khaimovich, private, missing 11/25/1914

Schnayden, Nachman Moshkovich, private, went missing 08/06/1914

Schwartz, Khaim Zalmanovich, shooter, missing 11/11/1914

Shikhel, Boruch Nakhmanovich, private, went missing 08/18/1914

Shister, Ios-Moyshe Yudkovich, private, wounded 08/23/1914

Shlak, Wolf Moshkovich, private, went missing 11/20/1914

Shvets, Nukhim Shelmovich, private, wounded 10/12/1914

Surkis, Yankel Davidovich, shooter, missing 09/27/1914

Tabachnik, Aron Davidovich, private, wounded 08/28/1914

Trachman, Moshko Abramovich, private, missing 12/03/1914

Tsimbler, Srul Itskovich, private, wounded 11/22/1914

Zinger, Aba, private, missing 06/24/1914

Those who went missing mostly fell into German captivity, or died somewhere in the retreat.

YIDDISHLAND

So, having examined the period from antiquity to the early 1930s, it is safe to say that a conditional country was created - Yiddishland, which was scattered in different cities and towns, and which in the 20th century, in the truest sense of the word, turned to dust. It stretched across Ukraine, from North to South, from West to East, Poland, the Baltic States, Belarus, Russia.

However, long before the existence of Yiddishland, on the territory of modern Ukraine and, accordingly, on the territory of Bar, emerged Khazar Khaganate (empire), a powerful state in 6th -12th centuries. For the state structure resembled a modern federation, one of the subjects of which was Kievan Rus.

The Khazars were not an ethnic group or nationality. It is rather a generalizing name for the Turkic, Hungarian, Slavic, and Jewish people. The peculiarity of the Khazar Khaganate was that a significant part of its population (including Slavs) professed the Jewish faith.

The essential features of the Khazar empire were toleration and equality of citizens. That is, there was a Jewish component of Kievan Rus.

From the map it shows that the territory of the Khazar kingdom covered part of Eastern Podolia, where the campaigns were carried out in the Western and South-Western part of Ukraine with the capture of this area. Therefore, some politicians and our enemies are trying to draw a parallel Khazar Khaganate with Ukraine, where the Jews in the protection of the country and the state play an important role. What I'm saying is that we need to learn our true story by rejecting lies and various myths and falsifications. And all this will guarantee our freedom, sovereignty and defense.

Yiddish was spoken in Yiddishland, which was native to both European Jews and the Jews of Ukraine. On the territory of modern Ukraine, this language developed, because here lived the leaders of Hasidism Rabbi Baal Shem Tov, Rabbi Levi-Yitzhak from Berdichev and Rabbi Nachman from Bratslav, who raised the Yiddish language to the level of holiness, to the level of "loshn-koidesh". In the period between the two world wars, Ukraine had a network of educational and cultural organizations in Yiddish.

Since the second half of the 1940s, the centers of Jewish culture were liquidated, their leaders were repressed. The catastrophe of Jewry destroyed the majority of Yiddish speakers and broke the chain of transmission of the Yiddish cultural tradition, both religious and secular. Now most of Yiddishland is small pieces that are spread across Ukraine.

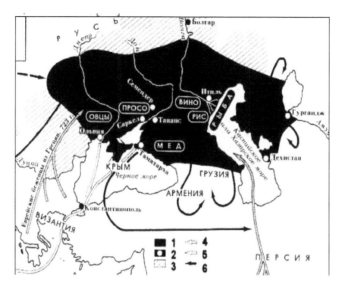

Map of Khazar Empire: 1-Khazar Kingdom, 2-Khazar cities, 3-tribes paying tribute to Khazar, 4-ways of resettlement of Jews in the Khazar, 5-trade routes of the Khazar, 6-military campaigns of the Khazar

The life of European Jews was very difficult. Pogroms with hundreds, and even thousands of Jews killed in England, France and Germany were a habitual phenomenon.

And only Poland was waiting for Jews. And then it's not a case of humanism, and that is not a master's business-trading, this was the gentry, except the system of trade was poorly developed in Poland. Therefore, the Polish and Lithuanian magnates for this cause invited Jews from all over Europe.

In Poland Jews had privileges granted by kings Boleslav II and Casimir III in the 13th and 14th centuries. Experiencing oppression and persecution in Western Europe, people began to move actively to the Kingdom of Poland. By the end of the 17th century, 80% of all Ashkenazis lived in Poland. After a certain period, Poland began to decline, and, accordingly, the Jewish pogroms began, and enlightenment came to Europe.

In the 18th century Jews massively began to settle to the West, and to the East from Poland. But for some time Poland remained the center of Yiddishland. With the transfer of Jews to the Russian Empire, and here in the early 20th century, Jews became the great non-Slavic people of Russia, there were 5.2 million, which is 4.1% of the population of the Empire and 60% of the Jewish people. And Ukraine became the core of Yiddishland, where most Jews lived in the so-called "Pale of Settlement".

Jewish property is invisible, if about any of the nationalities we could say "centuries of oppression", then about the sorrow of the Jewish people we might say "millennium" in the terms of time. In such circumstances it becomes usual for the house not to be adorned, as maybe the Cossacks, during a pogrom, will not be impressed about whose house this is and will move on. Jews have created many architectural schools, but there was no one specifically Jewish.

You can tell, of course, and the role of Jews in the Great October revolution of 1917 and that after the abolition by the Provisional government the "Pale of Settlement", Jews began to settle throughout the former USSR.

Then the exit from Yiddishland was replaced by a terrible Holocaust -- a massive and consistent genocide of the Jewish people -- which promted further assimilation and departure to Israel, USA and other countries of the world.

Generations after the Holocaust are like a tree without roots. Two main reasons contributed to this: the Holocaust and the Soviet regime. If Hitler destroyed Jews physically, the Communist regime destroyed them spiritually.

Modern Yiddishland is a shell that was thrown off by the ancient people in the early 20th century, making a sharp turn in their lives.

Analyzing the above table, it can be seen that the percentage of the Jewish population employed in agriculture decreases dramatically over time. This is due to the fact that by the end of 1939 almost all Jewish collective farms were liquidated, and after the war the national Jewish districts, which were also engaged in agriculture, were liquidated. Over time, the number of unskilled workers also decreased, because Jewish families sought to receive a good education. Accordingly, the number of leaders of middle managers, middle managers and other specialists of the highest category increased. Trade was no longer a priority. In the party-state apparatus, the number of Jews has practically not changed since 1959, because there was an unspoken quota for the admission of Jews to work in the Communist party. Approximately such distribution of Jews in all spheres of activity was also reflected in the town of Bar.

At the same time, the creative and scientific achievements of Jews were widely known at the state level of recognition. Many of them in the 1940s-1950s became winners of the Stalin prize. Among them - writers: Samuel Marshak, Ilya Ehrenburg, Emmanuel Kazakevich, Margarita Aliger, Lev Kassil and others; film director Julius Raizman, singers and actors - Mark Reyzen, Igor Ilyinsky, Mark Bernes; composers Reinhold Glier and Matvey Blunter; violinist David Oystrakh; cartoonist Boris Efimov; sculptor Zair Azgur and many others. The heyday of David Dragunsky started at the beginning of the 1950s. Dragunsky opposed Zionism, identified it with anti-Semitism, often represented the USSR abroad, actively criticized Israel's aliyah and its politics. Later he realized the falsity of his views on life. Also, many scientists received the

Stalin prize: ophthalmologist Mikhail Averbach, mathematicians - Israel Gelfand, Felix Gantmacher, Leonid Kantorovich, Alexander Khinchin, physicists - Lev Artsimovich, Lev Altschuler, Yakov Zeldovich, Abram Ioffe, Lev Landau, Julius Khariton, aircraft designer Mikhail Gurevich, historian Eugene Tarle. The first world champions in the history of Soviet sport were Jews: weightlifter Grigory Novak and chess player Mikhail Botvinnik.

Social and professional structure of the Jewish population of the USSR in 1926-1989, in percent					
Year	**1926**	**1939**	**1959**	**1970**	**1979**
Party-state apparatus	0.3	1.3	0.4	0.3	0.3
Middle manager	2.0	8.3	8.7	8.5	7.6
Scientists and University professors	0.1	0.8	1.2	2.1	3.2
Other highly qualified specialists	6.5	12.8	20.1	26.5	31.4
Specialists of average qualification	5.4	16.6	20.2	20.9	18.9
Junior employees	6.2	10.2	9.2	7.3	6.2
Professionals in the field of trade	21.2	11.4	8.4	7.2	6.2
Skilled worker	35.2	24.2	25.4	21.7	21.3
Unskilled worker	11.4	11.2	5.8	5.2	4.7
Agricultural workers	11.7	3.2	0.6	0.3	0.2

A characteristic feature of Ukrainian Jews is such a parental attitude to the country where they live, a clear reassessment of their responsibility for its future. They say that if there is a meeting of two Jews, they will talk about Ukraine, or a somehow born union between a Ukrainian and a Jew wasn't noticed it as clearly as it was not expected.

Yiddish language is valued in the European culture. In 1996, the Council of Europe adopted a Declaration on this issue. Sweden, for example, allocates $ 100,000 annually for the development of the Yiddish language, which in 2000 received the status of one of the five minority languages.

It is necessary to support the idea that Yiddish is a part of both European and Ukrainian culture, and language support is a national issue and should be dealt with at the state level with the participation of various foundations and organizations. In the perspective of Ukraine's European integration, these problems are extremely relevant.

If special methods were earlier used for the destruction of the Yiddish language, now we also need special targeted measures to restore it. All that will create conditions for a possible restoration of Yiddishland, but it will be at a new stage of development.

And another interesting fact. In our times, the most densely populated Jewish city is Uman, the patrimony of the "Bratslav Hasidim", where tens of thousands of pilgrims come for the Jewish New Year each September. Here, on the outskirts, a real Jewish neighborhood comes to life on these days. Jews and locals interact as if in parallel worlds, sometimes crossing paths (yet thousands of visitors who are not aware of the local culture and customs of the holidays definitely create inconvenience), but do not seek to interact. So lives a certain type of small shtetl during Jewish New year (Rosh-Ha-Shana).

The world of Jewish places... There was nothing left of them, As if Vespasian had passed through the fires and the noise. The shoichet will not say his greasy jokes,

And, a coachman will not sing on the highway while lashing the horses

I'm used to it – it's impossible to surprise me.

But my old father, he still needs to ask

How people were taken away from the bright day to die.

And how the children cried and begged in vain for mercy. My blind father, this world is known and dear to him.

And with a trembling hand, because his eyes are blind,

He will feel the houses, synagogues and stones of the graves, -

The world of familiar paintings, from which he came once.

A world of familiar pictures -

Nothing would bring them back to him.

And let's give the Germans ten for each bullet,

The shoichet will not say his greasy jokes,

And, a coachman will never sing again while lashing on the horses.

Naum Korzhavin, *Time is given. Verses and poems.*

JEWISH COMMUNITY DEVELOPMENT, 1880-1950

To write about the 20th century we need to go beyond its historical boundaries.

By the beginning of the revolutionary events of 1917, the social-economic structure of Ukrainian Jewry had not undergone significant changes. The traditional occupations of Jews, which stood out in the pre-capitalist period, were preserved by the harsh conditions of the Pale of Settlement. Through its nationality and religion, Jewry, by the decision of the Tsarist government, had the opportunity to engage in only certain types of economic activity. The Jews of the towns were allowed to conduct intermediary trade between the town and the surrounding villages, to engage in certain types of craft. In particular, about half of the Jews in the "Pale of Settlement" were engaged in trade among the entire population.

In the industry that operated in the "Pale of Settlement", according to the census of 1897, about a third of the Jewish population was employed, and agriculture engaged 3-4% of Jews, employees of private companies amounted to 5%, those in public service and engaged in so-called "free professions" - 5%. This peculiarity of the social structure and economic activity of the Jews was, in fact, the main reason for the specific attitude towards them from the surrounding ethnic groups, as well as the emergence on this basis of a number of problems, the combination of which was called "the Jewish question".

At the end of the Civil war, the Jewish population was in a worse position than other ethnic groups in Ukraine.

A typical picture of the life of Jewish residents during the Civil war is described in a letter from a group of Jews from the town of Kopaigorod, Podolia province (located 25 km from Bar) in 1924:

We well know from life of former times that we, Jews, are scapegoats at all cases: the landowner will argue with the land tenant - to whom will not get justice? - the Jew. The bailiff will not get along with the constable - who is put in prison? - A Jew. The landowner argues with peasants about works - here it is clear business whom it is necessary to flog? - A Jew. And after such disasters, misfortunes, after so many pogroms, when our blood flowed like a river from one end of our country to the other, when our fathers were slaughtered, mothers were shot, children were killed, sisters were raped, brothers were tortured, property was looted, houses were burned and so on - and all this for what? We are all Jews - Communists-Bolsheviks. Also, in particular, in our small towns of the Polish-Romanian border, from where the landlords fled, during the imperialist war, the Austrians and Germans entered, then Petliura, damn him, then the

Poles, then again Petliura with his horde, there was nothing left to plunder. Killed, robbed, burned. The place consists of 142 houses, you probably think of actual houses. Nothing happened, just houses. 120 of them consist of one room and a kitchen, two rooms and a kitchen there are 20 pieces, 3/4 of them rooms with shops together. There are 195 families. Of these, 56 families of artisans who do not have bread, they have nowhere to earn a living. 32 families of widows and orphans - the inheritance of bandits-Petliurists and others, without any means of livelihood, 20 families of old men, looking into the grave without need and hunger, 35 families of the unemployed, 5 people are laborers, 8 former butchers, who do not have meat to sell, a Rabbi, two shoychets, who are paid by the water from the well. Thus, there remains our so-called bourgeoisie, and you know who it is: 15 families have patents of the first category, own one consumable sheet, and each of them has goods for five or six rubles: 2 dozen matches, 20 pounds of salt, 1 pound of Montpensier, 20 sheets of cigarette paper and several spools of thread. All this "commodity" he buys himself in cooperation and stands with it on the street right on the ground, or he goes to the nearest fair in order to earn a pound of bread. 11 families have the patent of the 2nd category, and such at us appear large bourgeois. He goes to Zhmerinka for some goods, such as a barrel of herring, 5 pounds of kerosene, 20 pounds of candy, 100 packs of matches - all this cost 50-60 rubles. The largest traders-owners of the 3rd category – 12 families. 3/4 of them own goods from 20 to 100 rubles. These are manufacturers, and the law is that if he has a production for 30 rubles, he must have a patent of the 3rd category. Having goods for 500 rubles - there are only six families. These are the 192 families of the place mentioned, and you can imagine the good life of the place.

In our town everyone is united by one desire: to destroy all Jews. Either during the day or at night our local leaders celebrate lush parties with plenty of drinks, and this requires a decent amount of money, but local chief of militia finds a way out. Money is necessary: "Now to issue 40-50 penalties for unsanitary acts and money will come." We keep our town pretty clean. We have nothing to do, so every day we clean the streets, they are much cleaner than in Moscow. But the authorities need the money, so they fabricate the protocols and transmit them to people's court, and there we are judged without witnesses, etc. The next day people bring the last remaining pillows for sale. All people are to stand on roofs and paint pipes, being afraid of penalties, then turn for shopkeepers. Why did they open their shops from noon to 4 o'clock? And after all this the order is issued requiring signs be painted with red paint and they should have 1 1/2 yards in width. For all inaccuracies of execution of this order fines are taken, and "the money goes into their own pocket". Besides, bribes from all sides are taken, parties are celebrated and they make to themselves such dresses, much more beautiful, than dresses of the former landowners. And this is done by all our good leaders of power.

Arbitrariness at all levels turned into the norm: "there are, then, these 38 remaining families of merchants, which we have already written about. Standing over their head, their chief of militia threatens them. If in a 24-hour period they will not contribute 120 rubles to 38 shops, and for synagogues - 150 rubles, he will show what the militia can do. For example: an unsanitary act, acts for signs, for pipes, then, to be sure, these acts will be more expensive in cost. And if a citizen allows himself to ask a question, he is told that this is counter-revolutionary agitation. Then the whole mass is intimidated, and out of fear the last shirts are sold, and everything is fulfilled. In addition, comes someone who calls himself an agent of Komtorg and shall convene a meeting of all citizens. Then they are told to leave the meeting, because they did not want to gather anybody, only the peasants, because at the meeting they must discuss how to torture and strangle Jews. There are no grain growers among Jews, for we lack land for Jews, it remains obvious that Jews must go to look for this land. The question is, on what means to go? Sell your houses for 200 rubles? And after all, it was recently written in the newspapers about such elements, that they should not budge. On the other hand, after all, that little house, as a matter of fact, is not even yours, and a thought will appear in head of the Executive Committee, and he will nationalize several houses. Appeal to the people's court, the answer will be that, however, in such places nationalization does not exist, but the Executive Committee is right.

This is only part of a letter that was sent to the Central Executive Committee by Jews from the Podolia province. This pattern was observed in many cities and towns of the province. There was no response to the letters, although we can draw some conclusions.

The number of Jews throughout the territory of Ukraine decreased. According to the demographer Ya.M. Schinsky, in 1919 in Ukraine lived 3.3 million Jews; of them in the territory of Soviet Ukraine – 1,577,000, in particular, on the right bank of the river Dnieper – 682,000, on the left bank – 198,000. Only 4.65% of Jews worked as workers, 4.11% as employees and 4.2% in transport. Among the Jewish workers, printers and tobacconists predominated, and among the employees - workers of the medical and sanitary sphere, 200,000 Jews were engaged in craft.

According to the survey of Jewish settlements of the border strip of right-bank Ukraine, the declassified Jews made up from 40 to 70%. In the towns, the majority were artisans who worked on scarce raw materials. The absence of the latter, and those markets closed by Bolshevik measures, further complicated the difficult situation. In Podolia the total number of unemployed was more than 30% of the total Jewish population living in the region. Most of the unemployed were women, only one in five of them had the opportunity to work. The group of unemployed included artisans and those who had no work at all or worked sporadically, as well as people who lived on the help that came from abroad.

In 1917-1918, suburban Jewish agricultural farms appeared, which were engaged in growing vegetables and processing dairy products purchased on the market. For many, agriculture was the only means of existence.

The coming to power of the Bolsheviks in Ukraine led to an even greater strengthening of the devastation of Jewish towns, because the labor activity of the Jews was based on small private property, trade, the right to which the new government usurped. The policy of "war communism", with its widespread practice of expropriations of property, directly affected the sphere of economic activity of the majority of the small-town Jewish population. The Bolsheviks banned private trade. An system was created which was to be responsible for the distribution of products in the city and the exchange of products between the village and the city. The need for intermediary trade, which the Jews were engaged in, disappeared. Jewish merchants, traders, artisans were faced with a choice: either to die or to change the sphere of activity. The politics of the Bolsheviks dealt a blow to Jewish artisans and craftsmen. The creation of a system of state orders for enterprises led to the closure of access to the market of handicrafts and artisans, and it was saturated with cheap factory products. "War communism" led to the prohibition of trade of artisans and peasants. Craftsmen and artisans found themselves in conditions where the alternative was one - to become a worker of Soviet enterprises or join the ranks of mass poverty.

The social-economic situation in shtetl did not change for the better during the introduction of the new economic policy in the USSR, which granted the right to individual producers, in particular peasants, to freely sell products, paying a fixed tax to the state. Similar rights were granted to artisans. In 1923, they were removed from the group of non-labor element and referred to the transitional group of "half-breeds", and in 1925 to the group of workers. The socio-economic state of Jews in cities and towns during the NEP depended on local specifics. The more economically developed the town was, the more middle-class and prosperous artisans lived in it. In the small towns, most of the artisans and traders were poor. The income of artisans and traders depended on the purchasing power of the peasants and residents of the town. If the town had its own industrial production (factory or factory), the artisans and traders could count on a larger contingent of buyers of their own products. The solvency of artisans depended on the seasonality, qualification and specialty of the artisan. So, big profits were received by leather workers and shoemakers. During the period of complete unemployment, low-skilled artisans were forced to live on casual earnings, traveling to the surrounding villages. The lack of raw materials, wear and tear of equipment and the lack of working capital had a negative impact on craftsmen.

By the mid-1920s, a layer of Jewish intellectuals and civil servants was forming. The ranks of the commissars were filled by young Jewish intellectuals, or representatives of the liberal professions, who sympathized with the Bolsheviks. After the announcement by the Communist party of the nativization policy, some Jewish employees were ousted from the local Ukrainian authorities by national cadres. The reason for the dismissals was the ignorance of the Jewish Soviet bureaucracy of the Ukrainian language. On the basis of statistical data of trade unions of Ukraine, the number of Jewish employees decreased to 180,000. That is, Jewish employees made up about 8% of the total number of the Soviet bureaucracy. Most Jewish employees worked in state institutions of economic commissariats.

In the early 1920s, the authorities did not pay attention to Jewish artisans. They were mechanically classified as unearned elements. The leaders of the Ukrainian Jewish section considered the Jewish artisans the main social base for the anti-Soviet, anti-proletarian activities of the Jewish bourgeoisie. The administrative institutions of the town neglected their problems. This led to discontent with the policies of the ruling party and the spread of Zionist ideology among the population of the towns. The situation that developed in the towns of right-bank Ukraine in the mid-1920s for the Bolshevik regime was explosive. In the towns, overpopulated by the impoverished Jewish people, widespread calls to fight the Bolsheviks were initiated. The Jews of the towns were looking for a way out of the situation, trying to emigrate abroad, or, in extreme cases, to migrate to the big cities and settle down there for industrial enterprises. Negative information was spread abroad. The actions of the ruling party were considered by representatives of the Jewish community as an open manifestation of state anti-Semitism. All this led to the growth among Ukrainian Jewry, especially young people, Zionist views and political beliefs.

Striking data on the participation of Jews in the national economy of the province (in the second half of the 19th century) is compared with the total number of people employed in these industries (recall that the Jews accounted for 12.2% of the total population of the province): educational and educational activities - 69.8%, science, literature and art - 46%, processing of plant and animal products – 73.9%, maintenance of taverns, hotels, clubs – 78.5%, trade mediation – 95.3%, maintenance of housing and construction works – 36.8%, production of clothes – 58.1%, trade - 85%, metal processing - 29%, agriculture - 0.3%.

In the early 20th century, the Jewish population of the Podolia region was concentrated mainly in cities and towns. Some Podolia towns, which had a significant number of Jewish populations, kept the Jewish flavor, which, in turn, determined their life, social and living conditions, and economic characteristics. In the zone of settlement, which also included Podolia, 43.1% of the Jewish population were engaged in trade. Of all traders – 809,000 people were engaged exclusively in trade of agricultural goods, grain and bread. 20% of the employed Jewish population were artisans, 11% of Jews (555,000) worked in industry, but 276,000 of them worked exclusively in the garment and shoe-leather industry. In the Pale of Settlement in the industry worked almost a third of the Jewish population, however, only 3-4% of Jews were engaged in agriculture, 5% were employees of private companies that were in the public service, and 5% of Jews belonged to other professions. As a result of the government policy, the Jewish towns of the right-Bank Ukraine turned into a kind of economic and socio-economic phenomenon. In the early 20th century in Vinnytsia county, Jews made up 30% of the artisans (of which: shoemakers - 41.5%, carpenters - 12.2%, bakers and butchers - 10.5%, blacksmiths - 6.3%, builders - 6.3%), while among the handymen in Vinnytsia Jews were only 4.1%. According to some researchers, high economic activity, managerial skills, dexterity, economy, and eventually higher educational level, contributed to the transformation of Jews into the central element of the economic complex of Podolia. In 1917 the Jews owned 21% of sugar factories, 86% of distilleries, 76% of the breweries. In the Jewish lease were 96% of the mills and grain scourers, 92% of all houses and shops that belonged to the state property of the province, 22.4% of all leased private land. Among the artisans of Podolia province Jews accounted for 72.2%. Thus, during this period, the Jewish population of Podolia constantly grew and became an important component of the economic complex of the region. As a result of restrictions on the part of the authorities and through certain features of national and cultural life, Jews in places of compact residence formed a socio-economic and cultural phenomenon.

Bar already had schools #1 and #2, a secondary school, a Jewish school, a post office, an inn (now they would say a hotel).

A synagogue was located not far from the Protestant and the Roman Catholic churches. The Rabbi was, as I have said, David Zaydman, who was also the chairman of the Jewish community, as well as Barlbarlach Zeidi. There were the kitchens of Khuna and Avram, the fire-house, the cinema, etc.

It is clear that all this goes in circles, throughout the decades of the 19th-20th centuries, until the beginning of the Great Patriotic war.

Let's go back to the 19th century. In the work "The Economic State of the Cities of the Russian Empire" it is indicated that as of 1861 of the provincial cities of Podolia province, only Bar was recognized as industrialized. According to the statistical commission in 1866 there were 19 factories - this was the fourth largest number in the province.

Here is the description of the Jews of Bar. From desk and topographical descriptions of the Mogilev district of Podolia province about the town of Bar in the late 18th and early 19th centuries only a draft version without a date has been preserved, but, given the spelling of the text and other materials on this topic, it is possible to consider the years of description were 1797 through 1802:

In this shtetl (there is) a Jewish wooden school and with it two winter beginner schools. The guest yard is made of stone, has a comfortable height; there are 57 merchant shops in it, including the wooden extensions. These shops contain goods of different kinds: cloth from foreign and local factories, baize and other thick cloth: and from Berdichev, Brody, Leipzig, Ravich and Bratslav: silk, paper, thread and woolen matter and different kinds of small goods. Moreover they bring from Berdichev iron, ropes, herring from Golany, from Korets - porcelain and various kinds of pottery. Out of the Turkish goods - groceries, coffee and sugar. Jewish merchants recorded and to Mogilev's magistrate belonging are 10, and this includes one of the 1st guild. Most of the above-mentioned places are engaged in foreign trade of certain goods, and sheep's wool, honey, wax and hot wine are taken back there, and sometimes cattle is also moved over there. But according to their assurances, most of them go there only to buy. Other Jews of the local town are petty sellers of raw and dried fish, salt, tar, some spices, and most of them are pub keepers and distillers. Of these, there are also artisans: tailors up to 50, meaning including furriers 16, shoemakers 15, goldsmiths and silversmiths 3, coppersmiths 17, watchmakers 2, glaziers 2, barbers 18 and for all of them a right bookbinder is needed. From their houses the Jews paid to the temporary owner the so-called tax rent from 3 to 14 zlotyh. From retail shops, in general, 1600 zlotyh and other collected income consisting in rent 45000 zlotyh. 11 fairs in a year happen in this place: 1st – the day of St. Nicholas; 2nd – St. George; 3rd – St. John the Evangelist; 4th – Intercession of the Theotokos; 5th – Simeon; 6th– Demetrius; 7th – St.Nicholas the Miracle-maker; 8th – Elijah the Prophet; 9th – in the New year; 10th – in Candlemas and, finally, the 11th – in the middle of Lent. Moreover, there are daily small trades. Russian merchants bring different furs, tea, iron, ordinary Russian canvas, and fish to the fairs of Russia, in addition to the mentioned goods. From Polesie of Volyn province tar, wooden utensils, from the province of Kiev varieties of oil, and other such goods. The settlers come from the surrounding and rather remote villages, and the merchants and Jews from the towns and bring ordinary and well-known products of growth. Cattle is also brought in small quantities, and other Jews buy it for foreign trade. There is no master's distillery here, but only 5 Jewish distilleries, in which 10 small and simple boilers produce wine. The proportion satiric tubs and the resulting effect on alcohol distilleries. There is also in addition Jewish mead, in which a small amount of honey is boiled. Master's brewery, it brewed light beer from barley malt, which is grown in consistent amount in the same plant in the malt house. Here was used malt 10 kortsov [1000 kg.] hops half of korets[500 kg.] and turns out quite tasty beer in 26 barrels [40 buckets - 491,9 liters], each measured in 25 garntsov [1/4 bucket] which are sold at 8 zlotyh per barrel. But this beer very soon oxidizes, because it is not well boiled. There are 2 of these weekly processes for the beer production. This plant is under the ownership. 3000 zlotyh in interest received from the local Jewish kahal. Well known Bar Confederation began here in 1767, it happened with great confluence of district and remote inhabitants, except 10,000 of regular troops under command Pulavsky and Pototsky. In this same year, the coming part of the Russian army under the leadership of General Apraksin destroyed their slightest intention, dispersing their rebellious crowd and entered this town in spite of their fortifications. Further, the plague appeared here, as residents remember, up to 3 times, but the former in 1770 killed the noble part of the inhabitants. In 1774, the town burned down almost to the ground and in the same year, most of the houses were still built.

There were large forests in Bar area. This contributed to the fact that they were engaged in the extraction of resin, production of potash, timber, beekeeping, and there were many distilleries. The development of trade was facilitated by the fact that roads passed through the town: the Black way, by which the Tatars used to make their attacks on the southern parts of Russia through Bar, Zynkov and other cities; the Kuchmansky way, which near the village Popelyukh and the town Khmelnik was connected with the Black way. There was also a waterway - on the southern Bug through a tributary of the river Rov you could get to Bar and Brailov. Also the merchants from Asia came here, usually they brought Asian goods and bought local products.

Through Shargorod there was a large trade in imported goods with Volokhs, Turks, Tatars, where town of Bar acted as an intermediary. There were many warehouses in Bar for this purpose.

Many Jewish families lived in Bar. Surnames began about 200 years ago. Here is what the number of the Jewish populations in years: in 1847 - 4442 persons, in 1856 - 2894 persons, in 1860 - 4026 persons, in 1897 - 5773 persons (58%), in 1910 – 10,450 persons (46%), in 1923 - 5054 persons, in 1926 – 5,720 people. (56%), in 1939 - 3,869 persons.

It was this expression among Podolia Jews: *Bar is a shut, un a Baranivka iz a pitsale pitsale shetele!* (in English: Bar - is a city, and Baranovka - is a small town). This term referred to the importance of the Jewish community in the town of Bar.

In the early 19th century, a Jewish printing house was established in the town, according to A. S. Barovia. In 1925 it was mentioned by A.S. Barovia in *Library News* while talking about the Jewish printing houses of Podolia. It is known that Empress Catherine II by her decree forbade in 1790 to import Jewish religious books into the territory of Russia, and in return allowed the opening of Jewish printing houses in Yiddish and Hebrew. But in 1836 these printing houses, except Zhytomyr, were closed by the Tsarist government.

However, no editions from this printing house have been found. Perhaps it was a small printing house and printed religious books and things for the local community.

In the Vinnytsia state archive on the history of the Jews of Podolia in the 19th century there is a City Council fond of the town of Bar (fond 501 list 1). It contains minutes of meetings, records of contracts, brokerage cases, characterizing the active participation of the Jewish population in the commercial, industrial, economic activities of the city. The most valuable and interesting are the family lists of Jews for 1852 (fond 262, list 3, item 18). These family lists were drawn up in accordance with the requirements of the "provisional rules of 1851", on the division of Jews into "useful" and "useless".

In the State archive of Vinnytsia region there are also the police reports for October of 1843 on Bar. They show what surnames existed at that time and which activity was conducted by Jews in the town. Here are some examples.

October 1st. The case of merchant from Bar, Shmuel Izakovich, contacted the town hall with a request which was written on the ordinary paper instead of the stamp paper.

October 2nd. The complaint of merchant from Bar Riva, wife of Khaim Kleiman, about the "innocent" arrested of her husband with a request of his release.

October 19th. About search and delivery to Odessa of the merchant Khaim Gershl Kleiman who owed to the Odessa city Duma 20 thousand rubles in silver.

October 20th. The request of the Letichev magistrate to send out merchant of the 3rd guild Nachman Serebriysky who owed to the Treasury.

October 21st. With a drum beat the police of Bar is calling people willing to buy property of deceased member of kahal David Levitas.

October 22nd. They listened to the report of Bar's bourgeois Jew Herschl Ostrovsky, to whom he informs that his wife was going with the Jew Boruch Hasmanov to Berdichev. And in the town of Hmelnik she was robbed.

October 23rd. The attorney of Bar's alcohol commission Abram Tseitlin reports that at a wedding of petty bourgeois Krivoruchko people drank vodka made in tavern (self-distilled).

October 29th. Appeal of Bar attorney of alcohol commission Abram Tseitlin stated that previously the sale of drinks was held in the house of the Jew Yankel Poltin, but Yankel was drunk all the time, so the pub is transferred to the house of the Jew Srul Leybovich Kolomir in the city center.

Storms in politics reflected the further arrangement of life of the residents of Bar; its attitude to ancient traditions, preservation of the past.

Disassembled so-called "walls" were destroyed as an unnecessary history of the town along with the people who inhabited it. During this period most of the buildings of the rich people in the past fell into disrepair. Doors of the former shops are boarded up with wooden planks, the exterior decorations of the houses disappeared, the facades are also not taken care of. The wooden or combined houses of other residents complemented the picture. Bar lived through another desolation, which quickly came after the rise in all spheres of life of the town. This was especially striking in its historical part.

The shopping area of Bar covered the area around the current bus station square and continued to the "Eternal flame" monument. It was the center of a business district.

In 1855, there were 131 Jewish merchants of the 3rd guild in Bar, according to the general census. In 1860 there was Shtok's distillery, which was engaged in the production of alcohol. This enterprise became the basis for the creation of Bar's distillery. But that was preceded by the following events.

On May 7, 1860 in Bar's police merchant Itsko Gulko appealed with a complaint about the seizure of his land by Mark Barabtarl for the construction of a distillery. He became its first owner. However, later a criminal case was brought against him for non-payment of taxes and in 1867 the plant was confiscated and put up for public auction. And the merchant of the 2nd guild Shtock bought it then.

Later, starting in 1892, this distillery belonged to the merchant Yossi Mosenkis. In October 1899, he sold the distillery to three merchants: two Odessa residents Jacob Zakharenkov, Moses Tsviling and the tradesman from Orsha Joseph Nickelshpurg. Then the company of "Nickelshpurg-Zakharenkov-Tsviling" became famous and further increased the production of alcohol. It was they who carried out a major reconstruction of the plant and brought the daily output to 300 decalitres of vodka from grain and potatoes.

The clerk at the factory was Aron Drabkin, and Josif Lande was responsible for the distillery laboratory which was located in the cellar. According to the survey of crafts in the town in 1904, it was written as follows: "Bar's No. 74 distillery – owned by Odessa merchant Ya. D. Zakharenko and Orsha tradesman I. Nickelshpurg". In 1917 this distillery was owned only by I. Nickelshpurg. In 1919, he signed a three-year lease agreement with Froim Malkiman, however, starting in June 1920, the nationalization of the plant began. Later it became known as Bar's distillery.

Wine processing plant, mechanical workshop, early 20th century

Also, in 1863 the merchant's guest house of the merchant I. Shtock was built. It had an area of 279 square meters, the size of 12 by 24 meters with a basement, that was a one-and-a-half-story house. It was the best house in Bar and was in a convenient location, the porch overlooked the market square, and nearby was a Protestant church, Catholic church and synagogue. The future Ukrainian writer N. Kotsyubinsky, whose father worked in the police department of the town, lived in this house during the years 1872-1875. At that time, the house already belonged to the police department. In the town it is known as "Kotsyubinsky's house".

The current state of the estate where N. Kotsyubinsky lived

In 1857 the town hall of Bar had representatives from the Jewish community – they were Volko Naftulovich Leyvant, and Luzer (Leyzor) Lemelevich Galkner. In the apartment commission of the town hall - Moshe Leybovich Rapoport-Friedland.

In 1858, according to the order of the Podolia Governor, the Jewish craft and shop councils were organized in Bar. They were divided into handicraft and non-local (cabs, housework, and so on). The number of registered artisans was 875. These justices were required to account for the people, but they did not reflect the actual picture because part of the artisans were shielded from registration. In 30 years they all will be canceled throughout the Podolia province by the government decree.

In 1886, in Bar about ten families of Jews wanted to create a credit consumer society like the Austro-Hungarian *Raiffeisen*. In the 1860s former non-commissioned officer G. Raifazen created a small credit union, which began to function, then also there were other societies, which began to be called "raifazenki".

On the charter of Bar's consumer society the general governor of Kiev imposed a resolution: "...illusions... return..." that is, it was refused.

Later, in 1893, on the initiative of the world mediator Mogilev county P. Okulov 22 "company stores" were opened in the county, including two in the town of Bar. However, after the death of P. Okulov all of them ceased to exist. The reason for this was the neglect of the basic principles of the institute of shareholders.

In 1895, as evidenced by the "Podolia address-calendar", as a part of Bar City Duma one of the members (that is, the Deputy) was a Jew - merchant Mordko Shimonovich Fuhs (according to the laws of the Russian Empire no more were allowed, 1/5 of all representatives could be non-Christians).

In two-class secondary school of town of Bar was a full-time caretaker (he is a teacher of history and geography) - Moisey Konstantinovich Krokhmalny, school's doctor - Semyon Moiseyevich Hertzman.

Among the freely practicing doctors Semyon Moiseevich Hertzman and Mark Moiseevich Moreynis were mentioned.

In Bar there were representatives of insurance companies: Russian – from fire and hail (petty bourgeois Nachman Serber), Northern – from fire (merchant Wolf Bronshtein), commercial - (merchant Yossi Mosenkis).

Merchant Yankel Ovshiya Katz rented the watermill (city property) and was its manager.

Nakhman Serber was appointed State Rabbi.

In 1900, after the elections to the city Duma, Nakhman Kiselevich Serber became a representative from the Jewish community.

The watermill was now leased to the merchant from Proskurov Solomon Marantz, and the mill manager was Markus Meerovich Gorenshtein.

Merchant Leib Landau was the representative of the insurance company "Anchor".

Nuta-Nathan Meshenberg remained the tenant of the pharmacies. He was also the manager of one of the pharmacies. The second was managed by his assistant Magda Bonuchar.

In the 19th century Bar also had a Zeltser water factory, the owner of which was a Strauss.

"Branded" bottle for water bottling, Bar Ukraine

A little history of medicine of the town of Bar.

In the documents of the archive of the Commonwealth in the mid 17th century there is a record of awarding the king Ya. Kasimir pharmacy owner Martin Gaase, who was from the town of Bar. Later in the 19th century, the name of a local doctor Friedrich Gaase was mentioned.

Bar was an established medical center in the 16th century as indicated by the metrics of the crown archives of Poland. In the early 17th century the town already had a hospital and in 1647 there was a workshop of surgeons in this hospital.

There was another pharmacy at the monastery, but at the time of Khmelnitsky, these two pharmacies were destroyed, and the practice of medicine itself fell into decline.

In addition, from the archives it is known that the town was repeatedly ravaged by the plague epidemic "pestilence", which led to human victims. The largest plague epidemic was in 1770. This was a natural selection – as there was no medicine.

In 1876-1885 the pharmacy of Strauss is mentioned in the Russian medical lists. In 1881 there was a pharmacy department. Since 1890, the nobleman Adrian Eduardovich Straus was listed as an owner of the pharmacy and pharmacy department, and Emil Robertovich Thom as was the manager and tenant.

At that time in the recipes of pharmacies it was written about the use of various herbs, roots, leaves, seeds, balms, infusions, concoctions. And all this was from local raw materials. And that's why the owner of the pharmacy A.E. Strauss addressed to Emperor Alexander II letter from 8 August 1878 year with request about providing him in lease of an island on the local pond for a pharmacy's garden and he is committed to pay on annual basis 60 silver rubles to the local Duma. But perhaps this request was never fulfilled.

Fragment of a letter to Emperor Alexander II

In 1892, Bar operated 11 other large enterprises:

1. Soap factory. Founded 1886. Belonged to Bar's petty bourgeois Aron Borukhovich Khariton
2. Tannery. Founded 1858. Belonged to Bar's petty bourgeois Aron Moshkovich Moreynis.
3. Tannery. Founded 1858. Belonged to Bar's petty bourgeois Leyb Fridman.
4. Tannery. Founded 1846. Belonged to Bar's petty bourgeois Moyshe Gelman.
5. Honey factory. Founded 1879. Belonged to Bar's petty bourgeois Pesya Samsonovna Levitova.
6. Honey factory. Founded 1886. Belonged to Bar's petty bourgeois Shendlya Lipovna Kiperman.
7. Cement plant. Founded 1840. Belonged to Bar's petty bourgeois Borukh Rosenblatt.
8. Cement plant. Founded 1840. Belonged to Bar's petty bourgeois Srul Averbukh.
9. Cement plant. Founded 1850. Belonged to Bar's petty bourgeois Gershko Felberg.
10. Cement plant. Founded 1876. Belonged to Bar's petty bourgeois Sheyna Zeltser.
11. Watermill. Build 1884. Rented by merchant Yankel Katz.

According to statistical information of 1894-1896, another distillery (owner was merchant X. Kantselson) and two small soap plants (merchants S. Latishman, M. Estsis were the owners) were operating in Bar.

There were three brick and tile factories owned by Jews:

B. Rozenblit plant - produced 10 thousand bricks and 10 thousand roof-tiles.

L. Felberg plant - produced 8 thousand bricks and 8 thousand shingles.

Z. Shafir plant - produced 8 thousand bricks and 9 thousand tiles.

There were seven leather factories in the town owned by:
1. I. Moreynis - production of 200 pieces of leather
2. M. Gelman - production of 200 pieces of leather
3. S. Mekhilovich - production of 150 pieces of leather
4. Sh. Fridmanzova - production of 100 pieces of leather
5. M. Oykher - production of 220 pieces of leather

   6. Sh. Razhen - production of 100 pieces of leather
   7. D. Farber – production of 200 pieces of leather

On 18 March 1898 the town Duma of Bar sold to Solomon Marantz, merchant from Proskurov and the owner of the sugar factory, 56 des. 1892 sq. fathoms of urban land for the construction of a sugar factory for 19,876 rubles.

According to statistics 60 foreigners lived in Bar in 1897. They were mainly from Austria-Hungary, Germany, Moldova, the Czech Republic and other European countries. They were merchants, businessmen, mechanics, blacksmiths, carpenters, locksmiths and people of other professions. They contributed to the further industrial development of the city. Thus, in 1900, representatives of the Austrian and Jewish money owners opened the sugar factory in Bar. It was then that its first product was released - sugar. They created a joint stock company to establish the work of this enterprise, which became known as "Joint stock company sand-refining sugar factory of Bar, City of Odessa." It was bought from the Proskurov's merchant S. Marantz. At the head of the joint stock was to E. Ashkenazi (native of Austria). The structure of JSC "Sand-refining plant of Bar" also included well-known Jewish and Austrian entrepreneurs: M. Rafalovich, B. Magner, O. Krivanek. The sugar factory employed 200 workers in the season.

And already in 1913 there were 400 workers and among them about 100 were Jews. The volume of production amounted to 354,223 pounds of sugar. The Board of the plant included at that time the brothers Zaitsev - the owners of the Yalta sugar plant and N. I. Kogan.

Another Austrian entrepreneur Aron Kovich in 1903 opened a tannery in the town using the latest technologies.

The school teacher is remembered in Bar, Rile Ida Frederika August, (born in 1857 Germany), who applied for Russian citizenship in 1915.

Probably the town was an attractive place to live and work for foreigners who managed to adapt here.

In the late 1890s the volunteer fire society was created. Ordinary members of this society were various artisans, workers, intellectuals, homeowners and others. According to the national composition there were Ukrainians, Poles, Russians, a large percentage were Jews. All of them remembered that in Bar in 1774 there was a major fire. Then almost all the houses burned down and there were many victims. In the town there was also a professional fire brigade and there, too, Jews worked as ordinary firefighters.

Bazarnaya street, Bar, 19th century

*Shopping area, near the present site of the bus station,
Bar, early 20th century*

Central street of Bar, the beginning of the 20th century

The building which housed the postal office. To the right side was a photo studio of Yurgilevich

The building of the Jewish school, Bar, 1930s

Fire brigade, Bar. Photo By V. Leybman,
a famous photographer in the town, 1905

In the Memorable book of the Podolia province for 1911 there are many famous people.

Thus, members of the town Council were Nachman Kiselevich Serber and Semyon Moiseevich Hertzman. The latter worked as a doctor in a Jewish hospital and also was a school doctor. Isaac Meerovich Finkelstein worked as a doctor in the sugar factory's hospital. Jacob Khaskelevich Kreyzo was the pharmacist.

Mark (Michael) Moreynis was noted as the private physician.

Kreyna Meerovna Ryzha, Isaac Khaimovich Sirkis and Shimon Lazarovich Shichtman were the dentists.

In village Luka-Barskaya was iron foundry of G. Abramov and Abram and Meer Frenkel. A. Frenkel was its manager. The office was located in Bar. The plant employed 59 workers, produced various parts for machines, valves, cranes, pumps. There was a 22-horsepower locomotive engine. Annual production was 36,950 rubles.

Joseph Nickelshpurg was the owner of a distillery, and its manager was Moses Snitserenko. The annual production of the distillery was 145,000 rubles.

M. S. Marantz was a manager of the sugar factory, which annual production was 1,430,000 rubles.

There were other manufacturing plants mentioned earlier, but they were less powerful.

Photographer V. Leibman worked in Bar in 1905. His main place of work was Gorodok in Kamyanetz county, and in Bar he had a temporary office.

In 1911 there was a photo studio of Mendel Fayvelevich Gershenzon in Bar, and in 1915, a photo studio of A.M. Yurgilevich began to operate there also.

Advertising postcard shop of Yurgilevich

The conditional complex included "trading houses" of famous merchants of the 1st, 2nd and 3rd guilds, there was also an inn with rooms for different levels of guests. A maidan (small square) for wagons and phaetons also was near this inn. And in the building, built in 1911 (now near the store "Grosh") the pharmacy was located and neurologist Trachtenberg lived there. This house has survived to this day but is abandoned.

The main purpose of this complex was to conduct the fairs. For their conduct it was necessary to obtain documents from the Russian Emperor. Even merchants from the capital came here to Bar for the fair, not to mention the residents from the local district and the Podolia region. All this points to the importance of fairs in Bar.

The homestead of neurologist Trachtenberg also contained a pharmacy in 1911. The date is visible atop the house's facade

B.Ya. Kats, a 1st guild merchant, lived in the house where the Social Security Department is now located. This merchant had watermills in the village Kleban, he bought wheat from the peasants and milled flour, and carried flour by railway cars to various provinces, even as far as Austria.

Kats was also was a member of the Board of Trustees, which constructed a Jewish school and a secondary school, engaged in charitable activities, and allocated funds.

B. Ya. Kats planted a pine forest on his lands in village Mateykov, thus creating special environmental conditions. In the summer at his business's own expense, he constructed tents to heal patients with tuberculosis. Kats was a respected man, distinguished by intelligence. He died on the eve of the October revolution. His son Leybish Bentsionovich Kats inherited his father's business and after expropriation in 1926 escaped persecution at the construction works in Moscow. He was financially poor, but managed to help his son to study and to become an aircraft designer. B.Ya. Kat's grandson worked in the design bureau of S.A. Lavochkin. He defended his thesis to become a candidate of technical sciences, and one of the developers of the aircraft wing.

The former trading house of the 1ˢᵗ guild merchant, B. Ya. Kats. Built late 19th century.

Other great events took place in this arena of the economic life of the town. Many rich Jews lived here, who formed the "business climate" of the town and laid the foundations of charity, which created their very principles. Even then they independently applied the principle: the rich to share with the poor, with such efforts paved yourself a way of life.

B.Ya. Kats also was the owner of a factory which produced cigarettes. They consisted of a tube of thin paper and a mouthpiece. There were several such factories in Ukraine. The factory of A. I. Duvana in Kiev was the largest, it represented the highly mechanized production of cases at that time. In 1891, A. Duvan with A. Katin (known in Moscow as a factory owner, which also produced cigarettes) had built a tobacco firm *Dukat*.

In 1856, Bar had 6 synagogues, three Jewish schools, a cemetery, and in 1910 there were 12 different synagogues in the town. In 1913, a Jewish women's school was opened, where they studied Russian, French, German, arithmetic, history, geography, and sewing trade. Preserved in the archive is a list of persons who in 1913 completed the full course of the 7ᵗʰ grade of the women's school (Central State Archive of Ukraine, Fund 459, inventory 14, case 91):

1. Rukhlya Waynberg
2. Golda Geylman
3. Hone Levit
4. Sheyndlya Natanzon
5. Bronya Rosenblith
6. Khaya Serebriyska
7. Esther Felberg
8. Rukhlya Shikhman

Between 1910 and World War I, the Jews opened factories in Bar for the processing of agricultural products - sugar beet, flax, tobacco, wine and vodka. They also had many different shops, owned the only pharmacy in the town, and engaged in transportation. In the 20th century Jews in the town were engaged in handicraft, tobacco cultivation, there were three mead factories owned by merchants Leyzer Eisenberg, Levitov, Waynberg.

There were many cabs in the town at that time.

Jewish cab driver - the balagula, early 20th century

The Jewish butcher, early 20th century

Many people were engaged in pottery. So, in the book "Creativity of Potters of the Town of Bar", the author V. Gudak recalls the masters of pottery, among whom were Jewish masters.

In the early 20th century in Bar was the private Jewish school of Zilberman, a Jewish hospital for 10 beds. The community retained a doctor and a medical assistant, and there also was a private practitioner (in the later time it was M. Moreynis).

The hospital was very important for the town and for its residents. That's why the Mayor of Bar, V.M. Shpakevich, was elected as a Chairman of the hospital council.

Stamp of physician Moreynis

In 1920, the hospital was nationalized and operated as a state hospital. The doctors here were Shamis, I. D. Burshteyn, F.M. Burshteyn.

The building housing the Jewish hospital is currently empty, 2017

On April 7, 1899 the public library was opened, which was maintained at the expense of the town. In 1900 on its development 900 rubles were given, in 1901 - 600 rubles. Chairman of the Executive Committee of the city library was Athanasius Dwornitsky. In 1901, according to his report, the income of the library amounted to 518 rubles. 54 kopecks., that is, the services of the library were paid. The main part of the library fund were books from the section "Literature", from periodicals were such: "Kievlyanin", "Odessa Leaf", "Russia", "Field", "Peace of God", "Children's reading" and others. On 1 January 1902 the library fund had 923 books of 350 titles, subscription to 18 periodicals, it had full-time librarian (with salary of 120 rubles per year). However, this library did not suit the Jewish community, because there were almost no books in Hebrew or Yiddish. Therefore, the question arose about the opening of an additional branch of the library. It was opened in 1913. The library had about 500 books in Yiddish, Hebrew and there were books in Russian, there were periodicals in Yiddish "Latest news", "Time", "Working voice". The library was maintained at the expense of the Jewish community. The books were first handed over by everyone, and then books were bought for the library. The library had various types of books including fiction, references, religious, scientific and educational literature. That is, now it suited both Jews and non-Jews.

Also, the honey factory of Sh. L. Kiperman, weaving factory of M.I. Frenkel, printing office of Sh. Shvets, more than 100 shops, 22 inns were opened - all this was owned by Jews.

Respectable Jews of Bar,
Leah and Peysakh Zilberman, 1882

Jews were always active in the public life of the town, although they were forbidden to be the Chairman of the town or the Council acting on behalf of the Chairman, according to the government circulars at that time.

Here is an example. In 1883-1884 the Ministry of Internal Affairs considers the complaint of the bourgeois from Bar the Jew Sh. Barskover on the admission of abuses in the local public administration: the head of the city council Charnitsky, Deputy Epstein and the town council secretary Dzikovetsky.

The actions of the town council was dissatisfied with Jew M. Fefer that accused the heads of the council of bribery and removal of stamps.

The complaint of merchant Saltrennikov confirmed: "..the extortion from the members of the Council, especially from Dzikovetsky". The merchants Katzman and Rapoport, S. Trinkman, A. Heev and others were the witnesses in this case.

The situation in Bar changed for the better only after the next elections.

The Jews not only worked, but were engaged, like the rest of the population, in a class struggle for their rights.

In the revolutionary events of 1905-1907, part of the Jewish population of the Russian Empire, primarily young people and members of political parties, took an active part. It manifested itself mainly in the conduct of anti-government agitation among the population, the distribution of literature and leaflets, the organization of political strikes, rallies, illegal gatherings, and the like.

In early 1905 in Bar the following party cells were created: the social Democrats of the RSDLP, the Jewish-Bund (Jewish socialist party of the working class) and the Poalei Zion (translated from Hebrew as "Workers of Zion"). These parties sometimes acted together.

So, in September 1905, a meeting of Zionist-minded Jews (members of the party Poalei Zion) was conducted in the house of the director of Bar's sugar factory M. Marantz. The subject of the meeting was the establishment of a committee for the elections to the Duma. Representatives of the Bund were present.

In the city Newspapers were distributed: "Proletarian", "Social Democrats", proclamations of "Down with the Autocracy!"

During the summer of 1905 they distributed a proclamation among the workers of various enterprises and residents of the city "To the workers and workers of the city of Bar."

They called for a strike to increase wages and reduce working hours. In 1906, the bourgeois B. G. Chemerovsky campaigned and distributed leaflets among the workers of Bar's distillery, for which he was detained by the police.

The Zionist organizations of Bar were also active during 1910-1914. This indicated growth of the national consciousness of Jews and the spread of ideas among them about the restoration of the Jewish state.

Bar group of the RSDLP numbered 30 people, half of them were Jews, and this group operated during 1905-1907.

Members of political parties took part in the organization of a strike in the spring of 1905 at the sugar factory. The strikers demanded a reduction of working hours to 8 hours, pay regardless of age and put forward other demands. The administration of the sugar factory was forced to partially make concessions - the working time was set 10 hours, wages were equalized.

In the period 1906-1907 revolutionary work declined and was carried out passively, although during this period in the town there were cells of parties of social revolutionaries and radicals.

1913 was a year of great economic growth in the Tsarist Russia. It was the year before the World War I, and then came the tumultuous years of revolution and devastation.

In Bar also felt the rise of production and activity in all spheres of life and, accordingly, successfully developed the Jewish community.

Well respected man and doctor S. M. Hertzman was elected as a head of the Jewish community, E.S. Nordshtein was appointed the judicial investigator of the department No. 3. There was a state rabbi, a synagogue and 12 houses of worship in the town.

Ya. N. Ryzhiy owned the drugstore. Pharmacy stores have kept: M. Kh. Koyfman, Ya. A. Koyfman, R. M. Koyfman, V. V. Lukacher, M. I. Tanenboym, A. M. Tselinker.

Doctor M. M. Moreynis was the head of the hospital at the sugar factory, and doctor Simon M. Hertzman was the head of the Jewish hospital, he was a doctor in a secondary school.

Sh. Goldenberg was the midwife.

S. M. Hertzman, E.M. Ryzha, Sh. Ya. Shechtman – all of these dentists had a private practice.

M.S. Marantz continued to work as the managing director of the sugar factory. Steam-powered mill of the sugar factory was leased by M. I. Frenkel.

Another town's steam roller mill was again leased by the merchant Ya. M. Katz, the annual grinding volume was 120 pounds.

The mead factory was owned by Mendel Kiperman. M. S. Finkelstein was the manager of the candle production plant.

The warehouse-store of agricultural machinery and equipment was very popular between residents of Bar, its owner was Shlomo Moshkovich Bronshtein. This firm was founded in 1896. Here you could buy both domestic and imported equipment, as well as spare parts for them and get the necessary advice. There was also a workshop to learn how to repair this equipment.

The cooperage production in Bar was located in the rented house of the well-to-do merchant of the 1st guild Ryzhiy, who was also a great patron in the town.

It was located on the street Meschanskaya (now the street Sobornaya). It was a large two-story house. Rental fee was 75 rubles per year, and 4 workers produced casks for 3000 rubles. Y.E. Nikelshpurg was the head of production there, he was also the owner of distillery No. 74. It employed 25 workers, alcohol was produced from bread and molasses. In 1910, production was 236,850 buckets of product, which contained 40% alcohol.

Advertisement of commercial products, Sh. M. Bronshtein, 1913

The town had well developed leather industry due to the fact that the peasants were engaged in cattle breeding. Here they bought leather, tanned it and made various products from it. The following residents of Bar were involved with tannery and leather production:

Gelman, Beyla Moshkovna
Gelman, Gersh Menashevich
Gelman, Meer Menashevich
Gekhtman, Gershl Shlemovich
Greenberg, Iosif Chaimovich
Krasner, Leib Berkovich
Felberg, Yudko Abramovich
Shkolnik, Mordko Davidovich

The wealthiest people in the town had large shops and engaged in the manufacture trade, but there were also small manufactory shops that were kept by:

Averbukh, Shimon Chaimovich
Barabtora, Ikhiel Ovshievich
Bromerg. Haya
Broyt, Sura Davidovna
Fayfel, Dobrish Zayvelevna
Fishman, Ruhlya Leyzerovna

Fishman, Khaya Manusovna
Fitermaler, Mikhlya Mordkovna
Fleischer, Shimon Noyachovich
Fogelman, Berko Abramovich
Gerenshtein , Mendel Vigdorovich
Gerenstein, Freyda Leibovna
Gershenson, Perl
Gibel, Leya Froimovna
Goldberg, Mireya Aronovna
Krahmalnik, Brucha Abramovna
Leifer, Leya Fridel'na
Luk, Itsko Usherovich
Magazinik, Rivka G. and Ko.
Okopnik, U. A.
Rif, Malka Smulevna
Rosenthal, Leyba Leyzerovich
Sas, Volko Luzerovich
Shiringen, Shulim Volkovich
Shtulboym, Perlya Elevna
Zack, Itsko Moshkovich
Zeltzer, Volko Yankelevich
Zhovner, Dvoira Moshkovna
Zlotnik, David Yankelevich
Zuckerman, L. G.
Zuckerman, Manya Shmulevna
Zuckerman, Mordko Gershenovich

In the area of Bar there were a lot of forests, and the demand for wood was constant and accordingly, the forest industry developed quickly here, there were also warehouses of wood. The following residents of Bar were engaged in forestry:

Epshteyn, Rivka Leybovna
Goltsman, Shmul Khaimovich
Oksman, David
Pekerman, Motel
Peldesh, S. M.
Polishchuk, Moses Leybovich

Involved in haberdashery trade deal were:

Beditman, Yekhiel and Ko.
Bril, Moshko Alterovich
Greenman, Itzko Leibowitz

Zaydman, Josif Moiseevich

Zeltzer, Sosya Ovshievich

Mintz, Basya Shmulevna

Perelmuter, Shulim Srulevich

Stolyar, Ida Khaimovna

Tabak, Khaim Gdalevich

Frenkel Moshko, E.

Tzelman, Maryam Iosifovna

Shelmover, Shmul Shemshovich

Shteinberg, Leyb Iosifovich

Jews were also engaged in wine production and distribution. Wine shops #265, 266, 1366 were in town. They also were selling "Hungarian" wines from different fruits and berries. Dints Yankel Gdalevich, Leykikh Itzko Srulevich and Leya Shterenberg were the main distributors.

Iron products, always in demand, were distributed by:

Einshtein, Nakhman Manuilovich

Galperin, Zus Leybovich

Pildish, Khaim Khunovich

Pildish, Shmuel Itskovich

Shteinberg, Genia Ovshievna

Shteinberg, Ides Moshkovna

Shtrik, V. S.

Many people were engaged in the grocery trade:

Belfer, Gersch Leybovich

Berenshtein, Shendlya Mordkovna

Evel, Moshko Abramovich

Eyltershamis, Moshko Abramovich

Fershteyn, Mordko Abramovich

Fuchs, Yankel Mordkovich

Gershenzon, Zlata Gershkovna

Gerwitz, Srul Abramovich

Goldis, Zlata Khaimovna

Katz, Pinkhas Davidovich

Leiferman, A. I.

Leiferman, Shifra Khaimovna

Mediap, Sura Abramovna

Ryzha, Gitlya Leybovna

Ryzhiy, Noakh Ionovich

Sanits, Reizya Srulevna
Shnaider, Golda Shmulevna
Shterenberg, Ovshiya and Khaim
Skipka, Esther Shlemovna
Spector, Abraham Shmulevich
Tabachnik, Sura Volkovna
Tinkevich, Yona Markovich
Volyoreld, Mintzya Abramovna
Weiss, Enja Iosifovna
Zaydman, Fishel
Zeltser, Yankel Volkovich

Yekhiel Santernik was engaged in the grain trade, Srul Shimshonovich Pechker was selling and repairing watches. The following residents of Bar were selling various kitchenware:

Guberman, Khaim Izrailovich
Katzman, Ruhlya Gitlyovna
Mints, Sh. Yankelevich
Rafalovich, Perlya Yakovlevna

The tobacco trade was owned by the prestigious Shtock, S. D., and the weaving factory was owned by Bekelman, Pesya Khaimovna.

A famous jeweler in the town was Tsirlis, Isai Gershkovich. Rapoport, Borukh Itskovich owned the beer warehouse.

Petty trade:

Barer, Josef Ruvinovich
Berger, Itsko Shamovich
Bonyak, Moshko A.
Efshtein, Yudko Menakhimovich
Fiks, Josif Shamovich
Fiktelshteyn, Sura Khaimovna
Fishova, Luba Yankelevna
Gelman, M. M.
Genadivik, Yudko Srulevich
Khazin, Esther Markovna
Kiperman, Sheyndl L.
Krasner, Ruhlya Shamovna
Leyfer, Reyzl V.
Lobe, Abram Iosifovich
Tabachnik, Khaya Noakhovna

Teper, Ruvim Simkhovich

Vayner, Zlata Leybovna

Zilberman, Rukhlya Shamovna

Ryzhiy, Gershl Nahmanovich was a director of the loan office.

Many more Jews were engaged in craft, and we cannot count all of them.

In 1913 it was planned to hold 16 fairs and market days were scheduled every two weeks on Thursdays.

Trade occupied a very important place in the life of the town and was almost the main occupation of the population after handicraft.

Jews took part in the revolutionary events of 1917-1920. The Secretary of Bar's revolutionary committee was B. Kleyman, and it was during the period when the head of the revolutionary committee was M. E. Vrublevsky.

Due to the lack of stable money and towns' frequent change of power, money collapsed frequently. IYaltushkiv, on the market day of November 14, 1918, goods sellers carefully selected currencies. Each trading area independently established it's accepted currency. On pork "torgovitsa" accepted only Ukrainian money, on horse - krohns, on voloviy- "kerenki", and sellers of milk, oil and other products - "Nikolaevka". Even Ukrainian money could be buy everything. In the tumultuous year 1919, Bar had its own money.

A change ticket worth one ruble, not yet signed or numbered by the town administration

The following images show exchange tickets worth three, five and ten rubles:

The reason for the appearance of town money was that in 1918-1919 in Ukraine there were no money changers. And then began the rapid release of cash surrogates in the places, including in the Podolia (banknotes, exchange marks, credit marks and others).

They were made by a printed set on ordinary paper with the signature - the original. Sketches for surrogate money in Podolia were developed by a brilliant artist George Norbut.

In Bar were issued 27 varieties of tickets, with a nominal value of 1, 3, 5, 10 rubles. In Bar on the change tickets of the town duma on the reverse side was printed: "By order of Bar's Town Duma on January 10, 1919 No. 5 the change tickets are used for small retail payments, give's council on demand instead of cash, and can be exchanged back to cash at any time and fully secured by cash".

The revolution of 1917, the national liberation competitions of the Ukrainian people, as well as Soviet innovations changed the usual way of life of Jews, they were allowed to take an active part in the social and political life of Podolia, and sometimes they became an influential force in the creation of the party and state. The habitual Jewish self-government was finally destroyed and significant changes in their social and economic life took place. The authorities tried to instill in Jews a love for new professions, including agriculture.

Jews also united in industrial associations-craft production collectives: shoe making, baking, cooperage and others, organized credit societies.

In 1920, 300 Jewish families were artisans, 28 were employees, and 150 were agricultural workers.

The socio-economic situation of Jews in cities and towns during the NEP depended on local specifics. The more economically developed the town was, the more middle-class and prosperous artisans lived in it.

Income depended on the purchasing power of the peasants and residents of the town. In addition, the solvency of artisans depended on the seasonality, qualification and specialty of the artisan.

At that time Bar was industrialized. There were many factories of different profiles and plants of different capacities.

The largest trade union in the town were weavers, because in addition to the cartel of weavers there was a weaving factory.

A measure of the wealth of the artisan in Bar was weekly revenue of 15-20 karbovantsiv (Ukrainian currency), and for poor person the weekly revenue was 3-4 karbovantsya, this was in 1923.

Financial assistance to Jews was provided by loan and savings societies established in 1923 with the help of "JDC". On average, artisans received 40 rubles for 5 months at 6% per annum.

Four districts were created in the town, including one Jewish district. However, in 1923, the Podolia Executive Committee instructed them to be eliminated as they were not meeting the requirements of the time.

It is interesting that people themselves gave certain names to certain areas of the town. So, the area near the Jewish cemetery was called "Kaptsanivka" - from the Jewish word *kaptsunim*, which means poor, beggar, naked man. Very poor people lived there in those days.

In 1921, in Bar 5 tobacco factories artisanal cartel type were registered by the Podolia's department of finance, that is, Bar became the center of tobacco processing in the province. There were such factories: "Noblex", "Hope", "Industrial Goods", "Revival", "Anchor". The owners or tenants of these factories were Jews. In the same year the district union of labor cartels was created. And the union of professionals led and integrated them.

In 1924, 30 employees of all factories, as well as suppliers of leaf tobacco, commissioners for the sale of finished products and 5 inspectors of the district inspectorate were arrested. 1,500 pounds of shipped tobacco products were found, which were not included in the reports. In this case, the Vinnytsia district brought criminal charges against 100 employees of this industry and the tax inspectorate.

And certainly these factories were liquidated, and in their place in 1925, the factory *Zorya* of Barsky agricultural society was created.

At the end of the 1920s the number of employed Jews was: in the handicraft industry - 41.6%, in trade - 17.5%, and in the civil service - 17.7%, in transport - 4.3%, in agriculture - 2%, other amateur trades - 9.9%.

The main regions of Jewish agrarian resettlement in Ukraine were Kherson, Krivoy Rog, Mariupol, Zaporozhye, Melitopol district. It should be noted that in such places of compact settlement of Jews there was a need to create administrative-territorial units that would take care of the interests and needs of visitors. Therefore, a number of Jewish national village councils and three national districts were established in the South of Ukraine: Kalinindorf, Stalindorf and Novozlatopol. If we examine more deeply the origins of this problem, it should be noted that the encouragement of the Jewish population to agricultural labor was one of the directions of the social policy of the Soviet government in the field of national relations. One of the reasons for this was the difficult economic situation of the Jewish population, primarily the parochial poor, due to the artificial curtailment of the NEP (decline of crafts, restriction of small trade). The political goals of this planned experiment can be seen here. In rural areas, the Bolsheviks sought to obtain an additional social base, because they had great doubts about the reliability and loyalty of the Ukrainian peasantry to communism. So, this large-scale campaign to attract the Jewish population to the labor market was politically best for the party and the Soviet government. The resettlement of Jews in the southern regions of Ukraine and Crimea was not a concern for their social protection and the development of Jewish agriculture. This resettlement process was forced and brought social tension among local residents, Ukrainian and Russian peasantry, and caused mass discontent on the part of the Jews themselves.

In 1926, the natives of Bar (10 families) organized the Jewish agricultural colony *Glakhgayt* in the Kherson region.

In 1936, settlement of these regions by Jews began after the establishment of the Jewish autonomous region, centered in Birobidzhan, the. It took place not as the leadership of the country wanted. There was a Jewish resettlement plan for each area. Thus, the Vinnytsia region had to send 400 Jewish families and 450 singles to Birobidzhan, including those from Bar 10 families and 15 singles. This work was carried out mainly by force.

In the 1930s economic reforms in the USSR significantly changed the structure of socio-economic life of Jews. According to the 1939 census, the number of employed Jewish population (excluding the unemployed and those who received scholarships, military personnel) was 58% compared to 46% in 1926. The proportion of Jews employed in trade gradually decreased, but the number of Jews employed in industry and agriculture increased.

Famous milliners who could sew everything for every taste were: Khayka Bonyak, Beyla Tkach, Dvoyra Tkach.

S. Sh. Pachkar, N. L. Pukhemovich, Sh. L. Blayman were the watchmakers.

Good photos were made by photographers: I. Geller, M. Korenfeld.

There was a whole team of tinsmiths who could do anything at your request: I. Moshel, N. Moshel, Sh. Moshel, B. Roiter, A. Usherov, V. Kolomoisky, N. Kolomoisky, M. Kraitman.

Jews worked in various jobs. Among them were carpenters, locksmiths, turners, casters, masons, cabmen, cobblers, shoemakers, clerks, hairdressers, weavers, beekeepers, bakers, agricultural workers and many other professions.

In 1930, 1,000 Jews worked in various enterprises, 400 – in industrial cooperatives, 53 families worked in the Jewish agricultural cartel.

In Mogilev-Podolsky district, which included Bar for example, in the late 20s, 3,768 Jews worked in agriculture, accounting for 31.6% of the total Jewish population of the district. This was the largest figure in Podolia. There were 22 Jewish collective farms, 5 mixed (Ukrainians and Jews) collective farms and an agricultural cartel in Bar.

This agricultural cartel was established in 1929 with an allotment of 200 hectares of land. It was called "The Jewish farmer," and in Yiddish *Der Idisher poyer*. Chairman of the cooperative was first twenty-five-thousand – former worker of the Odessa port, A. Kushnir, later - local Ya. Raidun. The land was cultivated by horses, but there were also tractors, sowed grain and industrial crops, vegetables. In the cartel was a thresher with a drive, a winnower and many other equipment. The farm had cows and pigs of elite breeds. It had a strong economy, which helped to survive and work despite the famine and criminal obstacles of the authorities in the period 1932-1933.

This cartel was multidisciplinary. In addition to the main agricultural production there were auxiliaries. Thus, the department of meat processing for sausages and other meat products, as well as leather dressing was created at the livestock farm. Next to the gardens was organized wine shops and they produced dried fruit. Tobacco was grown and processed. There was a big smithy where various forged products under the order and many other productions as a part of this agricultural cartel were made.

From this it is clear that the collective farm was ahead of its time in the development of agricultural production, and is also an example of the selfless work of the Jews on the land, which they did not have before.

Indicative is the statistics of financial income of different groups of the population. The maximum earnings for an artisan in the 1920s in the town was 5-7 rubles per week, the average - 3-4 rubles, and one workday in the Jewish collective farm was 1.5 rubles and 1.5 kg vegetables, which is about three times higher than earnings in the Ukrainian collective farm. Therefore, the peasants tried to get a job in the Jewish collective farm, their number was about 10% of their members.

Collective farmers worked selflessly in the fields and farms.

Brigade of Frima Melamud (1907-1961) was one of the best in the cultivation of sugar beets in Bar's collective farm. In early 1939, the brigade called all beet growers of the district to start a socialist competition in honor of the XVIII Congress of the All-Union Communist Party of Bolsheviks (leaders of the revolutionary working class in Russia). The brigade fulfilled its obligations with honor. For obtaining a large harvest of sugar beets Frima Melamud was awarded a government award. In 1939-1940 she was a participant of the all-Union agricultural exhibition in Moscow. Her life was described in the Central Jewish newspaper *Der shtern* (Star), as well as in regional and local periodicals in the period 1938-1939. In particular, in the newspaper *Komsomolskaya Pravda* No. 32 for 1939 the decree on rewarding of foremost workers of agriculture of the USSR where under No. 119 it is printed about rewarding of Frima Melamud Order of the Red Banner of Labor: "Melamud Frima Isakovna – head of brigade of the collective farm "Der Yidisher poyer" Bar district, Vinnytsia region. Her brigade for 3 years harvests 500-660 quintals per hectare." The decree was signed by the Chairman of the Presidium of the Supreme Union of the USSR M. Kalinin and the Secretary of the Presidium of the Supreme Union of the USSR Gorkin on February 8, 1939.

Melamud family, Frima sits rightmost. 1956

F. Melamud, by her work exalted the Jewish community of Bar, and the town itself. They became known not only in Ukraine, but throughout the USSR. After the war, she continued to work in the Jewish collective farm. She was buried in the Jewish cemetery of Bar.

In 1950, Bar's collective farm, named after Mikhail Frunze, and Bar's agricultural cartel "Jewish agriculturalist" were united in one collective farm named after Mikhail Frunze.

In pre-war Bar, some Jewish believers went to the synagogue in traditional Jewish clothing, and no one was surprised. On the streets next to Ukrainian and Russian, the Jewish language was heard. Then there were Jews who spoke Ukrainian poorly. And there were Ukrainians who spoke Yiddish. The Ukrainians who brought products for sale from the villages to the market knew a few dozen Jewish words. In the Soviet Party branches, in the Prosecutor's office, the court, the police, Jews worked efficiently. This ability to work was important here.

In 1921 the Department of Evsection (Jewish section of the all-Union Communist party of Bolsheviks) was created in Bar. The resident of Bar A. Chemerisky, who was a participant in the revolutionary events in Russia and the founder of the Evsection, helped to organize it in Bar. In 1926 Greenbaum worked as the head of department of finance in Bar district, and in 1927 I. S. Blinder worked there.

In the 1930s, the Chairman of the Executive Committee in the town was M. Balaban, a Jew who was later repressed. Before World War II, the Chairman of the Executive Committee was M. I. Golberg.

Also at that time such well-known physicians like Katz, Joseph Faygol, David Kuperman worked in the town. Such a respectable dentist as G.Sirkis was known to everyone in Bar where he worked before World War II and after the war he had his private office. B. Sirota worked as a dental technician for him both before the war and after. These doctors were participants of World War II.

Also doctors in the town in the prewar period in different years worked: Ida Kildish, Abram Mitbrayt, Lev Mitbrayt, Ida Plivdish,, dentist Anna Leiferman; midwives: Fanya Mitbrayt, N. Kaplun, Basia Kleinerman; pharmacists: Nina Soyfer, Nina Schnayder; dental technician - Isaac Leyferman.

In the 1923-1924 school year in Podolia province operated 88 Jewish schools, which amounted to 17% of all schools in Podolia guberniya. With further Ukrainization, by 1926-1927, the number of Ukrainian schools in Podolia increased to 61.4%, and Jewish schools - 21.5%.

Doctors of Bar's district hospital and clinic during the departure of Dr. Kuperman to Moscow. Bar. May 1933. Pictured left to right are: Vereshchagin, Katz, Sklyarevsky, Sirkis, Faygol. Third from the left sits Kuperman

At the same time, not all Jews sent their children to study in Jewish schools, instead they were sent to Russian or Ukrainian schools.

In October 1921, a sub-department for work with national minorities (Polish and Jewish) was created under the department of education of the Executive Committee in Podolia district. In December 1921 in the report of the committee of Podolia it was reported that this Jewish department arranged court over "cheder", conducts fight against Zionist currents, distributes literature in Yiddish. Such sub-departments existed also at county and some of the cities' departments of education. Also, such a sub-department was in Bar where many Jews lived.

In the 1920s and until the mid-30s, a seven-year Jewish school operated in Bar. A literacy center was established at the school. The committee for parents worked on various interest groups and attention was paid to educational work, training was carried out at a high level. In the period of 1932-1938, the school was located in the building where the Greek Catholic church is now located.

Bronya Mayfman, Faina Polishchuk, Dina Rapoport, Khayka Rafalovich, Segal, Nadezhda Sosina, Bertha Spector, Sofa Stolyar, Joseph Leviman and others worked as teachers in the Jewish seven-year school. After its closure in 1938, almost all the teachers went to work in the Ukrainian schools of the town, where they transferred all the children. Jewish teachers also worked in these schools. Here are just a few names:

Luba Tkach, Maria Fayngit, Sura Friedman, Eugene Schuster. All of them were executed by the Nazis in 1942.

Before World War II in school No. 2 S.M. Lerner, A.M. Rosenblatt, L.Z. Tarnapolska and others worked as teachers.

Women's gymnasium (now school No. 2); building belonged to the merchant from Riga, early 20th century

HOLODOMOR JEWISH PAGES

Until the early 1930s, Ukraine had 25 national districts: seven German, three Bulgarian, three Greek, three Jewish, eight Russian, one Polish.

There is documented evidence of starvation in three Jewish national districts - Kalinindorf, Novo-Zlatopol and Stalindorf. Now it is the territory of Dniepr, Zaporozhye, Kherson.

At the beginning of the 1930s, Jewish agricultural settlements were quite strong and profitable farms. They had tens of thousands of cattle, more than 10 thousand units of agricultural machinery and modern equipment at that time.

In March 1933, the leader of the Ukrainian Communists Kosior noted the difficult situation in these national areas.

In one of documents it was reported:

The inhabitants of the village Voroshilovgradskoye of the Stalindorf area are starving. In the house of collective farmer Braverman, who was arrested for stealing collective farm grain, four children aged 5 to 10 years died. They laid motionless with open wounds of the initial stage of physical decomposition.

In this national district there was another message:

The situation is very difficult. People are no longer waiting for help, but lie in cold, unheated houses and wait for death.

The facts of famine were recorded in other areas, especially in towns and cities with a high percentage of the Jewish population: Zhytomyr, Berdichev, Korosten, Belaya Tserkva, Kamenets-Podilsky, Odessa, Bar and other small towns.

Especially difficult was the situation of Jewish artisans who worked in the Ukrainian village. Usually, Jews baked bread, repaired, sewed, engaged in trade. In 1933 the rural place was dying, death came into the Jewish homes.

From the materials of the Vinnytsia State Archive: "Unsatisfactory condition in Jewish towns: in Ilintsy, Zhornyshche, Dashev, Kitaygorod from 5 to 10 cases of starvation occured daily."

Any actions that were aimed at preserving the seed or subsistence fund were punished immediately.

Under these methods of struggle were Jewish collective farms of the southern Ukraine: "Sidorf", "Red Bessarabets", "Foroys " and others who carried out plans to deliver bread.

If the Jews died less from hunger than their Ukrainian neighbors, it is thanks to the help of each other. There were still *Torgsin* (the exchange store) where it was possible to carry any jewelry, or other clothing (if it was) for trade of a kilogram of flour or a piece of butter, or for a pack of tea. They became operational in 1931 and were liquidated in 1936.

Vinnytsia's regional office *Torgsin* as of May 15, 1933, had 11 department stores, which included 41 reception places and stalls for shopping, and it only covered 55% of the districts of Vinnytsia region. Hunger forced citizens to bring gold jewelry, Royal coins, silver jewelry, antiques, as well as melted silver coins of the Soviet sample (in the form of coins that were not accepted) and this way people escaped from the imminent death.

During the 4 years (1932 – 1936) of *Torgsin*, the regional association of Vinnytsia received from the hungry population about 6 million gold rubles, 2 tons of household gold, 25 tons of silver and other jewelry. The scale of this activity is stunning. And there is also a share in this contribution of Bar department store, which did not lag behind in its activities. In the days of receipt of food products there were huge queues in which it was necessary to stand for 1 to 2 days.

In May 1932 Commercial director of the Vinnytsia branch of the all-union office *Torgsin* A. Zhovtis sent a letter about the economic feasibility of opening points in the cities of Bar, Mogilev-Podolsky, Tulchin. On December 12, 1932 such shop Torgsin was opened in Bar where most of its workers were Jewish. This store had several stalls in the towns of the district.

An anonymous narrator from the Vinnytsia region recalled:

People gave what they had, because in that torgsin, there was everything - flour and oil, everything was available. But you had to have something to trade in order to buy. America sent food in bags. I saw it in the window. I still remember how I wanted that cornmeal, that cornmeal flour. So I think I would have eaten it all! How it is - cornmeal and white flour and then such big pieces of smoked bacon, wool sweaters, shoes. Everything was there, everything was sent from America.

The name of the shop *Torgsin* in Bar so deciphered by conscious Jews in another way:

Comrades, look around, Russia is dying, Stalin tortured the people.

It was a call to the people to fight for their freedom. However, it should be noted that in the conditions of the genocide of 1932-1933, the absence of *Torgsin* would further deepen the tragedy and there would be more victims of the Holodomor.

The famine was also in Bar, but it was not the same as it was in the villages around. During the second Holodomor of 1932-1933, 15 people died in the town. The first Holodomor was in 1921-1923. In the materials of the Mogilev district in 1925, it was noted that in Bar district there is a famine and peasants express their dissatisfaction with the Soviet government.

However, small artisans of Bar began to protest against the exorbitant taxes that swept the war-weakened city.

Announcements of the activities of Torgsin and food prices, 1930s

To replenish local budgets, the government resorted to manual methods of managing the economy. So, in the year of 1925 a shop is opened in Bar to sell vodka. In two days 90 buckets of vodka were sold in there. That is, the last penny was extracted from the starving population.

In the autumn of 1925, the reports of the State Political Directorate was noted that 50% of the population of Bar district is already hungry, some have bread for 2-3 months, others have no bread at all.

Here, those who worked at the enterprises were given food cards, which were support for workers and their families.

In 1928 in Bar 1/2 pound of bread was given only to those who worked in enterprises, other poor people did not receive, and it elicited anti-Soviet sentiments. On June 28, 1928 this was written in the report of the head of the Mogilev-Podolsky district department. Anti-Soviet leaflets were also posted here.

Memorandum of the deputy chief of Mogilev-Podolsky district the State Political Directorate of the Ukrainian SSR, the deputy chief of Mogilev-Podolsky border detachment # 24 Zaitsev to the secretary of Mogilev-Podolsky district committee of Communist Party of Bolsheviks of Ukraine about anti-Soviet performances of Bar citizens on June 26, 1928.

Top secret. Lately in town of Bar of our district, ½ pound of bread was given by the local co-operative exclusively to the working population, i.e. to the members of trade unions, artisans, etc. The rest of the poor declassified population does not receive bread at all to this day. On this basis among the latter mentioned population was noted a strong indignation, expressed in the fact that on June 13 this year a crowd of local poor broke into the building of the Executive Committee with a demand for the release of their bread. The authorities called the police, but before the arrival of the latter, the crowd was calmed down by a promise of issuing bread to them and then the crowd dispersed. However, the bread to the latter category of the population is still not given, which could cause new excesses. It should be noted that on the basis of food difficulties the activity of the anti-Soviet element increased. It's evidenced by two leaflets which were found: the first at the building of the Executive Committee, and the second at the entrance to the garden.

Leaflets are written in printed letters by hand, using the colored pencil in the Ukrainian language and quite competently. The content of the leaflet is as follows. The first leaflet: "Great achievements in 10 years of Soviet power led us to a great way to wait in line for bread." "The grain procurements have resulted in starvation". The second leaflet: "Brother, having listened to the cooperative, having given bread you had - you starve. Do not let yourself be deceived in the future. You feed the parasites with your bread, thanks to a pack of leaders of the cooperation. Cooperation makes a fool ignorant peasants". Reporting on the order, we ask about the action you have taken to inform us. Deputy chief of Mogilev-Podolsky district the State Political Directorate of the Ukrainian SSR, the deputy chief of Mogilev-Podolsky border detachment # 24 signature Zaitsev. Vrid. Of the Chief UCHOSO signature Schnayder. State Archive of Vinnytsia region, fond P-31, list 1, item 379, page 13.

More prosperous families shared a piece of bread with their neighbors, and if it were not for the traditional Jewish mutual aid, it would be very difficult for poor and large families.

In 1920s in Ukraine there was American Jewish Distribution Committee aid to Jews - "JDC". Representatives of this organization signed an agreement with the Soviet government on the establishment of the European Committee, which distributed American charitable assistance to the population.

In 1922-1935, during the famine in 35 provinces of Soviet Russia, including the Podolia province, "JDC" provided direct assistance to areas of Ukraine where many Jews lived, and donated $ 4 million to the American Administrative Assistance Fund, which also operated at this time in areas affected by famine.

In Bar these organizations assisted three orphanages, and in 1922, about 45% of the city's population received assistance, regardless of their nationality.

In 1926 "Agro-Joint" helped ten families of Jews from Bar to create agricultural colonies in Kherson region.

But still the famine was cruel and did not divide its victims by nationality. Here's a small information of the large trouble, which endured together Jews and Ukrainians.

In the spare time during the peaceful period, the long winter evenings in Bar were about the "gatherings" of Jewish grandmothers with their grandchildren. Over a glass of fragrant tea they told stories about the Jewish boys - cantonists, about pogroms, about Petliurists, about Denikins, Bolsheviks and other meshimeydim (bandits), they told about the terrible cases of cannibalism in hungry years.

And here I want to remember about a Jewish boy from Bar who was kidnapped at the age of 8 to send to the cantonists. Let's give him the name "Arn" -- perhaps, he had another name, but it is unknown. He converted to Christianity, graduated from military school, served and fought. He received a high officer rank and awards, but in 1883 he remembered his native town. General Arn went to Bar to find Arn-Bersh Hammer's father, brothers, sisters, and all his relatives. But his relatives did not accept him for his apostasy and for the loss of ties with the family. This is such an unusual story for Jews. The present name of this General (and perhaps not the General, who among the Jews could understand these ranks?) was forgotten in the maelstrom of events and hardly ever mentioned in the family. This was written by one of his relatives, writer Efim Hammer in the magazine *Mishpaha* #22.

There was also talk of miracles associated with the name Baal Shem Tov. In addition to this name, mentioned the names of Hasidim and tzaddikim: the Rabbi from Chernobyl, the Rabbi from Skvira, the Rabbi Tversky. And, as an anecdote, there finally were a large number of jokes and anecdotes about Herschel Ostropoler. However, not everyone knew that this was a real person, a Hasid, a connoisseur of the Torah and Kabbalistic books.

Herschele lived in the second half of the 18th century, and because of the name of his hometown Ostropol in Volhynia he received the name Ostropoler. Herschel was a very capable boy and no one doubted that he would become great. However, life has disposed differently. Herschel was orphaned early and had to make his own way in life.

Due to the urge to ridicule, he gained many enemies in Ostropol and so he left the town.

After long wanderings Herschele became a court jester and a funnyman at the court of the Hasidic tzaddik Rabbi Boruch Tulchinsky, also known as Rabbi Boruch Medzhibozhsky. The Rabbi was respected and loved by the Hasidim. Sometimes the Rabbi had notorious fits of temper and the Hasidim were looking for someone that could cheer him up. And then they remembered Herschel, who studied with the Rabbi.

Herschel managed to cheer the Rabbi up and stayed close by him, amused him, and could get him out of melancholy.

Herschel sometimes left Medzhibozh and went to different shtetls. The Jews fed him, laughed at his humor. The relationship between Herschel and Rabbi Boruch has been the subject of many stories and anecdotes. It is said that for his evil mockery the Hasidim threw Herschel down the stairs and he soon died of his injuries.

In popular memory, Herschel remained a bright ray that illuminated the meager world of the Jewish town.

POST-WORLD WAR II COMMUNITY DEVELOPMENT

The war changed the usual life of everyone. However, for Jews it led to the fact that they lost forever the originality of the organization of social life. The structure of the Jewish population of Podolia changed dramatically, because a significant part of Jews was destroyed.

After the liberation of Bar from fascists and the end of World War II Jews began to return to town. They were those who survived in these dire conditions: some came back from evacuation, some returned from Romanian zone occupation, and some returned alive from the war, and newcomers were many.

After the Nazis left Bar, Jews who survived this war began to return to their homes. And here they had to face the hatred of a certain number of local residents. These residents though that all Jews are buried, and then they rose up, came to their houses and even started to demand their belongings.

And, despite this, the period of restoration of the town and adjustment of peaceful life began.

In 1950-1970s the Jewish population in the town was still significant, and it played a certain role in its development. Doctors, teachers, lawyers, trade workers, engineers, employees of different ranks, builders, mechanics - all of them rebuilt and developed Bar.

Interestingly, a high percentage of Jewish students were in school No. 3.

Jews worked in different spheres of production, organizations, there were many teachers, doctors, engineers, and simple workers on all objects of the town. I will only dwell on some of the colorful and famous Jews of the town, although everyone deserves to remember them.

In the postwar period, S. Khovichthe was the director of the sewing cartel "May 1st". This cooperative was established on the basis of the cartel "Coop-textile" in 1944. Khovich served in this position until 1957. It was a period of formation, modernization, improvement of garment production and preparation for the establishment in 1957 of the enterprise "Garment factory of Bar", but with a different director.

 T. D. Komarova worked as an ophthalmologist for many years, now her children also work as doctors.

 I. Anshin was the chief of the TETs at Bar's sugar plant. A veteran of World War II, P.L. Tarnopolsky worked as the head of the PMK-47. During the years of his leadership, the vast majority of new buildings of the social sphere of the town and residential high-rise buildings were built.

Ya. B. Gumpel, who was a participant of World War II, worked as a dentist in the district hospital.

S.M. Felberg, in fact broke out of oblivion, she escaped from Bar ghetto. After the war, she graduated from medical school and became a well-known children's doctor in the town. In the period 1945-1950, Vulman worked as the chief physician of the district hospital in Bar.

In the post-war years, many Jews worked: in the trade system – S. Burshtein, I. Kelman, I. Leyfer, I. Mitelman, M. Mintz, F. Noer, T. Sumina and others; doctors – A. Tozer, A. Farbman, the Maidman family, in which the husband worked as a dentist and his wife worked as the head of the pediatric department of the hospital, E. Felberg, T. Schlafman, R. Mishuk, K. Faibishenko - pharmacist; medical staff - I. Faygol, K. Waynman, D. Greenshtein, Z. Shusterman, R. Kremin, O. Schuster.

S. Prince was a respected lawyer. D. Noer and M. Vul were engaged in filling of siphons and service of automatic machines of sparkling water in the town.

R. Tsarfis was in charge of Bar's branch of the Mogilev-Podolsky Bureau of technical inventory for many years.

Also, Jews worked in the banking system, construction offices, they were various employees and the like.

For many years Elya Anshin was in charge of the mill, which provided the residents of Bar with high-quality flour. The mill worked on the site of the present bakery which is now closed down. E. Anshin was a respected man.

After World War II, D. Fishelevich worked in the town as a private tailoring master. He returned from the war disabled without a leg. He was a famous master. One of his students F.V. Novakovsky later became the best specialist in tailoring of any clothes in clothes factory.

M. Tarasovsky was a leader of Bar's inter-farm enterprise "Incubator station" for several decades. He put a lot of effort into the modernization and development of this station and brought it to the forefront. At first it was an incubator shop from a poultry farm but then stably independent production "The master's hatchery station". Here, even in the 1960s, there was a small quail farm.

Everyone in town knew the tinker G. Prityka. He worked for many years in house management, could do the job of different complexity without drawings. He was invited to cover the roof of the Catholic church and he performed it himself.

Esya Luk was in charge of the iron and hardware store.

As there is no Odessa without aunt Sonya, so there was no Bar without aunt Esya. And even now, when someone is interested in where you can buy this or that thing by domination, the answer is obvious - in the store where aunt Esya traded.

A well-known mechanic in the town and beyond was A. M. Mook, who worked for the local district consumer union. In the early 1960s he made himself a car - dump truck with a capacity of 500 kg and used it for various transportations. Below is a photo of this car and the master himself Abram Mook next to the car.

Truck of A. Mook

I want to remember the kindness of Shpiegelman. He was the director of the pig-rearing complex, the so-called "America" and an avid hunter. Here is the reason where this complex's name came from. Eyewitnesses say that during the years of Nikita Khrushchev's leadership, in response to his slogan: "let's catch up and overtake the United States", this complex was built on the site, which now borders on the East with the cannery. Human wisdom has invented a concise name. On a question: "Where did you go?", was the answer: "Going to America." So the area called "America" arose in Bar.

Now back to Shpiegelman. Hunters once told the story. One day he forgot his gun at home, and went out to nature with a crowd of cheerful friends. When the time came to start hunting, there was nothing in the motorcycle's carriage, except for snacks. Since then, among the hunters' jokes went about it for many years. Shpiegelman even became a hero of local anecdotes.

Abram Mook along with his own project

With the election of the chief accountant of the machine-building plant I. Luk to the position of Chairman of the Board of VAT "Barsky machine-building plant", the company is technologically updated, changing product mix is witnessing radical changes in personnel, there is a requirement to improve the production efficiency.

The company operates stably, acquiring a modern appearance. Chairman of the Board and chief engineer E. Khoda become academicians of the Ukrainian technological Academy. In the corresponding category I. Luk is determined to be the best employer in Ukraine. As a philanthropist, he always helps those who are in trouble, and people respect him for it. With the direct participation of Ilya Grigoryevich, memorials were installed at the place of execution of Jews in the villages of Popovtsy, Mateykiv and a memorial complex near the village of Migalivtsi. He also takes an active part in the life of the Jewish community of Bar.

His son G. Luk is a head of "Altair", which specializes in the implementation of the mineral water "Barchanka".

In the period from 2012 to early 2014, Luk was the Chairman of Bar district state administration, and before that he was the Deputy Chairman of Bar state administration.

Naum Sirota was the director of the local enterprise *Belvodokanal* for many years. During the period of his leadership, the organization became modern, worked steadily, expanded the network of water pipes, improved water quality. The staff of the enterprise respected the head and do not forget him now that he is retired.

During the construction of the cannery, the Directors at different times were M. Mintz and G. Kesler. Kesler worked as a Director in the first years after the commissioning of the first stage of the enterprise. By the way, father of G. Kesler worked as chairman of the collective farm in the village Mal'chivtsy.

There were many Jewish teachers in schools of Bar: the Yanovsky and Belfer families, Ya. Kortsenshteyn, G. Sirota, B. Treser, D. Herzenstein, A. Gontmacher, Polyak family, Kh. Meidbraer, E. Feldberg, P. Anshina, L. Kleban, S. Rabinovich, S. Gluzman, S. Kogan, M. Gerzenstein, P. Zack, F. Perelman, K. Zeltzer, K. Gontmacher, S. Abramenko, S. Chakos, A. Markizon.

I have already told about D. Gerzenshtein, but I also want to recall his social activities. As a teacher of German, he made many efforts in establishing friendship between students of school No. 1 and the builders of gas pipelines from the German Democratic Republic. Meetings were organized, trips were made to the builders, who were located outside the city. Gerzenshtein helped the students communicate in German. He took part in the musical design of the school literary theater, because he played the violin perfectly.

In school No. 1 were many talented pupils - artists. O. Tselman was noted among them. She was a participant in many theater productions of the school. Tselman graduated from the theater institute. Recently she worked in the Russian theater in Israel. Wife of D. Gerzenshtein, Malvina Oskarovna, made certain contributions to the cultural life of the town. She was a soloist at many concerts and worked at school No. 3 as an English teacher. She also knew German, Hebrew, Moldovan. She was secretary of the party organization of the school. The teacher S.P. Gluzman with her 50 years of party experience helped Malvina Gerzenshtein with this public work.

B. Sitnik - physical education teacher, he played for a while for the football team *Podolia* in the Ukrainian football championships. His young pupils won prizes at different levels of football tournaments.

Roma Weisman and Lenya Kesler played in the town's youth football team in the early 1960s.

Pupils of the coach S. K. Chakos - Bar athletes, successfully performed at various regional, national and international competitions. So, M. Tabak was the winner of many marathon races.

The head of the methodical office of the department of district education was R. Lando.

The head of the kindergarten of the machine-building plant was M. M. Vinokur. There were still many benevolent, decent, talented Jewish teachers and many others who taught more than one generation of Bar's residents, gave them a start in life. In 1953 394 teachers were working together in Bar and in its district, including 25 Jews, representing 6.3% of the total number of teachers. You can tell a lot about them, which is enough for a separate collection of memories.

Many Jews worked at the machine-building plant, they were engineers, heads of departments, shops, skilled workers. Here are some surnames of the Jews who worked there in different post-war time: the deputy director - Ya. Lakhterman, chairman of the trade union committee - M. Estershamis, head of the department of labor - B. Schatz, lead engineers - S. Belfer, M. Pankevich, A. Ephroimsky, M. Mook, Miller family, production manager - Ya. Ephroimsky, chief technologist - L. Felberg, shop manager - O. Alexandrovsky, turners - V. Garber, K. Greenshtein, milling – A. Moshes. The foreman of locksmiths was V. Lando, and his father A. Lando worked in the department of labor, E. Kleyman was a fitter in the plant. Tamara Mook Engineer worked for many years at the plant as the engineer of the development of the metal-cutting tools. She came to work there after the college graduation, and it was her only job before retirement.

Different jobs in the factory work: B. Greenshtein, Ya. Greenshtein, Ya. Schnayper, O. Gonikman, M. Elokim, I. Ozerovsky, P. Belfer, Prokhorets family.

The head of the club of the plant was G. Mishuris. Later, after retiring, she received the title of Honored Worker of Culture of Ukraine and is still the head of the club "in the evening".

Many other famous residents of Bar went through hard career paths.

In the memoirs of the pilot V. G. Lutsak, who was a Bar resident, he recalls his classmates - Jews who attended school in the late 1940s and early 1950s. They were the original individuals. L. Kaplunovsky - the son of the deceased soldier, was the best mathematician; G. Bergman was best in the drawing and always wore ironed clothes; Ya. Felberg - he was respected for his humor and worldly wisdom. But the most interesting figure was Mark Bizyaev - the son of the deceased soldier. He was a very talented man with a difficult character, in school and outside of it always sought to achieve the truth. And he succeeded, though he had to go to truth using the hard way. Khaya Belfer is also mentioned because she was the first school love of V. Lutsak.

S.A. Kuts was the director of the grocery store *Druzhba*, 1960 – 1990s. He was a respectable and well-known man in the town.

In the early 1970s a branch of the Simferopol KB *Prodmash* was opened in Bar. It existed until the middle of 1990s. During this period many Jews worked here as leading engineers and technicians. If the average number of employees was 60 people, then 15 there were Jews. Here worked at different times: S. Belfer, M. Pankevich, E. Khoda, M.

Moock, I. Anshin, S. Kupershtein, A. Elokim, G. Feldman, E. Belfer, R. Feldman, R. Krasnyanska, M. Anshin, B. Khmelnitsky, B. Naftulishin, T. Miller. Head of department V. A. Vakar even agreed with his workers and made days off to celebrate the big Jewish religious holidays - Pesach (Passover) and Rosh Ha-Shanah (New Year).

The famous confectioner and head of the confectionery shop of Bar's consumer society was Moshes Polina. A. Ryzhy was in charge of the catering system. For many years I. L. Sekuler, doctor of the agricultural sciences, worked as the chief agronomist of the agricultural administration in Bar.

I, Michael Kupershtein, the author of this book, came to Bar in 1973 from Kamenetz-Podolsky to work at the cannery, which became for me the only place of work in the town of Bar. I worked my way up from the master of the production shop to the chief engineer.

There was almost no such enterprise or institution where Jews did not work in different positions, they worked well, glorifying their enterprise with their work. Honor and praise to all of them!

Everyone, regardless of who he was and what he did, glorified the Jewish community *Rahamim* of Bar, which means "mercy"; everyone was a worthy and merciful successor of community traditions, a role model for descendants. So it has always been and so on it should be.

Since Ukraine became the independent country, many Jews moved out to different countries of the world. This was due to both political and economic conditions.

In connection with the beginning of departure of Jews to Israel during the existence of the USSR there was a wave of agitation, but aliyah (departure for permanent residence) had to be stopped. In the late 1970s - early 1980s there were performances of lecture groups with a variety of topics: "Zionism-illusions and reality", "Zionist propaganda in the service of imperialism", "Zionism in the system of imperialism", "Zionism-the ideology of anti-communism", "Ukrainian bourgeois nationalists and Zionists are enemies of peace, progress and socialism". These lectures were based as part of the anti-Zionist propaganda and agitation in the country. For the most part, Jewish communists and representatives of the creative intelligentsia were assigned to fight with Zionist propaganda.

So, in 1979 the teacher of the secondary school No. 2 A. Gontmacher only criticized "international Zionism" about 40 times in various enterprises of the town and district. I, the author of these lines, was also invited to criticize Israeli policy towards the Arabs back in 1973 in Kamenetz-Podolsky, where I was a secretary of the Komsomol organization of the cannery plant. However, I under any pretext refused to do so until I transferred to work in Bar.

Aliya managed to slow down, but it did not stop. In total, more than 51,000 people left the USSR in 1979, more than any subsequent year until Perestroika. The 1959 census in Bar counted 763 Jews; 1989 - 357; 1993 - 199; 2001 - 68; 2017 - about 40.

It is also necessary to tell about the cohort of Jews – residents of Bar, who, due to certain circumstances, left the town of Bar both during the Soviet Union and during the independence of Ukraine. That is, they are in the diaspora in relation to their hometown. These people live in different cities of Ukraine, Russia, USA, Germany, Israel, Canada.

By their work and public position, they glorify the country of their residence, but they do not forget their native land. Whenever there is a possibility, they come to Bar to bow to their native land, visit friends and put a stone on the graves of their relatives, to visit the graves of dead Jews during World War II. I want to name Jews who left Bar, however, this list is not complete.

In Russia live: M. Kelman is the owner of a construction company, N. Pateshman works at the same company as the head of the financial department; S. Kuts resides in Nizhniy Novgorod, worked in the field of agronomy, G. Polyak, O. Segal, M. Trachtenberg and others.

In the USA live and work: B. Khmelnitsky is the owner of the building company, the Ozerovsky brothers. By the way, Ya. Ozerovsky before leaving for America worked as an operator at the film studio in Odessa, and Michael was a sculptor. In the United States, there are also T. Getsilevich with her son, family Moshes, Kharzis, Markizon, Petrogradsky, Vayser, Teperman, Maydman, Sobol, Raydun, Moshkovich, Goldman, B. Pustilnik and others.

In Germany: family Yanowski - N. Yanovskaya worked for a long time as a teacher at the school, M. Polyak, Botvinnik family, M. Tusk, K. Ryzha, and the families of Gerberg, Gvozdev, Shusterman, Sumin, Monyak, Leifer.

Immigrate to Israel: the families of Kordonsky, M. Khovich, L. Garber, M. Mook, V. Belfer, S. Belfer, G. Elokim, R. Schlafmann, L. Felberg, Karetnik, P. Anshin, R. Gontmakher, L. Gertzenshtein and many others.

The families of R. Vaysman, M. Noer, E. Vinokur live in Canada.

There are now more Jews, residents of Bar, who live abroad than in the town of Bar. Therefore, it is long overdue to establish centers of the Jewish community in the countries of residence and maintain constant communication with Bar Jewish community. Then this connection will never be broken and will pass from generation to generation.

MODERN JEWISH COMMUNITY

With the proclamation of Ukraine's independence in 1991, the Jewish community began to change.

During the Soviet era, it was not cohesive. In the report of Commissioner for the Religion under the Council of Ministers of the USSR in the Vinnytsia region it was indicated that in early 1971 in the town of Bar there was an unregistered Jewish religious community of 20 people. Here is a surprising small and rounded number of members in the community. But whether it really existed is unknown. If there was, it was most likely in the 1950s to the midddle of 1960s. After all, back in 1947, the Jews of Bar appealed to the authorities to open a synagogue in the town. Jews did not receive permission to open a synagogue, and therefore they had to carry out religious ceremonies and pray secretly. There was need of minyan (10 religious men) here. In the absence of minyan, religious ceremonies were not conducted.

There were separate initiative groups that were engaged in the care of the cemetery and mass graves. People who were not indifferent to this gathered near graves, and they also helped the poor both morally and financially. So, until 1976, D. A. Bunarsky cared for the cemetery and afterwards B. Miller, B. Greenshtein, S. Kuts took care of the graves.

In 1993, the Jewish community of Bar district "Rahamim" (Mercy) was officially established, which had 150 members. Its registration took place in 1995.

M. B Pendler was elected as the first Chairman of the Jewish community of Bar district, and, V. D. Garber was his deputy.

The period of self-affirmation of the community began. Financially, the community was supported by sponsors, its members themselves and Jewish residents of Bar who went abroad for permanent residence.

In 1994, a Jewish school for children and ulpan (courses) for the study of the Hebrew language were organized. These courses lasted only one year, but they provided an opportunity for those wishing to understand the language, and were also useful to those, who needed to prepare for going abroad. Classes at the ulpan were conducted by a teacher from Vinnytsia L. Vinnitsky. They happened once a week on a Sunday.

The school existed for two years and was closed due to the beginning of mass aliyah (departure). Jewish traditions, culture, literature, religious rites, the order of the holidays and Hebrew language were studied in the school. P. Anshina, G. Mishuris, P. Gontmacher, M. Pendler taught at the Jewish school. Not only Jews attended the Jewish school and ulpan. They were open to all comers.

Attended this Jewish school: V. Veselskaya, D. Veselsky, N. Mints, L. Kupershtein, E. Kuznetsova, R. Kordonsky, R. Mishuris, O. Treser. All of them took an active part in the life of the Jewish community.

Purimshpil performed by children from the Jewish school. Pictured, left to right: L. Kupershtein, E. Kuznetsova, N. Mintz

Jewish school students sing for the Bar Jewish community during the Passover celebration. Pictured, left to right: I. Drizik, L. Kupershtein, D. Veselska, V. Veselska, E. Kuznetsova, N. Mintz.

Students of the school helped in the preparation of the holidays and performed various concerts during the celebrations of the Jewish holidays. This was a period of active perception by children and adults of their Jewish way of life.

After M. Pendler left abroad for permanent residence, V. Garber became the Chairman of the Jewish community. He was the leader of the Jewish community of Bar from 1996 to 2009.

It was the time when everyone realized that when people are together, they are a great force.

In 2009, after the death of V. Garber, G. Ryzhy was elected as the Chairman of the community. During this period goes a full assertion of the Jewish way of life and its knowledge. Since that time, three people had become full members of the community, having passed giyur (converted to Judaism). G. Ryzhy is one of the founders of the public Association in Bar district - sports organization "Football club *Storm*, is engaged in trainer's work. He previously played for the local football team "Storm" in the regional championships and was its coach.

The representatives of the rabbinate always come on holidays Rosh Hashanah (New year) and Pesakh (Passover) to conduct services the way their grandfathers and great-grandfathers once did.

Last preparations for Passover, 2018

During the other Jewish holidays community representatives also visited city of Vinnytsia where they participated in services in the synagogue, and also visited the museum of Jewish culture and life.

Every feels pride for himself, for the community, for what we are, for what we exist. In 1996 a Jewish charity center *Hesed Emuna* (Care and Faith) was created in Vinitsya.

It takes care of all Jewish communities of the district, including Bar. Currently there are 4 representatives of this organization who help the Jews-former prisoners of the ghetto and not only them.

For many years the library from this charity center comes to Bar, usually it happens about once a month. Meetings take place in the district library of Bar. The district library became the basis for the implementation of the initiative "library on wheels" of the regional society of Jewish language and culture and the charity center. Its organizer, Lyudmila Voytenko, holds various events for the Jewish community of Bar. Participants watch documentaries about artists and the life of writers; listen to various concerts of Jewish singers; and view movies about the cities of Israel, galleries, national holidays, about neighborhoods with ancient stone buildings, bazaars, and the like.

The Jewish community visiting the charity library, 2017

At these meetings, L. Voytenko also holds interesting conversations about the outstanding Jewish figures of culture and science, shows novelties of literature. The visiting charity library also provides a variety of Jewish literature for reading during the familys' gatherings.

Non-Jews also attend these events with pleasure.

So, the life of the Jewish community, despite the small number of its members, continues.

Cemetery is cared and still taken care of with help of S. Kordonsky, N. Sirota, O. Karetnik, L. Mintz.

Jews in the modern history of the town occupy a certain place. They work, they are engaged in public work.

Thus, the plant has been saved thanks to the public position of the chairman of PAT

"BMZ" I. Luk. And the plant works, still providing more than 300 people with jobs and money to feed their families.

Everyone knows the auto shop of L. Mints, which carries out high-quality repairs of cars of different brands.

Members of the Jewish community review literature, 2017.

At different times during the years of Ukraine's independence, Jews worked as teachers, engineers, mechanics, office administrators. They opened their own coffee shops of various kinds and small clothes shops.

In August 1989 the expedition of St. Petersburg's Judaica Institute visited Bar. Meetings were held with some members of the Jewish community: T. Sumina, the Maydman family, S. Dunaevich, S. Kutz, with local historian I. Barladin, with the priest from the Roman Catholic church – father Bronislaw, and with other people.

The representatives of the expedition inspected the Jewish cemetery, the place where the old cemetery used to be, the Jewish buildings that have survived, memorial complexes that were built in memory the Jewish people who died during World War II. They also took pictures of the various objects that are in one way or another related to the life of Jews in the town of Bar.

In 1997, the representatives of the Steven Spielberg Foundation came to Bar. They met and interviewed members of the Jewish community who had survived the Holocaust (about 20 Jews). Later, each was sent a videotape of their stories. This videotape is a memory of those people who survived the Holocaust and lived through it. They can always be seen, heard and remembered.

Everyone who took part in this project received a letter of thanks signed by Steven Spielberg.

Also the contacts are maintained with charitable organizations: *Shalom Ukraine* from Auschwitz Poland, *Christians for Israel Ukraine* from Holland. Representatives of these organizations have repeatedly visited Bar, met with the Jewish community, conducted various conversations, helped with food packages to members of the community.

Letter to interview participant Anyuta Koifman (my mother) from Steven Spielberg

Fragment of the newsletter of the charity fund "Christians for Israel - Ukraine"

In November 1999, US Congressman Eliot Engel visited our town. His family ancestry comes from Bar. His grandparents are buried here.

Eliot Engel

In the town's council, the Congressman met with representatives of the authorities and the Jewish community of the town. Eliot Engel was interested in the life of the town and communicated with the Jewish community. The delegation visited the Jewish cemetery and the graves where Jews were shot. The guest was accompanied by the director of the representative office of the American Jewish Joint Distribution Committee "JDC" in the Central and Western regions of Ukraine Vladimir Iosifovich Glozman, who was also interested in the life of the Jewish community. Congressman Eliot Engel presented special souvenirs from the US Congress to the local government and the Jewish community.

There were representatives of different countries who once had family ties with Bar, and they had many other interesting meetings.

In 2017 there was also a Jewish community meeting with OBSE representatives, whose mission is located in the city of Chernovtsy.

In March 2017, there was a meeting of the Jewish community and the town's residents with Holocaust researcher K. Roos, who presented two books *Rama* and *Born to Suffer?*. This was a testimony of living witnesses – prisoners of ghettoes and camps.

Information letter of the OBSE mission

*Meeting with Holocaust researcher K. Roos
in the district library, 2017*

On September 29, 2016, events were held throughout Ukraine to honor the victims of the Holocaust and to mark the 75th anniversary of the mass shooting of Jews by Nazi occupiers in the Babi Yar tract in Kiev. The leadership of Bar and its district, members of the public and the Jewish community laid flowers and observed a minute of silence in memory of the victims of the Holocaust. It happened on the outskirts of Bar and at the site of the mass shooting of Jews in village Yaltushkiv, near the village Myhalivtsy.

On April 28, 2018, the 95th anniversary of the creation of Bar district was celebrated in Bar. This great event in the life of all the inhabitants of Bar region became possible thanks to their ability to work fruitfully in their native land and to direct all their knowledge and strength for the benefit of their native land, thereby creating its history.

A solemn award ceremony of the town's residents took place in Bar. Among the awardees were members of the Jewish community of the town. Thus, for a significant contribution to the development of the town and district and active participation were awarded the Honorary badges the chairman of PAT "Machine-building plant of Bar" I. G. Luk and the former head of the company "Barvodokanal" and now a retired N. I. Sirota.

N. Sirota receives the Honorary award

Medal of Honor "for services to district of Bar" is given to I. Luk

In July 2018, the American journalist and writer Robin Blumenthal met with the Jewish community and members of the public of Bar. Blumenthal's great-grandfather, Joseph Menachem Mar'yanovsky was born in Bar.

At the meeting, the journalist told about the history of her family. Even in the early 1920s her great-grandfather with family from Shargorod, where they lived at that time, traveled to Romania, and then to the US. This was the period of Jewish pogroms of 1918-1920s.

The guest visited the cities and towns where her ancestors lived: Krivoy Rog, Shargorod, and our town of Bar. Now she is writing a book under the provisional title *The Last Place* and collects material about life of her ancestors in Ukraine. This meeting once again confirms that the link between generations will always exist.

Despite being few, Jews of the town take part in public city events because they do not just stay here, but live here. The town's Jewish community operates and preserves the traditions of its people. Good luck to all of them in independent Ukraine!

Robin Blumenthal

R. Blumenthal meets with residents of Bar, 2018.

PROMINENT JEWS FROM BAR

I will only mention a few names of prominent people who were born in Bar and almost forgotten.

Baron Akiva (1909-1965) was a prominent Israeli politician and public figure.

Berezovsky Boris Abramovich (1923-1993): Ukrainian physiologist, Master Degree, Professor of Vinnytsia Medical Institute.

Dmitry Afanas'evich Magazanik (1896 – 1948): the author of various Russian-Turkish, Turkish-Russian dictionaries and Turkish expressions published in 1930s - 1940s, a well-known expert of the Turkish language.

Alexander (Solomon) Chemerisky (1880-1942): active participant in Russia's revolutionary movement, publicist, public figure, repressed in 1939.

Shlomo Gilels (1873-1953: Israeli writer and teacher.

Berezovsky B., Baron Akiva, and Shlomo Gilels

Jacobo (Hacobo) Timerman (1923-1999) - emigrated to Argentina in 1928, a well-known Argentine journalist and politician. He was repressed by the junta during the "dirty war". His son, who a few years ago came to Bar, worked as a Minister in Argentina's government.

Mark Isaakovich Frenkel (1909-1982) - Soviet scientist in the field of mechanical engineering, Doctor of Technical Sciences, Professor, founder of the theory and engineering method of calculation of piston compressors.

I. Timerman, M. I. Frenkel

Aaron Markovich Arnoldov (Sheinfayn) (1894-1937): local historian, railway man, head of the Karelo-Murmansk plant, chief of the South Eastern railway in 1937, people's commissar of railways.

Emmanuel Froymovich Nelin (Freydzon) (1925-2012) - Russian actor and entertainer, honored artist of Russia (1995).

A. M. Arnoldov, E. F. Nelin

Batsheva Katsnelzon (1897-1988): member of the Knesset of Israel, member of the international Zionist movement.

B. Katsnelson, J. Barondess

Joseph Barondess (1867-1928) - U.S. politician, member of the Paris peace conference 1919-1920.

Moses Alexandrovich Berchenko (1933 -): specialist in the field of solar energy and semiconductor technology. Author of about 100 scientific works and inventions. Engaged in literary activities, published in Russia, USA, Israel.

Lev Stepanovich Keller (Lev Shepelevich Zilberman) (1899-1971) was born in Bar in a merchant family, well-known Communist party worker, journalist, member of the regional committee of the Communist party in the city of Gorky.

Semyon Arkadyevich Chernomorets (born 1938 -) - Professor, Doctor of Law, Honored lawyer of the Russian Federation, Dean of Ugra State University, authored hundreds of publications.

Alexander Naumovich Razhener (1921 – 2010): World War II veteran, well-known artist, portraitist, painter. He studied under I. Rubanov, I . Gurvich, and K. Morozov. Bright representative of the socialist realism. He painted still lives and contemporaries. Currently he lives in Moscow.

S. A. Chernomorets, A. N. Razhener.

There is much to be told of a cohort of eminent teachers, engineers, physicians, and ordinary workmen who exalted by their labor the town of Bar, in which they were born and lived, though they might afterwards have resided in other cities or countries.

Before the war, Dr. M. Moreynis (1864-1930) lived in the town. In the reception book for 1870 of Bar's school there is an entry under the number 91: "Mark Moreynis 3 group". Interestingly, Moreynis was a friend and classmate of N. Kotsyubinsky and wrote memoirs about him "from his student years", which formed the basis of the book about N. Kotsyubinsky, written by M. Ivashevskiy - *Mikhail Kotsyubinsky during his studies in the town of Bar*. This book was published in Vinnytsia in 1929.

M. Moreynis owned three houses in the town, one of which is currently the office of the military commissariat of Bar district. The Bar district police department is located in another building, and another building was not preserved. Two of Moreynis' private pharmacies and his doctor's office were located in this building.

Although the Jewish cemetery was destroyed during the war, no one dared destroy the grave of Moreynis. This shows human respect for the doctor and gratitude, because he saved more than one life and treated patients of different faiths.

Grave of Moreynis at the old Jewish cemetery, Bar

A large family Bogoraz, four sisters and four brothers, had roots in Bar. Their mother Anna Abramovna Bogoraz was born in Bar in the family of a merchant in 1839. After a while she moved to Ovruch in Volyn province, where she married a teacher from a Jewish school. Anna was small, but agile, she had a tough character, purposeful. Her children converted to Christianity, but her parents remained faithful to Judaism:

Perlya Mendelevna Bogoraz (Praskov'ya Maksimilianovna Shabalin Bogoras) (1860-1885) - an active participant in the movement for people's freedom, died in Moscow in a transit prison.

Nathan Mendelevich Bogoraz (Vladimir Germanovich Bogoraz) (1865-1936) - revolutionary, ethnographer, writer, professor, public figure.

Henry Mendelovich Bogoraz (Nikolai Alekseevich Bogoraz) (1874-1952) - revolutionary, Russian, Soviet surgeon, winner of the Stalin prize. He is the only surgeon in the Soviet Union, who conducted surgery on his prostheses. In 1920 his legs were cut off after he was hit by a tram.

M. Bogoraz, V. Bogoraz

Lazar Mendelevich Bogoraz (Sergei Maksimovich Gubkin) (1868 -?) - participant in the movement for peoples' freedom, doctor, one of the revolutionary teachers of V. Ulyanov at the University in Kazan, emigrated to France, where he was engaged in medical business.

Alexander Maksimilianovich Bogoraz (1877 -?) - revolutionary, died while working hard.

Bera Bogoraz and two other sisters studied at the conservatory, Bera died in 1922.

L. Kleban (born 1936) worked as Deputy Director of school No. 1 for educational work. His singing voice entertained at many concerts in Bar, its' district, Vinnytsia region, "Solar clarinets" of Ukraine. The author of several collections about the outstanding people of the town. He lives in Israel.

A history teacher with fifty years of journalistic experience A. Gontmakher (1922-1991) arrived in Bar in 1950. Then he worked as the head of department of culture in Bar.

A. Gontmakher

In the 1970s, F. Schuster worked as the director of the Palace of pioneers. It was a period of active development of the Palace of pioneers.

I. Kortsenshteyn (1931-1985) worked in Bar after graduating from pedagogical college in 1950s. As a talented mathematics teacher in school No. 1, he instilled the love of mathematics in many students.

The headmasters of the school at different times were K. Nudelman and B. Treser. They were famous teachers and organizers of pedagogical training.

I will dwell on the figure of K. Nudelman (1909-2000). Klara Izrailevna from 1945 to 1964 was the director of school No. 2. In 1945, it had only five classes and 200 students. She had a hard journey. From a simple worker of Bar's sugar factory to the head of the elementary school, she later became its director. Klara Izrailevna was born in Bar. At the age of 16, she began her career at a sugar factory, and then she, as an energetic and talented girl, was sent to work as the head of the first kindergarten. From 1937 to 1939, she studied by correspondence at the Vinnytsia State Pedagogical Institute, while staying in Bar and working in the middle school No. 3 as a head teacher. She became one of the first Komsomol members of our town, later - a member of the Bureau of the district committee of the Komsomol. When World War II began, Klara's husband went to the front lines, and she and her young children were evacuated to the East. She worked as the head of the evacuation hospital club in Mozdok and Tashkent. Later she was a history teacher and head teacher in Pekenti, Tashkent region of Uzbekistan. After the liberation of Bar in 1944, she returned with her children to her hometown. She worked as a history teacher at the middle school No.1 of Bar. At this time, she again studied by correspondence at the Vinnytsia State Pedagogical Institute, and later became the director of school No. 2. She was a public figure, a Deputy of the district and town's councils, a member of the district party committee, chairman of the district pedagogical society. Already a veteran of pedagogical work, she continued to participate in the public life of the school and the town. The local government highly appreciated the work of K. I. Nudelman, awarding her the medal "For valiant work in the Great Patriotic war of 1941-1945", the order "Badge of Honor", the badge "The Excellence in Public Education", twelve Diplomas of the Ministry of education of Ukraine. She died in June 2000, having lived a long and vibrant life.

The head teacher of the middle school No.1 was S.A. Dunaevich, and in the middle school No.2 - A. Yanovsky.

A. Schlafer was in charge of the children's sports school in Bar. He brought up many talented athletes.

M. Bonduryansky for many years worked as the chief technologist at the alcohol plant in Bar. This was the period of formation and approval in the country of the business brand of the plant.

You won't remember them all at once, because everyone is talented, outstanding. Every person has something that adorns him or her, making them unforgettable.

WHAT IS A JEW?

And now, when the last pages are turned, it is necessary to stop on a question: "And what is a Jew?". This question is not new, it has been written about a lot, and therefore I only summarize some observations.

For centuries, the question "what is a Jew?" just didn't exist.

Belonging to the Jewish people was associated with the adoption of a certain way of life. A Jew was a person who accepted the beliefs and the way of existence that Judaism dictated to him. Any conscious deviation from this way of life either in theory or on practice, was regarded as a betrayal of Judaism in all its manifestations, and it is not only about those Jews who have adopted another religion.

This state of things, which had existed for a long time, began to change in the 19th century. More and more Jews began to partially or completely abandon the fundamental precepts of historical Judaism, but nevertheless these Jews did not convert and continued to consider themselves Jews.

If in the 19th century the number of such people was insignificant, and sometimes even went to null, then in 1930s they were already, no doubt, the majority of the Jewish people. There was a serious problem: how to define their Jewishness? What is a Jew - in relation to these people?

If we turn to ancient historical times, then the Jewish people descendent from Abraham, whose name originally was Abram, but G-d changed his name and fate.

Abraham was born after the creation of the world (in 1812 BCE) in the town Cutha, Mesopotamia. His name Abraham that means "father of many nations", but it is Abraham who is the first person whom the Torah calls the word "Ivri " (Jew): "And the fugitive came and informed Abraham - ha-Ivri ..."(Genesis 14:13).

After the Flood, Noah's spiritual path was continued by his eldest son Shem. Shem's great-grandson Ever was the last righteous spiritual leader to mix languages and the only one of Shem's descendants who did not participate in the construction of the tower of Babel.

Ever's great-great-grandson was Terah - the father of Abraham. G-d revealed to Abraham and told him to leave his homeland - Ur Kasdim (Ur of the Chaldeans) and move across the Euphrates river, in the land of Canaan, which will become the eternal fate of the Jewish people and will be called Eretz Israel (land of Israel). G-d made an alliance with Abraham, then with his son Yitzhak, and then with Yitzhak's son – Jacob.

Jacob had 12 sons. They are the leaders of the 12 tribes (in Hebrew "shvat") of the Jewish people. In the Tanakh ("Jewish Bible") the Jewish people are called differently: "ivrim" (Jews), "Judah" (Jews), and also Israel, "bnei Israel" (sons of Israel) and Yeshurun.

The word "ivri" is associated with the name of the righteous Ever - Abraham's ancestor. Another explanation is "came fromthe other side": in the land of Canaan, Abraham was a stranger from the other side of the Euphrates river. Abraham, in contrast to Noah, Shem and Ever, took an "active life position", preaching faith in one God and denying idolatry. Our sages, interpreting the name "Ivri", explained that the whole world was on one side, and Abraham - on the other.

The word "Judah" originally meant a person from the tribe of Judah or, in a broader sense - a resident of Judah (Judah, the Jewish Kingdom in the South of the land of Israel in the era of the First Temple), and after this power ceased to exist, so began to call all Jews in general. Hence the term "yahadut" (Judaism) that emerged after the Babylonian captivity.

Jewish people are often named "the twelve tribes of Israel", but here it is necessary to make a number of clarifications. The Jewish people have 3 forefathers - Abraham, Isaac, and Jacob, and 4 matriarchs: Abraham's wife - Sarah, the wife of Yitzchak - Rivka and wives of Jacob - Leah and Rachel. The latter gave their maids to Jacob to be his wives as well and whose sons are, in some sense, considered children of Leah and Rachel respectively.

Let us list the 12 tribes of Israel as first mentioned in the Torah:

-     the six sons of Leah: Reuben, Shimon, Levi, Judah,   Issachar, Zebulun
-     the two sons of Rachel: Joseph, Benjamin
-     the two sons of Bilhah, Leah's maidservant: Dan, Naphtali
-     the two sons of Zelfa, Rachel's maidservant: Gad, Asher

Jacob, his children and their families - 70 in all - descended into Egypt, of which Jacob's son Yosef was the de facto ruler. At the end of the Book of Genesis (the first book of the Torah -) it is told how, while on his deathbed, Jacob blessed his sons, gave a separate blessing to each of them. The subsequent fate of each of the twelve tribes corresponded to the received blessing.

The two sons of Yosef – Menashe and Ephraim – Yaakov appointed the ancestors of the independent tribes:

And now, your two sons, who were born to you in the land of Egypt before I came to you in Egypt, they are mine! :Ephraim and Menashe as Reuven and Shimon shall be mine. - Genesis (48:5).

After leaving Egypt, the tribe of Josef is not considered by the Torah as a separate tribe, now it is two tribes – Ephraim and Menashe. Thus, the tribes becomes thirteen.

At the same time, the tribe of Levi (Levites) after leaving, occupies a special position, how to fully devote themselves to the service of G-d. The Midrash says that the Levites, unlike other tribes, were never slaves in Egypt - they were made overseers over other Jewish slaves, and they, protecting and covering their brothers, were punished for their "misdeeds." Unlike other tribes, Levites even in the most difficult situations did not cheat on the Almighty and did not worship idols - neither in Egypt, nor during the events with the Golden calf in the Sinai desert.

When the children of Israel received the Torah on mount Sinai, it finally turned them into a people. The Torah regulated the question of the definition of Jewry for all generations. According to Halakha (Jewish religious legislation) a Jew is a person born to a Jewish mother, or a proselyte who has accepted the Torah and the commandments in accordance with the established procedure in a recognized rabbinical court ("giyur").

In 1871, the work of G. Gutman in Yiddish language "What is a Jew?" was published in "The Jewish Library".

In 1908, the authors of the work were replaced when they were published in Warsaw in the weekly *Teater Welt*, but in Russian language. The famous Russian writer L. Tolstoy was listed as the author. Later this work was reprinted with mistake in "The General Jewish encyclopedia"(1943). And so this mistake remained to live, as the cry of the soul of Lev Tolstoy, for more than a century.

This article is certainly relevant now. And so I submit its full text.

This question is not as strange as it may seem at first glance. Let's examine this free creature that was insulated and oppressed, trampled on and pursued, burned and drowned by all the rulers and the nations, but is nevertheless living and thriving in spite of the whole world.

What is a Jew that did not succumb to any worldly temptations offered by his oppressors and persecutors so that he would renounce his religion and abandon the faith of his fathers?

A Jew is a sacred being who procured an eternal fire from the heavens and with it illuminated the earth and those who live on it. He is the spring and the source from which the rest of the nations drew their religions and beliefs.

A Jew is a pioneer of culture. From time immemorial, ignorance was impossible in the Holy Land, even more so than nowadays in civilized Europe. Moreover, at the time when the life and death of a human being was worth nothing, Rabbi Akiva spoke against the death penalty which is now considered to be an acceptable punishment in the most civilized countries.

A Jew is a pioneer of freedom. Back in primitive times, when the nation was divided into two classes, masters and slaves, Moses' teaching forbid holding a person as a slave for more than six years.

A Jew is a symbol of civil and religious tolerance. 'So show your love for the alien, for you were aliens in the land of Egypt". These words were uttered during distant, barbarian times when it was commonly acceptable among the nations to enslave each other.

In terms of tolerance, the Jewish religion is far from recruiting adherents. Quite the opposite, the Talmud prescribes that if a non-Jew wants to convert to the Jewish faith, then it has to be explained to him how difficult it is to be a Jew and that the righteous of other religions also inherit the heavenly kingdom. A Jew is a symbol of eternity.

The nation which neither slaughter nor torture could exterminate, which neither fire nor sword of civilizations were able to erase from the face of the earth, the nation which first proclaimed the word of the Lord, the nation which preserved the prophecy for so long and passed it on to the rest of humanity, such a nation cannot vanish.

A Jew is eternal; he is an embodiment of eternity.

   - Count Leo Tolstoy, 1891, St. Petersburg, Russia

AFTERWORD

Here is the last page of this small book which we turn over. There was something to remember, perhaps with sadness and pain, but probably with pride and joy.

In general, this is not a book, but only facts, events, quotes. It is the search for different eras in the ashes of the great Jewish losses. This is the repayment of our debt, it is a topic to be discussed, these are questions that must be understood.

Here, in our town, good, wise and tolerant people lived. Many Jews went to other countries, but remember their county, their land on which they ran barefoot during their childhood. In letters, conversations, they say that they do not forget their town, try not to forget the Ukrainian melodic language, which they consider their native.

We all always thank sincerely and bow low to those who are still alive, and to those who have not lived to our time, and bow to those who in the terrible days of the occupation provided assistance to the Jews who were in big need.

I have no doubt that only real Ukrainians - residents of Bar could do so.

Of the last generation of Holocaust victims, there are currently about 2,500 people left alive and they live in 42 cities, towns and villages of Ukraine, including several people who live in the town of Bar.

More than 75 years have passed since the last tragedies, and the Jews still continue to search for the Righteous Among the Nations, find and thank those people who helped them during the war. Let humanity, goodwill and respect for all people reign in every home, and God for honesty will give abundance.

Despite the contradictions that arose at different times between Jews, Ukrainians and Poles, they together repeatedly defended their hometown from a common enemy. And so therefore an idea arises to perpetuate these events by establishing a memorial sign "To all the defenders of Bar who fell on the walls of the town" in the historical part of the town and to consecrate it by the representatives of different denominations. And to make the inscription in three languages: Ukrainian, Jewish and Polish. After all it is impossible to separate Jews from the history of Ukraine and vice versa.

Sholom Aleichem, peace be upon us Jews, in our Ukraine, in our town, far across the ocean, in the land of Israel, in mass graves and under black gravestones in the cemetery.

As long as you live, remember! Peace to you all!

DICTIONARY

Action - an operation against Jews, mainly in the ghetto, to concentrate them and send them to destruction.

Anti-Semitism - a form of national intolerance (xenophobia), which is expressed in hostility to Jews as an ethnic or religious group, often based on prejudice and bias. There is a difference between state and domestic anti-Semitism.

Assimilation (from Latin - assimilation) is the process by which members of one ethnic group lose their distinctive features and borrow the identity of another ethnic group with which they are in direct contact.

Babi Yar, near Kiev, Ukraine - mass grave where the Nazis first killed Jews and then Soviet prisoners of war, Gypsies, communists and underground workers. There, during two days, 29 and 30 September 1941, Sonderkommando 4A under the command of P. Blobel killed 33771 Jews, not counting those killed infants and children who were less than 3 years old. In total, during the years of occupation, in Babi Yar were killed from 100 to 200 thousand people, most of whom were Jews.

Cantonists (from French "canton" - corner or district) - so called educated young children who were in military service in Russia during the reign of Tsar Nicholas I. In 1827, compulsory schooling of 12-year old Jewish children was introduced. Authorities abducted Jewish children, took them to school of cantonists, and forced them to acceptance Christianity.

Chevra, in plural Chevrot (from Hebrew "society") – one of the examples is chevra kadisha – a burial society, which assists with funerals of its members in accordance with Jewish customs and traditions.

Collaboration (from French - "cooperation") - conscious, voluntary cooperation during the war with the enemy in his interests and to the detriment of his state. The word mostly applies in the narrower meaning, as a collaboration with the occupiers.

Concentration camp - a place of isolation and detention, mostly under inhumane conditions for "undesirable elements", declared enemies of the Third Reich. The camps were so named because the prisoners were physically "concentrated" in one place. According to historians, in Europe, the Nazis created 1634 concentration camps and more than 900 labor camps.

Einsatzgruppen (from German - entry in combat) - punitive groups of special purpose, created for the destruction of prisoners of war, mass executions of the population in the occupied territories. Four operational units accompanied the army, which carried out the invasion of the territory of the USSR on June 22, 1941 the Main task of the Einsatzgruppen was the destruction of commissars, Jews, Gypsies, partisans and other "undesirable elements". Divided into

Sonderkommando and Einsatzkommando during 1943-1944, the Einsatzgruppen were disbanded.

Fascism (from Italian "a union") - the generalized name of a specific extreme right-wing movements, ideologies and the corresponding form of government dictatorial type, the characteristics of which are the cult of personality, militarism, totalitarianism.

Forced labor camp for Jews - a place of imprisonment of Jews for the purpose of their use in heavy work, converted from the ghetto or filled with able-bodied Jews from the ghetto, subordinated to the leadership of the police and SS. On the territory of Vinnytsia region in the German zone of occupation for the construction and repair of the strategic road Lvov-Rostov was created about twenty Jewish labor camps. More than 10 thousand Jews died there during the construction of the Vinnytsia-Uman road section.

Gendarmerie - a part of the German police, which carried out police duties in rural areas.

Genocide (from Greek "genos" – family, tribe and Latin - to kill) is an extreme form of discrimination, targeted destruction in whole or in part of certain groups of the population on national, ethnic, racial or religious grounds. The definition of the concept of "genocide" was first given in his book "Principles of government in occupied Europe"(1944) R. Lamkin. He escaped from Poland to the United States during the time of Nazis' persecutions. From 1948 genocide is considered an international crime.

Ghetto (from Italian "getto nuovo" - new foundry) - an isolated part of a medieval Western European city, reserved for Jews. The term appeared in Venice first in 1516 and came from the name of the foundry, near which the Jewish quarter was located. In the course of the Nazis' "final solution of the Jewish question", ghettos were created as places of isolation and destruction of Jews by depriving them of their means of subsistence, or as places of temporary detention for further destruction in death camps or by firing squad.

Holocaust (from Greek "holo kauston") - burnt completely, sacrificial offering) persecution and mass destruction of the Jews of Europe by the Nazis and collaborators in 1933-1945. The term was first used in the 60s in journalism by writer E. Wiesel, as a symbol of gas chambers and crematoria in death camps. The term "Holocaust" in a broad sense is the persecution and mass destruction by the Nazis of representatives of various ethnic and social groups (Jews, Gypsies, gays, Freemasons, terminally ill and others) during the Third Reich.

Havdalah (from Hebrew "separation") - Jewish religious ceremony that marks the end of Shabbat and the beginning of the next week.

Judenrat (from German "Jewish Council") - Jewish self-government body, in 1939 created in Poland on the initiative of the German occupation authorities in each Jewish ghetto, and later on the territory of the USSR. The authority of the Judenrat: the management and provision of economic life and order in the ghetto, the collection of funds; selection of candidates for work in labor camps; the execution of the orders of the occupying power.

Kahal (from Hebrew "Qahal" – a group) - a local governing body of a former Ashkenazi Jewish community administering religious, legal, and communal affairs.

Kristallnacht (from German "Reichkristallnacht" - night of the broken showcases) - pogrom against Jews in all Nazi's Germany on November 9-10, 1938, carried out by special teams and civilians. At the same time, the streets were covered with shards of glass from the windows of shops, houses, synagogues, which belonged to Jews.

Lapserdak (derived from Hebrew "layb" and Ukrainian "serdak" words) – the 1st part is translated as "upper body garment, and the 2nd part of the word means "men's outer garment". In other words, is was kind of outwear for men.

Matzsevah (from Hebrew "pillar" or "monument") - a headstone or tombstone marking a grave.

Mezuzah (from Hebrew "doorpost") - a piece of parchment paper with the inscribed verses from Torah. It is enclosed in the decorative case and attached to the doorpost in a Jewish house as a sign of faith.

Mikvah (from Hebrew "from water") - a small bath for the ritual bath of the body with the purpose of ritual purification. The volume of water in the mikvah is from 250 to 1000 liters of water. Water when used of rain, or from the source. If the community had a choice to build a synagogue or a mikvah, the first priority has always been the construction of a mikvah. It was very important to the Jews.

Mishnah (from Hebrew "study by repetition") - the first written text containing religious interpretations in Judaism.

Mohel (from Hebrew "circumciser", in plural "mohalim") - a Jew who is trained to perform a process of Brit-Mila ritual circumcision for Jewish newborn boys.

Parnasse (from Hebrew "livelihood" or Yiddish "income") - ability to support yourself and your family, making a living.

Ramban (an acronym in Hebrew רמב"ן) - a leading medieval Jewish scholar, Sephardic Rabbi Moshe ben Nachman, commonly known as Nachmanides. His name is abbreviated as RaMBaN.

Reichskommissariat of Ukraine (RKU) an administrative entity (since August 20, 1941) that covered part of the Ukrainian and Belarusian lands during the occupation in 1941-1944. The capital of the RCU was the city of Rovno. The position of Reichskommissar was held by Erich Koch. The Reichskommissariat consisted of six General districts. Part of the Vinnytsia region was part of the General district of Zhytomyr. Here were created the districts (EBT), managed Gebrselassie.

Righteous People of Nations (from Hebrew – "Hasidey Umot ha-Olam") - according to the Israeli law on the memory of the Disaster (1951). This honorary title is given to non-Jews who during World War II saved Jews, risking their lives and did it for free. In honor of each recognized righteous person a ceremony is held, at which the righteous or his heirs are awarded an honorary certificate and a nominal medal, which in two languages – Hebrew and French is engraved with the inscription: "In gratitude from the Jewish people. He, who saves one life, saves the whole world." In Ukraine, there are about 2,500 people who received this title of righteous, including more than two hundred representatives accounted for the Vinnytsia region.

Segregation (from Latin "secession") - the policy of forced secession of any group of the population on religious or racial grounds.

Shabbat (from Hebrew "to finish the activity") - Saturday, the seventh day of the week, in which, according to the Torah, it was forbidden to work.

Shoichet (Yiddish variant from Hebrew "shochet") - ritual slaughterer or butcher.

Shtadlan (from Aramaic "to intercede on behalf of") - a representative of the Jewish community with access to high dignitaries and legislative bodies.

Shtetl (from Yiddish "a town", Jewish place) a small settlement, sub-urban type, or a certain area in the city, where the Jewish population mainly lived.

StAVR - abbreviation for State Archive of the Vinnytsia Region. Contains documents from Eastern part of Podolia region from 18th century until the present day.

State Rabbi - an elected position in 1857-1917 in the Jewish communities of the Russian Empire. He was approved by the provincial government and officially represented the community in the city authorities. The government assumed that the state Rabbi would be the spiritual leader of the community, but usually he was poorly versed in Judaism. Therefore, the traditional rabbis were the spiritual leaders of the Jewish community, in addition, they were considered as scientific advisers to state rabbis.

Tehilim (from Hebrew "psalms") - verses of King David.

Torgsin - the Soviet organization that served guests from abroad, and Soviet citizens with "currency values" (silver, gold, precious stones, antiques, cash) which they could exchange for food and other consumer goods. It was created in January 1931, and liquidated in 1936.

Tzadik (from Hebrew "righteous, pious") - spiritual guide of Hasidic Jews, a man who enjoyed a special position before God.

VUAN (in Ukrainian) - abbreviation translated as Ukrainian National Academy of Science.

Yad Vashem (in Hebrew "a memorial and a name") – Israel's national memorial of Holocaust and heroism. It was founded in 1953 by the Knesset to perpetuate the memory of Jewish victims of Nazism in 1933-1945. The area of the memorial is 18 hectares, 1 million people visits this complex per year.

Yellow star (from Ukrainian "lata" a riband) - special distinctive sign, which was ordered by the Nazis to be worn by Jews in German-controlled during the Holocaust. This sign was made of a piece of yellow cloth in the form of a six-pointed star.

Yiddishland (from Yiddish "Jewish country") - so conventionally called areas of compact residence of Jews in shtetls, which stretched through Eastern Europe, the Baltic States, Ukraine, Belarus, Russia such a long belt and existed before the Holocaust, that was until the middle of the 20th century.

Zhyd (from Polish "a Jew") - the ancient name of the Jews in the Russian/Ukrainian languages, later acquired an offensive meaning.

REFERENCES

1.　　　Altman I. A. Victims of hate. The Holocaust in the USSR, 1941-1945 / I. A. Altman. - Moscow: Foundation "Ark", 2002. - 543 p.

2.　　　Disasters of times. In memory of the disasters that befell on the Jews in 1648-1649 in Ukraine, Podolia, Lithuania and Belarus from the united rebels under the command of Bohdan Khmelnytsky. / [comp. Ehoshiya; transl. M. Berlin] / / Readings in the Imperial Society of Russian History and Antiquities at Moscow University. 1859. January-March. The first book / University printing house. - Moscow, 1859.

3.　　　Boyko O. The construction of synagogues in Ukraine / Oksana Boiko // Bulletin of Institute in Ukrzapadproektrestavratsiya. - Lviv, 1998. - Part 9. Pages 5-33.

4.　　　Brockhaus F. A. The Jewish encyclopedia : in 16 books / F. A. Brockhaus, I. A. Efron. - St. Petersburg, 1908-1913.

5.　　　Web portal of the World Holocaust memorial center Yad Vashem/ - Mode of access: https://www.yadvashem.org.

6.　　　The great famine in Ukraine 1932-1933: in 4 volumes / [Executive Director of the Commission James Meys]. - K.: Kyiv-Mogilyanska Academy, 2008. - T. I: The testimony of the eyewitnesses to the Commission of the U.S. Congress. - 2008.

7.　　　Verstyuk V. F. Ukraine from ancient times to the present. Chronological reference. / V. F. Verstyuk, O. M. Dzyuba, V. F. Reprintsev. - K.: Naukova Dumka, 1995. - 687 pages.

8.　　　The entire South-Western region. Reference book Kiev, Podolia and Volyn provinces. / South-West Department Russian Chamber of Export; comp. M. V. Dovnar-Zapolsky; under editor A. I. Yaroshevich. - Kiev: Fish and Volsov, 1913.

9.　　　Volovik M. V. Ethno-cultural landscapes of Podolia towns. / Volovik V. M. - Vinnytsia: PP "O. Vlasyuk", 2011. - 270 p.

10.　State Archive of the Russian Federation. Inventory. R-1339. Fund 1, List 415, Item 3. Copy. The Author Denikin A. I.

11.　　　Galchevsky Ya. Against the red invaders. / Ya. Galchevsky. – Kiev: Medibori – 2006, 2011. - 360 p.

12.　　　Gisem O. V. The Holocaust in Ukraine (1941-1944): dictionary-reference / Gisem O. V.-Kiev: Sphere, 2009. - 92 p.

13.   The Holocaust in Ukraine: the search for answers to the questions
of history. : textbook / [compiled by: Eromenko G. et al.]. -
Dnepropetrovsk: Tkuma, 2012. - 148 p.

14.   Guldman V. K. Podolia province. Experience of geographical and
statistical description. / Guldman V. K.-Kamenets-Podoliay: Printing
house of Podoliay provincial Board, 1889. - 510 p.

15.   Gusev-Orenburgsky S. I. The Crimson book. The pogroms in the
Ukraine 1919-1920. / S. I. Gusev-Orenburgsky. Harbin: DECAPO, 1922. -
252 p.

16. StAVR - Fund.1 - List. 1 - Item. 496 (1925-1926) - 262 pages.

17. StAVR-Fund.-227 - Podolia provincial government 1796-1919 - Item.
35,9 thousand.

18. StAVR -Fund.-33 - List. 1 - Item. 17 - page 185

19. StAVR -Fund.-501 - List . 1 - Item. 43 - page 80

20. StAVR -Fund.-532 - List . 1 - Item. 83 - page 65

21. StAVR -Fund.-532 - List . 2 - Item. 33 - page 147

22. StAVR -Fund.-63 - List. 1 - Item.5 - page 184

23.   StAVR -Fund. P-425 - List . 1 - Item. 136 - pp.
63-64.

24. StAVR -Fund. P.-136 - List. 3 - Item. 371 - page 16.

25. StAVR -Fund. R.-925 -List. 8 - Item. 58 - page 81.

26.   State Archive of Khmelnitsky region. Fund 115 (Podolia provincial
drawing). - List 1 - Item 11 - pages 154-170.

27.   S. Dodik. The fate and life of the boy from the shot ghetto: memoirs
/ S. Dodik - Moscow: Kaleydoscope, 2004. - 128 p.

28.   S. Dodik. Echoes of the Holocaust / [Electronic resource] S. Dodik.
- Moscow, 2009. - Mode of access:
http://shorashim.narod.ru/case_dodik1.htm.

29.   M.G.Dubik. Handbook of camps, prisons and ghettos in the
occupied territory of Ukraine (1941-1944) / [compiled by M. G. Dubik] -
Kiev, 2000. - 320 p.

30.   V. V. Dyachok. The town of Bar and its suburbs in the cameral and
topographical description of the Mogilev district of the late XVIII - early XIX
century. V. V. Dyachok, O. Ya. Dyachok// Scientific notes of Vinnytsia
State Pedagogical University named after Mikhail Kotsyubinsky. Vol. 19.
Series: History: Collection of scientific works. - 2011. - Pages 277-280.

31.   Jewish Soviet encyclopedia. / compiled by I. M. Levitas. - Kiev: Stal,
2007. - 704 p.

32.   Jewish chronicles of the XVII century: scientific and historical literature./ Moscow: Geshirim, 1997. - [Electronic resource].-Mode of access: https://www.e-reading.club/bookreader.php/1017594/Evreyskie_hroniki_XVII_stoletiya._Epoha_hmelnichiny.html.

33.   L. T. Ezioransky. Factory enterprises of the Russian Empire for 1914 / L. T. Ezioranski. - Petrograd: D. P. Kandaurov and son, 1914. - 1612 p.

34.   S. Yesyunin. The town of Bar, Mogilev district in the second half of the XIX-early XX century : Socio-economic aspects // Third Mogilev-Podolia regional conference - Mogilev-Podolsky, Kamenets-Podolsky: Oiyum, 2009. - Pages 116-122.

35.   Jewish genealogical research on-line service JewishGen [Electronic resource]. – Mode of access: https://www.jewishgen.org.

36.   B. Zabarko. We wanted to live. Certificates and documents. / B. Zabarko. - K.: Dukh and literatura, 2013. - 592 p.

37.   Yu. A. Zinko. The first half-century in the history of distillery in Bar/ Yu. A. Zinko, A. K. Lysiy//Scientific notes of Vinnytsia State Pedagogical University. Series: History - 2011. - Vol.19. Pages 48-52. - Mode of access: http://nbuv.gov.ua/UJRN/Nzvdpu_ist_2011_19_11.

38.   Internet version Russian Jewish encyclopedia / [Electronic resource]. – Mode of access: http://www.rujen.ru.

39.   History of cities and villages of the Ukrainian SSR. : in 26 books / Vinnytsia region. - Kiev: The main edition of the USSR Academy of Sciences, 1967-1974. - Vol. 3: Vinnytsia region. - 1972. - 630 pages.

40.   M. Yoltukhovsky. History of the native land: a textbook. / M. Yoltukhovsky, I. Barladin. - Bar, 1991-1992.- part 1. - 70 p., part 2. - 60 p.

41.   M. Yoltukhovsky. Between nothingness and the joy of hope (from the history of medicine of our region) / M. Yoltukhovsky // Podolsky Kray. - 2015. 13, February 27.

42.   M. Yoltukhovsky. The Magdeburg Law and self-government of Bar and its suburbs in XVI-early XX centuries. [Electronic resource]/ M. P. Yoltukhovsky // Scientific notes of VSPU. Series: History – 2011. - Vol.19. - Pages 11-15. Mode of access:http://library.vspu.net/bitstream/handle/123456789/2940/2.pdf

43.   F. Kandel. Essays of times and events. From the stories of Russian Jews. / Vol. 6. - Jerusalem, 1994.

44.   Disaster (SHOAH) and Resistance. Vinnytsia region: Testimonies of Jews - prisoners of concentration camps and ghettos, participants of the guerrilla movement and underground struggle. P. Agmon, A. Stepanenko; comp.: S. Malyar, F. Vinokurova. - Kiev: the RIF; Tel-Aviv: Beit Lohameyha Ghettaot, 1994. - 191 p.

45.   L. Kleban. For the rest of my life: a documentary novel. / L. Kleban - Israel, 2000.

46.   The book of memory about the Holodomor in 1932-1933 years in Vinnytsia region. / Ukrainian Institute of National Memory [authors-compilers: V. P. Latsiba, V. V. Vyzhga, P. M. Kravchenko, I. P. Melnichuk et al.]. - Vinnitsa: GP "DFK", 2008. - 1102 p.

47.   The book of Memory of Jewish soldiers who fell in battle with Nazism 1941-1945 / [comp. M. F. Maryanovsky, N. A. Pivovarova, I. S. Sobol - Moscow: Sud'ba. - 1994: Vol. 1, 1995: Vol. 2. - T. 1: 548 p. - T. 2: 657 p.

48.   Books of memory of Ukraine. Winners. Vinnytsia region [Text]: combatants of the Second World war and the Great Patriotic war, who died in the postwar period, and those who live in the region. T. 1: City of Vinnytsia. Vinnytsia region. Bar district /comp. V. E. Kharchuk et al. - Vinnytsia: state enterprise "State cartographic factory", 2007. - 512 p.

49.   M. Kostomarov. Bohdan Khmelnytsky: a historical sketch. / M. Kostomarov. - Kiev: Veselka, 1992. - 93 p.

50.   E. Kotlyar. Ukrainian Judaica by Pavel Zholtovsky: folk studies notebooks, journal. / E. Kotlyar. // Ethnology notebooks No. 2. - 2016. – Pages 418 – 450.

51.   V. Yu. Krushinsky. History of Ukraine: events, facts, dates / V. Yu. Krushinsky - Kiev: Zodiac-Eco, 1993. - 176 p.

52.   A. Kuznetsov. Babi Yar: third Soviet edition. / A. Kuznetsov. - Moscow: Soviet writer Olymp, 1991. - 336 p.

53.   The chronicle of Samovydets at the newly opened list. With the Appendix of three little Russian Chronicles: Khmelnitsky, "Brief description of little Russia" and "historical collection" / [ed. Josef s. Semo. Levitsky].- Kiev, 1878. - 584 p.

54.   Chronicle of the Colonel Grigory Grabyanka / Translated from old Ukrainian. - K.: Znannya, 1992, - 192 p.

55.   V. Lukin. Jewish communities of Podolia: one hundred years after khmelnichchina: a historical guide. / V. Lukin. - Issue 2: Podolia. - St. Petersburg, 2000.

56.   V. Lukin. 100 Jewish towns of Ukraine: a historical guide / V. Lukin, B. Haimovich. – Issue. 2: Podolia. - St. Petersburg: Jerusalem, 2000. - 704 p.

57.   V. Lubchenko. Jews of Podolia and Ustim Karmalyuk: analysis of relationships / / Bulletin of the Hebrew University in Moscow, 1997, No. 2 (15).

58.   D. V. Malakov. Eastern Podolia: (from Zhmerinka to Mogilev-Podolsky). - Moscow: Iskusstvo, 1988. - 167 p.

59.   Ya. Matviishyn. Picturesque plans of three castles-fortresses from the XVII century. (Bar, Medzhibozh, Chigirin) in the Diplomatic archive of the Ministry of foreign Affairs of France. / Ya. Matviishyn. // Historical cartography of Ukraine. - Lviv, 2004. - 200 p.

60.   M. V. Mikhailyuk. Memoirs of Semyon Dodik and Efrem Tarlov as a source for the study of the tragedy of Jews in Bar in the years of occupation. [Electronic resource] / M. V. Mikhailyuk. Mode of access: http://bar-city.com.ua/gromada/krayeznavstvo. html?news=666.

61.   D. Mordovtsev. The Tsar and the Hetman. / D. Mordovtsev. - Moscow: Kniga, 1990. - 293 p.

62.   M. Nosonovsky. Ancient Jewish cemeteries: stories, monuments, epitaphs. [Electronic resource.] - Mode of access: http://library.eajc.org/page70/news13435.

63.   O. Guagnini. Chronicle of the European Sarmatia. / [head editor V. A. Smoliy; translated from Polish by Y. Mutsyka]. -Kyiv: Kyiv-Mohylyanskaya Academy, 2007 - 1004 p.

64.   I. B. Orlov. Between domestic and state anti-Semitism: the Jewish population of Russia during the Civil war and the NEP. // Armageddon - 1999. – volume 5.

65.   S. S. Ostrovsky. Jewish pogroms of 1918-1921 - Moscow: School and Books, 1926.

66.   O. Plamenytska. Bar's castle. / O. Plamenytska. // Military-historical almanac. -2002. No.2 (5). - pp 100-107.

67.   Podolia during the Civil war (February 1918-December 1920): Documents and materials. - Vinnytsia: Vinnytsia book and newspaper publishing house, 1959.

68.   A. Podolinniy. Town of Bar. Guide: second edition. / A. Podolinny. - Odessa: Mayak, 1990. - 62 p.

69.   Podolsky Jewish almanac. - Vinnytsia: Sens-SV. - 2007. - No. 5. - 164 p.

70.   Podolsky Jewish almanac.- Vinnytsia: Sens-SV. - 2011. - No. 7. - 120 p.

71.   Problems of Holocaust history: a scientific journal. - Issue 2. – Kiev: The Prime Minister, 2005. - 218 p.

72.   V. Putyatin. Life. History. Given. Kharkov. / V. Putyatin - Kharkiv: DIV, 2006. - 320 p.

73.   Russian medical list of the Ministry of Internal Affairs for 1904. - Medical Department of th Ministry of Internal Affairs - St. Petersburg, 1904. - 682 p.

74.   Ruth Samuel. On the trails of Jewish history. / R. Samuel. - Moscow:Biblioteka-Aliya, 1991. - 380 p.

75.   I. Svarnik. Ukraine through the eyes of a foreigner. Ulrich von Werdum. Diary of a journey of 1670, 1671, 1672 through the Kingdom of Poland / [translated by I. I. Svarnik]. - October, 1983. - No. 9 (467). - pp 84-100.

76.   M.Svetlov. Favorites. / M.Svetlov. - Moscow: Pravda, 1990. - 478 p.

77.   E. Sitsinsky. Defensive castles of Western Podolia XIV-XVII centuries: historical and archaeological essays. / Ukrainian Academy of Sciences. - Kiev, 1928. - 99 p.

78.   O. Smetanskaya. Fakty. (Vinnytsia-Kiev). 16.08.2002/ [Electronic resource]: [Website]. - Electronic data. - Mode of access: https://fakty.ua/85754-vlyubivshis-v-lizu-zhornickuyu-s-pervogo-vzglyada-komandir-partizanskogo-otryada-ksenofond-yacyuk-spas-ot-vernoj-gibeli-30-evreev-Name from the screen.

79.   Old photos of the town of Bar [Electronic resource]. – Mode of access: http://www.etoretro.ru/city2476.htm.

80.   O. Subtel'ny. Ukraine: History: Study help. / O. Subtel'ny. - 3rd ed. - Kiev: Lybid', 1993. - 720 p.

81.   Modern photos of the town [Electronic resource]. - [Website] - Access mode: http://photogoroda.com/photo-goroda-bar-photo-city-9910.html.

82.   E. I. Tarlov. The Holocaust: two testimonies. The tragedy of the Jewish community of Bar. / E. I. Tarlov, S. D. Dodik. : Zaporozhye city branch of the society "Ukraine-Israel". - Zaporozhye: [b. I.], 2003. - 110 p.

83.   E. I. Tarlov. The Holocaust: eyewitness testimony. / E. I. Tarlov. - Zaporozhye: Zaporizhzhya regional organization of all-Ukrainian Association of democratic forces "Zlagoda", 2001. - 80 p.

84.   G. S. Tkachenko. The myth of the Holodomor - the invention of manipulators for consciousness / [Electronic resource]. - Mode of access: https://kprf.ru/international/ 61342.html.

85.   M. I. Tyagly. Righteous people of the world [Electronic resource]. Mode of access: http://www.history.org.ua/?termin=Pravedniky_svitu.

86.   Photo Materials P. F. Timoshenko, O.M. Kolyada, M.P . Yoltukhovsky, L. Bazaya from the photo album "Old Bar". -[Electronic resource].- Mode of access:
https://www.facebook.com/media/set/?set=oa.15411843525 80106&type=3.

87.   Khmelnitsky local history studios. Scientific and local history collection. / [ed. Bazhenov L. V. (Chairman), Blazhevich Yu. I. (co-chair), S. Esyunin M (resp. SECR.), Zakhariev V. A. (compiler), etc.]. - Khmelnitsky: PE Miller A. A., 2015. - Issue 5. - 256 p.

88.   I want to know everything [Lim.Edition. "Vinnichina»;Ukr. language] //"vinnichchina". - September 10, 2005-P. 5.

89.   The chronicle of Nathan Hanover. Deep silt./ [editor: N. Yakovenko]. - Kiev: Spirit and literature, 2010. - 179 p.

90.   P. P. Chubinsky. "Proceedings of the ethnographic-statistical expedition to the West Russian region, equipped by the Imperial Russian Geographical Society. South-West Division. Materials and research: [in 7 volumes]/ collected by P. P. Chubinsky. - St. Petersburg: [b. I.], 1872 – 1878.

91.   A. I. Shneer. Captivity. Soviet prisoners of war in Germany, 1941 – 1945. / A. Shneer. - Moscow: Mosty cultury, 2005. - Vol.1-2. - 624 p. - [Electronic resource] .- Mode of access:http://www.jewishuniverse.ru/RED/Shneyer/index.htm

92.   I. Ya. Schupak. The Holocaust in Ukraine: the search for the answers to the questions of history. - Dnepropetrovsk: Tkuma Center, 2009. - Second edition. - 148 p.

93.   Electronic Jewish Encyclopedia [Electronic resource] / world ORT; sponsors: the Foundation "ava high" and the European Rothschild Foundation (Ha-Nadiv). - Mode of access: https://eleven.co.il

94.   Electronic archive of the St. Petersburg Institute of Judaica. 2nd Medzhibozh expedition 1989.- [Electronic resource]. - Mode of access: http//91.234.155.99/delo.jsp?delo=82.

95.   Electronic database "Feat of the people in the Great Patriotic War of 1941-1945" / [Electronic resource]. – Mode of access: http://podvignaroda.ru

96.   Lynne Viola. The best sons of fatherland: workers in vanguard of the Soviet collectivization. - Oxford University Press, US, 1989. - ISBN 0-19-504262-X – p.53.

Index of People

C

H

I

J

K

M

Table of Figure Photos, Maps

Ingram Content Group UK Ltd.
Milton Keynes UK
UKHW032259080523
421436UK00008B/309